MY TUNE

My Tune

Simon Bates

Virgin

To Rob and Sue,
for opening my eyes,
and to Martin for
always collecting the tapes

First published in Great Britain in 1994 by
Virgin Books
an imprint of Virgin Publishing Ltd
332 Ladbroke Grove
London W10 5AH

Copyright © Simon Bates 1994

The moral right of the author has been asserted

A catalogue record for this book is available from the British Library.

ISBN 1 85227 483 2

Typeset by TW Typesetting, Plymouth, Devon
Printed and bound in Great Britain by
Mackays of Chatham plc, Lordswood, Chatham, Kent

Foreword

Drive across the border from Somalia into Ethiopia and take the road that crosses the Ogaden and then winds on to Addis Ababa. If you follow your nose you'll come to the town of Jijiga. The town's name is spelt a dozen different ways on a dozen different maps so please don't write.

Jijiga is a sprawl of a town, dumped at the edge of the desert. It's a natural crossroads for trading and the camel trains sway through the city streets loaded down with wood or anything else that is in demand.

In the centre of the town is a bar called 'Bar'.

To find 'Bar', just go down the main street, turn left and walk for about fifty yards. There it is, behind a doorway set in a wall that runs by the side of the road.

On a Friday night early in 1994, I'd driven into Jijiga with an overpowering thirst and been advised that 'Bar' was the place to see and be seen. To be honest, both are nearly impossible after dark. The street outside has no lighting and inside there are two rooms with a bare electric light bulb in each. The effect is a little like one of those old Expressionist German films, with faces being suddenly and frighteningly illuminated and then disappearing into the shadows.

This is one of the last frontiers, where the aid workers who are scattered all over the desert drive into town on a Friday night to mix and mingle. The night I was there the place was packed with shadowy figures shouting and laughing at each other in English, French, Norwegian, just about every European language. I squeezed inside, bought myself a beer and leaned up against the wall talking to a mad American who claimed he was in the CIA, but who actually turned out to be a convoy driver.

There was a little ripple as a couple more people forced their way into the bar and a very clean and sharp, rather Sloaney accent cut through the air like a knife.

'Is Simon Bates here, I've been told that Simon Bates is here?'

My companion turned and said 'Yeah he's here, who wants him?'

The voice belonged to a slim and tough-looking woman of about thirty with bright eyes who said, 'I want to meet him. If it really is Simon Bates, then this is the biggest thing to happen in Jijiga for years.'

As we drove back to the UN compound later, my companion said drily, 'I guess you've really made it to international stardom now. You could put that on your publicity and your CV. "Simon Bates, the biggest thing to happen to Jijiga for years." ' He paused and added gravely, 'Maybe it would make a good epitaph.'

Chapter 1

YEARS AGO, a young, fresh faced producer, eager to contribute to his chosen profession, walked into his radio station. As he turned the corner into the newsroom, a typewriter sailed over his head. It was not one of the new, light electric sort: this was an old Imperial, built from solid steel, to last. Not surprisingly, our young producer ducked but caught a nasty blow on the backside by a second Imperial being thrown from the other side of the newsroom. He had walked into the dying embers of a passionate lesbian affair being carried on by two highly talented young journalists, both of whom now have significant careers. The producer bears the scars of their relationship still.

Every radio station I have ever worked in has been a madhouse, a tower of babel, a monument to the ego, a tribute to the survival of the individual. The daily battle has always been between the psychotics who actually go on air, do the talking, the presenting, or whatever you like to call it, and the management. In between the two is the rest, which usually consists of neurotic, deranged, manic lunatics, all of them quite unfit for the real world. In fairness, they have usually come into the business as sweet, pleasant people who have subsequently been driven mad by those on the air or in charge. Most of them, though, have the best intentions and love what they do with a desperation bordering on mania.

The producers, engineers, secretaries, doormen – these are damaged people; creative, funny, hateful, exasperating, wacky people. I've worked with and for hundreds of them. I've drunk with them, slept with some of them and even fought with a couple. Drunk or sober, they are splendid people for the most part. But you would not want any of them going out with your mother. And I cannot think of any of them with any style or quality who could be called truly sane. Nearly all of them are splendidly larger than life and yet they are sandwiched between the crazy voices and the buffoons who run the joint.

It has always surprised me that the murder rate in radio stations is so low. I usually like to check that any colleagues I am with aren't armed. If they are, and I turn my back on them, I would be asking for trouble and inevitably one day, I would get it. The point is that they look fairly ordinary and often they behave quite rationally. But under the surface there is real lunacy waiting to break out.

Anyone who works in radio has a heightened sense of drama. No one worthy of the name broadcaster, no one of stature, would ever dare fail to make a dramatic entrance. That entrance has to be a good one, it's the only chance that one ego has to be noticed amongst the herd of other egos. Which is why trying to make a big entrance into a radio studio can lead to disappointment.

On this one day in the autumn of 1993, while I was sitting behind the panel at BBC One FM doing my job – which was then *The Simon Bates Show* – the door would have burst open, if that were possible. But that's a technical impossibility in most radio stations and more so in the BBC, where gaining entrance to a radio studio is like taking part in *The Krypton Factor*.

For each studio there are two substantial doors, hung in parallel and weighted to improve the soundproofing. On occasion, I have mused that if one got the timing right and enlisted the help of an associate on the other side, it should be possible, by waiting for the right moment until a member of management found themselves in the space between the two doors, to seal them in for ever. A few nails and a couple of hammers would finish the trick. It would take a while for them to die of course, but at least they would go with the sounds of their favourite radio station ringing in their ears. Maybe in years to come, archaeologists would find them and conclude that the skeleton was proof perfect of the twentieth-century habit of sac-rificing an executive to the gods to guarantee great programming.

This particular occasion was like a million others when 'things corporate were going wrong'. In other words, all was not in control. There had been an air of chaos building at Radio One for a couple of years, and now the tension was tangible.

It was about midday and I was sitting in the studio playing the role of disc jockey when the door heaved slightly and then gave in gracefully.

In bustled a busy, red-faced and overheated figure, followed by a nervous and pale-looking humble character. The leader was a slightly plump man in his mid-thirties with the unconvincing wide grin of one who is either mightily annoyed, very harassed or both. He was clearly following the classic management technique of trying to appear 'very, very calm' when under stress.

The faithful retainer I knew – a pale, thin man with a damp handshake, with an uncanny knack of knowing which way the wind was blowing. He was the press officer for Radio One.

Half my mind was on what the BBC paid me to do – play music and talk – but the other half thought it recognised the leader, though it could not put a name to him. So for want of being more creative and aware that *he* thought I knew who he was, I fell back on the time-honoured broadcasters' last protective device – aggression.

'Who the hell are you?' I said.

'I'm the new Controller of Radio One.'

When I took a good look at him, so he was. Of course it had been absurd not to immediately recognise him, but he had made a point of not being seen around the building after being appointed and I hadn't actually met him in his new role.

It had been a messy few months since Matthew Bannister's appointment as Controller had been confirmed and I'd decided not to join the seemingly endless queue of paranoid broadcasters desperate to take Matthew for lunch. There was no point. The reason was quite simple: for a couple of years I had had a pretty good idea of which way the wind was blowing.

The BBC is nothing if not a renaissance organisation and therefore when the old guard are on their way out, the trumpets sound loud and clear, that is if you're prepared to listen. As in any large organisation, clear-outs happen every five to eight years and we were overdue for ours. The new management up on the fourth floor of Broadcasting House, just across the road from our studios, had been pretty effective in establishing an atmosphere of fear and distress as they set about trimming the staff list of the people who did not fit. Those who had spent the last two years with their hands covering their ears had been among the unhappy many who had been surprised when told to clear their desks and get out of Broadcasting House at once. Their shocked, pale, tear-streaked faces were a familiar sight in Oxford Street.

On a day to day level, it was difficult to deal with these rapid changes which naturally caused consternation. Often the 'thought police' would get to someone, chuck them out and not bother passing on news of their absence to mere mortals on the shop floor. The first realisation that someone did not exist could sometimes be an unanswered phone.

I had decided about nine months before that it was time to take stock and think hard about the future. I'd had a good run. In fact, it had been so good and so surprising that I was shocked to realise I was still there after all those years. It isn't always possible to be like the Vicar of Bray and shift allegiances each time the management changes.

Johnny Beerling, the previous Controller of Radio One, had been living on borrowed time for a couple of years. That had become all too obvious. A bright, entrepreneurial figure who lived his private and professional life in the full gaze of the staff, Johnny didn't have a place in the new BBC. He was a small vigorous man with a penchant for wearing blazers that clashed horribly with his ties, and he wore his heart on his sleeve. On a good day, the sun shone for him, on a bad day, his mouth turned down and he became the perfect Mr Grumpy. For all that, he was an honest man and the epithet 'you know where you are with him' could have been coined for Johnny though, as this is the BBC, one should add 'most of the time'.

Johnny was one of the old school and the new arrivals had piled work on him to the point where he became unable to be the boss of Radio One FM, because he was simply never there. The joke was that Beerling was the 'never present Controller'. As he had been forced to delegate more and more, so the morale of the station hurtled downwards. Even an idiot, taking a look at the new Armani suits and the studiously cool image cultivated by the next generation, versus Johnny's bright red blazer, or leather jacket with the Mao collar, would have sussed pretty quickly that he didn't fit. In fairness to him, Johnny did make a last-ditch stand, wearing a black shirt without a tie, but it wasn't convincing. His extrovert manner, which was given to expansive gestures and, with a few drinks inside him, a deeply emotional response to almost anything, didn't tie in with the new style. Somehow it wasn't possible to imagine Johnny hugging John Birt with delight at something going really well. On reflection, it was easier to imagine Johnny hugging the Director General than imagining John Birt reciprocating.

The flags had been up for some time. About a year before, in a matchless piece of ill-judged planning, Radio One had held its annual day-long conference at the Café Royal. The omens for a successful day were not good. For a start, these events were always loathed by the staff, half of whom liked to bunk off as early as they could after a short day in the office, so the other half, those who did the actual work, were forced to put in long hours before the conference begun simply to keep up with their schedule.

Such events were properly regarded as an opportunity for the management to flex their muscles and their egos. 'It's a day for the suits to show off to the boiler room,' the then producer of the evening programme said to me. Added to this, some bright spark had decreed that this was to be a 'no alcohol' affair. So we all trooped gloomily down Oxford Street and took the lifts in the Café Royal to the third floor, where grown men and women proceeded to stand around in sombre groups debating how to escape the prohibition. Another bright spark had conceived the idea that the event would take the form of a mock trial in which the staff would be presented by members of management giving evidence which justified their various roles in the running of the station. It was a farcical idea.

First, Johnny got up with a face like thunder and a voice of doom and ran through a catalogue of how things weren't going well and were undoubtedly going to get worse. His personal antipathy to John Birt's style was well known, but to have a normally cheery character sunk in gloom when everyone was expecting some kind of Shakespearean rallying cry was very depressing. After Johnny had announced that there was worse to come, there was a lacklustre attempt to adopt the 'new' management style. Staff were made to sit and listen to an endless round of self-glorification as each of the management team in turn got up to speak. It was an astonishingly tactless exhibition from a bunch who were so self-obsessed that they thought it more important to spend a day clapping each other on the back than encouraging the staff and making them feel valuable.

Then an organisational expert was produced who proceeded to alternately patronise and puzzle the whole of Radio One staff. This was the first time that most of them had seen anything like a management adviser in their lives. It was the first time that the Coopers & Lybrand culture, the new attitude, had hit them square in the face. These people had spent most of their working lives up to their armpits in a culture of deep belief in the concept of Public Service Broadcasting. For all their inadequacies, they believed that their job was to produce programmes. Throughout their careers, they had been encouraged to be individualists, and often quirky ones at that. They had been told that their sole function was to use their skills to produce unique programming. Now, without warning, they were introduced to the new philosophy. It was a tough and insensitive way to do it.

In a speech he had made the previous year, John Birt had taken a pop at Radio One, saying that the station had to change and become more innovative and contemporary in its outlook. But his speech had been so overwritten and couched in so many code words that most of the staff had missed the message. Now, few of them understood a word the organisational expert said as he limped through an hour of gobbledegook. But when he paused for breath, the hall erupted. Everyone wanted to know what he was talking about and whether his style was a marker for the future. The poor man struggled to explain himself, but it was a hopeless case; they spoke different languages and there was no glossary of terms available for the astounded staff.

The effect of this catastrophic day was unsurprising. For the staff, it was a signal of an irreparable schism between them and the management. Worse, there was obvious deep division in the management team, as executives, confronted by the all too obvious future departure of Johnny Beerling, began setting out their stalls as his successor. A deep and inconsolable depression set in throughout the station. Two members of staff resigned shortly afterwards as a direct result, and studios and offices were littered with copies of the *Guardian* Media Section opened at Job Opportunities.

The word was out that Johnny's days were numbered and that the man numbering them was John Birt. So, I wasn't entirely surprised when Johnny took me out for dinner in March 1993 and marked my card. Only a fool wouldn't acknowledge that Elvis turning up to do a gig at the local Asda store was about as likely as the new management embracing me, my style and my methodology. The truth was that I had been at Radio One for too long. I knew that myself, but my only excuse for not getting out and finding a new job at the time was that my working day – along with that of my producer – was so long that I had simply never got round to it. It was also true that whoever the new boss was would want to stamp his own personality on the network and quite right too.

There is very little that an incoming Controller can do to demonstrate himself as a mover and shaker other than to change around a well-established slot or two. Hence, much insecurity was induced at the Pebble Mill studios, where *The Archers* is produced, when a new Controller for Radio Four was announced!

Although at this point Johnny didn't admit to me that he was leaving, we both agreed that I should give up the morning show in September, at the end of the summer quarter, well before the new Controller was to be appointed. It seemed logical, fair and very generous on Johnny's part. On top of that, he arranged for a new contract to be offered by the BBC taking me through to the middle of 1994. So there I was with at least six months' gainful employment before I had to even think about organising life after Radio One and a nice little earner to take me through into the next year.

There was a minor hiccup in this arrangement when Johnny's exit was hastened, and again Radio One was left in organisational chaos. A miserable-looking Beerling had been hauled off to a hastily con- vened press conference by Liz Forgan (Managing Director of Net- work Radio), who had made the announcement and then brightly and insensitively told the assembled hacks that she couldn't stay be- cause she was 'spending the day at Lords in the Chairman of the Board of Governors' box'.

Johnny called me as soon as he was able and asked if I would be prepared to stay on the daytime programme for another month or so, to fill the slot before the new Controller made his decision as to my successor. Although I wasn't terribly keen, it would have been churlish not to agree, so I said 'yes'. With this arrangement, as with most things that went on in my time at the BBC, we all swore to be discreet. The problem is, and always will be, that one man's secret is another man's pub talk, and of course the word got about in a mod- est sort of way and the battle to take over the morning show was on. It was a very public secret, anyway. Mark Goodier, who was doing the breakfast show until the end of the year, had been making very funny not-so-oblique comments about it on air during our conversa- tion at 9 a.m. for months. Only an idiot would not have got the message, and certainly my mail bag was full of querying letters. By this time the record industry and most of the Radio One staff knew. They would have to be very thick not to have cottoned on, but there's always a few. So the battle to be my successor was on.

For me and the two producers fully in the know, sitting in my little studio for three and a half hours a day and knowing that I was on the way out, observing the civil war that broke out was a delight. Three broadcasters believed themselves to be in line for the job and watching them tout for the gig was a hoot for me and for Fergus Dudley and Christine Boar, the two producers most closely involved. Most days some poor civilian would tiptoe nervously into the office and faithfully relate the latest stage in the battle and who was being tipped for the crown on that particular day. Don't forget each candidate falsely believed that he would have to vanquish me as well as the other two.

Simon Mayo had told a couple of other disc jockeys a year or so before that he was determined to have the mid-morning programme for his own. The poor bloke also tried to initiate a minor press campaign attacking the kind of programming I'd been doing and the kind of image I had, whatever that might have been. The press officer tried to calm him down, but a couple of profiles appeared with some of the sniping still intact. All a bit of a waste of time and maybe I should have told him that I was leaving, but it seemed rather pointless and quite amusing.

The other two broadcasters in the frame for the job were Nicky Campbell and Mark Goodier. Both of them were too busy to indulge in much politicking.

In fact, it was a rerun of the days when I'd taken over the show from Tony Blackburn. Then, back in the seventies, the press had universally tipped David Jensen as the man most likely to succeed. They had all been proved wrong to my intense surprise when the then Controller Derek Chinnery had handed me the baton at a lunch in a Chinese restaurant.

I had thought I was going to be fired, so I had to spend the rest of the afternoon frantically calling people to say 'no thanks' to the jobs I'd been touting for only a couple of hours before. But that was a long time ago, in 1977 when Radio One was more of a talking point than it had become in the nineties.

Now, apart from Paul Donovan at *The Sunday Times*, there were few spectators who really understood what was going on.

Martin Dunn, when he was assistant editor at the *Sun*, had told me that Radio One was becoming unimportant outside the music columns, and as the years rolled on, he seemed to have been right. In fact, Martin had argued strongly that I should leave Radio One in 1990. I often wondered whether that was for my benefit, or the listeners.

The kind of press attacks that were being made on Radio One by

1993 were general and usually pretty uninformed. There was so little interest or real understanding of what was going on that life developed a sort of phoney war feel. I went on working and the programme continued to do what it had always done – play music and do some quirky outside broadcasts from Croatia and Ethiopia. But then, all of a sudden, when things should have been winding down gently, there we were in the autumn of 1993 and one intelligent and well-connected journalist had added two and two and made four.

He had noticed that I had stopped broadcasting 'Our Tune'. Normally the slot returned after its summer recess and that is what head of programming Chris Lycett had wanted. I had refused to bring it back purely because there was a mere eight weeks left of the programme's life. Chris knew this and agreed that it would be unfair to mess about with the audience's expectations and revive a slot for just a few weeks. The point was that there was no way 'Our Tune' was going to stay on One FM as a regular feature. The slot had caused enough internal dissension to almost require the new Controller to remove it.

Hearing this, making a few phone calls and adding two and two together, one journalist came up with the right answer: Bates was, at the very least, leaving daytime radio. No big deal in the scheme of things, but it made a good headline and created an absurd level of panic at Broadcasting House. Which brings us to Matthew's presence in my studio that day.

Once I had turned the microphone off and the loudspeakers down, he looked furtively at me across the desk. 'I don't want to talk here,' he said. 'Perhaps you'll come and see me when you've finished.'

He had some grounds for his paranoia. Although it is frowned upon by those in power, the studio manager behind the glass can, if he wants, tune into what is going on in the studio whether or not the microphone is on. The motivation is often no more than a desire to escape the crashingly mindless output that he is monitoring. Usually all he hears by flicking the switch is the disc jockey calling his agent or his bookie, or long rambling conversations with boyfriends or girlfriends or sometimes both. But just occasionally there's something more juicy to listen to and that's what Matthew had in mind. So I wearily said that I would be along as soon as I could.

After I had finished the show, I pottered about doing disc jockey things, putting CDs away and wiping up the coffee I'd spilt, and then walked down the corridor, through the security door and into the

Controller's office. It was an odd place to be. In the days when it had been Beerling's office, the place had been littered with the bric-à-brac of twenty-five years in Radio One – garish awards on every wall, reproductions of *Radio Times* front covers and the odd photograph of Johnny's family. Now it was almost totally empty. After the *coup* that had deposed him, Johnny had stripped the place of all its memorabilia and legged it, off to his new home in Docklands. Matthew hadn't had time to bring in his knick-knacks, so the office was suitably minimalist.

Under the previous administration, being summoned to this office was an unpredictable business. The moment the phone call came, 'Ask Simon to come and see me, will you?', I would go into a huddle with my producer and our PA.

'OK, what's gone wrong and what have I said recently that could drop us all in the shit?'

Invariably we were all too busy to remember what had happened over the last few hours, let alone the last week or two, so in I would go, frantically racking my brain for the latest sin I'd committed. And hunting through the list of available excuses.

If, when I walked in, Johnny looked up with a grin and a wave, things mightn't be too bad. The problem might be no worse than a listener's perception that I was a rabid right- or left-winger, depending on his mood. Or there might have been another niggly statement from Teddy Taylor, who was just about the only MP prepared to comment on anything I ever did, regardless of the fact that he'd never actually heard my show. We could laugh, or sigh at that sort of thing. If, however, Johnny wore a defeated look, beckoned me in with a 'Shut the door, please', and offered me a drink things were really bad. This meant taking a stance very quickly and certainly before knowing the real awfulness of the situation. But taking a stance was all a matter of luck.

I could plump for instant and premature denial: 'I can't believe that you'd ever imagine that I'd do something like that on air.' But this might force him into producing an actual tape recording of the offence, followed by an embarrassing retreat from me. Or I could go for a grovelling apology too quickly, which could mean that other sins might be revealed. Years ago a particularly good disc jockey nearly lost his job when he tried the second option after being called in to the holy of holies. Earlier that day, to his horror, he had found himself playing 'Crawling From the Wreckage' after the announcement of a particularly nasty plane crash. It turned out that the Controller hadn't heard him commit this offence and had called him into the office for an entirely different reason. When the DJ huffed and puffed and mumbled something about it not being his fault, Derek Chinnery had asked what he was talking about. The resulting row when Derek found out about the crash and the record was not a pretty one.

No, the best route usually was a choice between overcheerful *bonhomie*, or relaxed confidence.

On this occasion, we both knew we were playing out a silly little scenario which should have been disposed of a couple of months earlier, when Matthew became Controller. The problem the leak had caused for Matthew was now apparent. I suppose what he wanted was to make a press announcement about his changes to the network before telling me, or indeed any of the staff, until the last move. I assume this was to give the impression to the staff and press that he was a mover and a shaker, and that the careers of broadcasters lay cupped in his hands. The journalist who had added two and two together and punted the story had unfortunately ruined that impression.

Jo Grace, at one time Beerling's PA and now Matthew's assistant, was wearing her slightly grim 'Oh God, this is going to be a confrontation' expression as I walked past her and into Matthew's office.

He still looked remarkably uneasy, despite – or perhaps because of – a desperately artificial smile that thinly masked his anxiety.

I could not for the life of me understand why he was so nervous, and I still can't. He had no reason to be. After all, we both knew the score and he held most of the cards. I suppose he might have had a suspicion that I would leap on him and cry havoc while plunging a bowie knife into his breast.

Whatever, he was a nervous man and seemed desperate to distance himself from the chaos that was going on around him. He spent a couple of minutes explaining earnestly that his actions reflected BBC policy before coming to the point. 'After you finish the daytime show in October, there won't be any more, er, shows.'

Fine. In fact, better than fine. I felt like a soldier in a tight corner who'd just been told 'for you the war is over'. I wasn't that surprised.

Matthew maundered on for a while about wanting me to propose some programmes for 1994 as an independent producer before getting to the point once again.

'Now, I know you have a long-term contract and we'll honour

that. What I'd like to do is shorten it and make a series of final payments to bring it to a conclusion by the end of the year. Obviously we'd like you to produce some programmes for us in that period, what do you have in mind?'

What did I have in mind?

It was quite clear from the way he spoke that he wanted me to keep quiet while the changes to the network were introduced and that suited me perfectly. Here I was apparently being offered *carte blanche* as long as I didn't talk to the press.

I'd always been bad at grabbing opportunities, and I failed myself again.

'Well,' I said, thinking to myself that three wishes should just about do it, 'I'd like to go back to Bosnia and Pittsburgh to do some recordings I have in mind with a girl refugee and her family. I'd like to re-edit a programme I've done with Billy Joel in the summer and I'd like to spend a week or so in New York around about Christmas time recording a gospel choir.'

Matthew didn't seem to be listening. He looked at me blankly. 'Yes, great, fine, OK.'

For a moment I was furious with myself. Yet again I'd misjudged the situation. If I had suggested an Outside Broadcast from the Space Shuttle he would have probably said yes. He would have agreed to anything at all just to keep me out of the way. I hadn't been prepared for such an easy ride.

Matthew had got what he wanted, me out of his hair without a confrontation or too much trouble, and my silence. For three months at least. I'd got the perfect Christmas present, a licence to make three programmes that I desperately cared about. Programmes that were expensive, highly uncommercial and programmes I wouldn't have to appear in. Bliss.

Matthew seemed to have lost interest and it showed. 'I'll get contracts to call you,' he said. His nervousness had gone.

It was time to leave. It was also the last time I saw Matthew. Jo looked at me quizzically as I walked out of the office. I could have kissed her, but it was definitely the wrong time and the wrong place. I had to tell the people who mattered what was going on.

Christine Boar, my producer, gave me an uncharacteristic hug and very sweetly burst into tears. So did my agent, *in memoriam* to his fifteen per cent. I spent the rest of the afternoon in the office calling friends and confirming that I would be off the air and out of the

Radio One daytime schedules by the end of October, before nipping across Regent Street to my flat for a large cup of coffee and a few minutes' peace and quiet, while I thought things through.

The peace and quiet never happened. The phone was ringing itself off the hook from the moment I let myself in. The calls came from two distinct camps. The first batch were from friends calling to say 'hi', to offer support and simply be nice. The second batch were from people who were 'horrified to hear that I was leaving but who wanted to know if the job was up for grabs because they could probably get themselves out of their contracts if it would help'.

I had started making notes on the different ways the second category had of getting round to the same subject, when the doorbell rang. It was Johnny Beerling and Chris Lycett (the previous boss and his deputy) with a sheepish look on their faces and a bottle of red wine in their hands. They had thoughtfully come to see if I was OK, which of course I was, perfectly, thank you.

A year or so before all this, when one of the tabloids had set up a story that I was leaving Radio One, Alan Freeman, who had a good deal more experience than I, said to someone, 'You'll only know Bates is going when he's gone. He's the type who's quite capable of stepping out on to the fourth-floor window ledge one day and chucking himself off shouting, "Fuck the lot of you".' I was suitably flattered by this.

Given these two glum souls sitting opposite me, I almost wished I had. At least they would have had something to be cheerful about. I sat there making polite conversation for a while, before the first bottle was emptied. Then my guests turned their attention to my wine, and as they drank that, waxed lyrical about the way the BBC was going down the drain and how badly they were being treated. I found myself sympathising with them out loud while thinking, 'Wait a minute, these two are supposed to be here offering counselling and support to *me*.' After a while, they got bored with me and sauntered off into the darkness of Regent Street.

I heard one of them curse Birt in a fairly desultory way as I closed the door and went back to the phone, which was ringing again. It was Jonathon King, determined that I must feel dreadful and equally determined to do something about it if I did.

The following day, I turned up at work as usual. The newspapers had picked up on the story and so had the BBC's commercial rivals on radio and television.

Handled properly, this would have been a quick story on page eight one day and forgotten the next. Unfortunately, however predictably, a high level of drama was injected. Radio One's news division was suffering from nervous collapse that morning. Although they knew that I was leaving, they didn't dare run the story until they had approval from Matthew himself and Matthew wasn't in the office. The poor newsreader was at his wits' end about what to do. Considering that this seemed to be developing into a replay of the last trauma – when Prince Charles and Princess Diana had been splashed all over the front pages but been studiously ignored by our news service – I could only giggle.

Eventually, when Matthew arrived, a form of words was agreed between the news department and him and the hot news was announced at nine thirty . . . half an hour after I had started my daily programme.

Later that day, when things had settled down somewhat and Head of News, Jenny Abramsky was interviewing candidates for jobs in her division, one of the questions she asked was, 'How would you have handled the Bates resignation?' As one of the prospective applicants said to me afterwards, 'The word "better" occurred to me, but I needed the job.'

I called Matthew to try and sort out how we would handle things that day and found him extremely angry. I had done a short and decidedly uncontroversial phone interview with Gaby and Chris on *The Big Breakfast* early in the morning. They had always been immensely generous to me personally and when they asked me to talk to them I had no qualms in saying yes. There was nothing in the least threatening in the conversation, but Matthew was still furious on the phone.

'I said no publicity!'

I tried to explain that it wasn't in my gift to guarantee no publicity. I also said that there wasn't much point in pretending that something wasn't happening when it palpably was, but tempers were running high, and it seemed best not to continue the conversation, so we called a truce.

As the morning wore on I got a phone call from the front office. There were a couple of camera crews and some scribblers waiting outside Radio One's studios for me. I called Matthew again and told him that it was almost inevitable that this would happen. What did he think was the best way to deal with it?

There was a snort from the end of the phone. 'I can get you a fast car,' he said.

I assumed he was joking. After all, the idea of my being hustled (under a blanket, perhaps?) into the aforesaid fast car and away from Broadcasting House at high speed was too ridiculous to contemplate.

'No, Matthew.'

There was a pause.

'OK, then,' and he brightened up a little, 'I'll send the press officer down to send them away.'

The prospect of the press officer marching up to a band of Fleet Street's finest and telling them to be about their business didn't seem very convincing. I could imagine the response he would get. Matthew and I finally agreed that I would have to walk through the door just as everyone else did. I'd have liked him to walk through it beside me, but he didn't see that it would serve any useful purpose, so I did the job on my own.

The press were very pleasant on this occasion and I was suitably bland.

I now had a few weeks left at Radio One and some problems to solve. First and most important, I still had a daily programme to do. Then there was the matter of the last programme. I dreaded the idea of doing the last show after seventeen years in the studio in London. Inevitably management would turn up with crocodile tears and champagne at the end and we would all go through a dreadful and terribly British series of handshakes and hugs, all of them wildly insincere. It didn't bear thinking about. There was also the matter of the staff.

I have always had a terrible tendency to tears and I get emotional very easily. Point me in the direction of a Walt Disney movie about a dog or a cat and I'm the idiot cracked up at the back of the cinema howling uncontrollably. The idea of having to say goodbye to the people I had worked with, some of them for seventeen years, at a moment when I was vulnerable, would be too much. I would be certain to bring up the Thames flood barrier. Besides, I didn't have the confidence not to make a total fool of myself and become wildly emotional if I was doorstepped by some worthy hacks, as I certainly would be, after the programme.

So, the last programme would have to be broadcast from some-where as far outside London as possible. The perfect location was the obvious one – New York. It was ideal, I knew the city well and had a good working relationship with the BBC office in the Rockefeller Center, and because of the time difference I would do the programme at five in the morning, in a coma, so it would be over by the time I came out of it. I could also go straight on to Pittsburgh and begin work recording the Bosnian refugees.

Getting the suits to agree was easier than I thought. I had an ally in Chris Lycett, who understood that it was better to have me out of the country on the last day and perfect to have me out of reach of the press when Simon Mayo started. There were a couple of conditions. The first was that the Radio One producer Fergus Dudley would not be present in New York, and the second was that the programme would not be broadcast from the Carnegie Deli. Fergus and I had scored a spectacular critical dud a few years earlier with a show we did together from the Deli. I agreed with Chris and then set about arranging that Fergus be one of the producers and that the Carnegie Deli should be the location. Small-minded of me, of course, but it didn't affect the quality of the programme and if it irritated management slightly, then that was no bad thing. There was no difficulty in arranging anything. The depth of unhappiness in the organisation meant that once people knew it was my last programme it became a matter of pride to achieve the impossible.

While all that was going on, there was one last chance for a practical joke. A couple of months before the changes at Radio One were announced, I had arranged for the first-ever live radio performance by Prince to take place on my programme. That's not entirely true. Prince had said that he would do one and I sank to my knees and said, 'Thank you very much', while thinking 'How the hell do I put on a live Prince gig in Broadcasting House with three days' notice?'

Fergus Dudley and I managed to achieve it. By working round the clock, keeping Radio One's management in the dark about most of the preparations, pulling all the favours we could and with unstinting help from everybody concerned at ground level in the BBC, Prince did a twenty-five minute set at lunch-time one day in September 1993 in the BBC Concert Hall slap bang in the middle of Broadcasting House. There had been a moment when Fergus and I thought we had bitten off more than we could chew as, three hours before the gig, two huge Edwin Shirley touring trucks drew up outside Broadcasting House and disgorged Prince's entire Wembley sound rig!

There was a story flying around Broadcasting House for a while that the only reason I actually managed to book the Concert Hall for this was that someone in studio bookings had spotted the words 'Prince appearance' and had assumed that Royalty was involved. I've learned to take good stories at face value and not automatically assume that they're apocryphal. There had also been a little local difficulty with one member of Radio One's management who had taken it into his head that he would like to meet Prince and have a photograph taken with him and who couldn't grasp that when I said it simply wasn't possible, I meant it. He was desperately concerned for his future and instead of backing off had become more insistent, adding that, 'Matthew would like one too.' Unquestionably, Matthew knew nothing about this, but I knew enough about Prince to eventually suggest that there were other fantasies the foolish executive could indulge himself in.

For the BBC it was an astonishing *coup*. For Fergus and me it was a great relief that it actually happened. The programme was a great success. In fact, it worked so well that Matthew praised the show as being an example of what he wanted for the future of One FM. And as most of my colleagues at Radio One told me, the idea of Prince and Bates on the same bill was a little hard to take.

I have never been nor ever want to be credible. It's a silly, self-indulgent ambition and has little or nothing to do with the business of day-to-day broadcasting. Credibility is a once-a-week luxury that only part-time broadcasters can afford. It can be a trap waiting to be sprung on the unwary. Being credible is hard to sustain and a crown that once worn can only slip. Take your eyes off the road for an instant and you'll do or say, interview or schedule something that is so uncredible that all that hard work of gaining yourself a reputation will seem like a complete waste of time. However, on this occasion credibility was forced upon me. I became the man who could get Prince when no one else could. For a short time the perception was that if Jehovah was ever to do a live personal appearance, it would be on my show.

In an idle conversation over lunch, Johnnie Walker had told me about a band called The Counterfeit Stones. Earlier in their life they'd had credibility as Broken English and had starved. So they'd cancelled their credibility, gone out on the road as a carbon copy of the old Stones and begun to make a profit. 'You've gotta see them,' he said, 'they are astonishing. They don't just *sound* like the Stones in the mid-sixties, they *are* the Stones of thirty years ago.'

I had subsequently caught the band live and Johnnie was right. They were also perfect for the ideal practical joke. The Rolling Stones would play on the penultimate Bates programme. I asked the band if they would do the gig and explained that their set would be on my penultimate show. They were perfectly happy, they were going to get a gig, publicity and get paid. What a *coup*! Then I talked to Fergus about the idea and we agreed that we would follow the pattern of the Prince concert.

This involved creating an in-house buzz at the BBC, the ingredients of which were a last-minute and panicky request for the Concert Hall and a carefully prepared rumour that the Greatest Rock and Roll Band in the World would be playing a secret gig. The rumour was delivered by Fergus and I to four BBC employees – lovely people but famous for their inability to keep a secret.

Although the event was intended primarily as an amiable practical joke, there was another motive. By doing the programme from the Concert Hall, I couldn't be in Radio One's studios and therefore I would avoid anyone who felt kind enough to rumble the fact that even though the programme was my penultimate, it would be my last in the UK.

The jape went better than we could have dreamed. The band played superbly, the audience of BBC staff rose to the occasion and played the parts of fans magnificently. Two members of senior management turned up and were completely conned until some kind soul pointed out that Brian Jones was in this line-up and that he had been dead for a quarter of a century! By the time the third number was under way the radio audience was also in on the gag.

I felt wonderful, the joke had worked and the music had been good. But, as happens with all great crimes, I hadn't covered every angle and there was trouble brewing. The problem with being on the radio every day, is that you sometimes forget who's listening. Across at Blackfriars Bridge and Wapping, the mighty British press had heard my warm-up to the Greatest Rock and Roll Band in the World and by the time the band hit the air, forty of Fleet Street's finest were milling around outside Broadcasting House's front door, ready to snap Mick, Ron and Co. as they left. They weren't at all pleased when the doorman at Radio One pottered up to them, and said limply, 'It was all a joke, fellas.' They mooched off down Regent Street muttering something about 'Bates, ropes and lampposts'.

I was unaware of this and on a high as I slipped across the road to the flat to pick up my overnight bag for New York. Everything had gone well and I'd avoided making a fool of myself having to say goodbye to friends at Radio One. When I let myself into the block,

I thought I heard some voices, but dismissed it from my mind as I sprinted up to the third floor. And there, sitting on the stairs, champagne in hand and waiting patiently, were what looked like half the PAs from Radio One. They had filed across the road before I finished in the Concert Hall and waited outside my front door to say goodbye. That's when the waterworks started.

The last programme from New York was fun. Jim Steinman and Cyndi Lauper came down to the Deli. The band Texas had flown over to be on the show and Charleen sang like a dream. There were friends from the BBC New York office and friends from the UK who'd come over to be there.

We had a final joke up our sleeve, which I thought highly effective. The previous night when we'd arrived in New York, I had recorded a sequence with an actress pretending to be a distraught fan. In the recording, which we were going to play live, she walked up to me and said something to the effect that, 'If I can't have you, then no one can', and then she shot me. We had a local difficulty with the sound effect for the shooting. The only gunshot noise we could find in the New York office sounded like a mortar attack, but by speeding it up slightly and adding lots of crowd noises the whole ended up sounding very convincing. Half the staff of the BBC New York office contributed to the extremely believable screams and mayhem that followed the shooting. I loved it.

My producer Christine Boar loathed the idea. She believed that it would upset a good proportion of the audience, but to me it seemed a darned effective way of getting me off the network. We had every intention of playing the sequence until we heard the early news from London. The engineer at the London end was in on our plot and it was he who warned us what was happening back at home. The IRA had perpetrated another atrocity, and sitting there safe in New York, we all agreed that it would be piling bad taste on an obscenity to broadcast a hoax shooting. A pity, though. If we had transmitted the tape, there could have been interesting repercussions in London.

For some reason, John Birt had decided that the programme was a risk, I can't imagine why. Adrian Juste was in the studio in London that I normally occupied, playing records and jingles as we in New York requested. So Chris Lycett and Paul Robinson, as the available management, were deputed to sit outside the studio and 'should anything untoward occur, take the necessary action'. Apart from looking faintly foolish and causing much mirth amongst the staff, it's difficult to see what they could have achieved. Maybe if 'something unto-ward' had occurred, one or the other would have leapt into the studio, through the nearly unopenable doors, and cried very loudly 'He didn't mean it and we deny any involvement.' Needless to say, no rescue bid was required or mounted. The public were safe.

After Adrian Juste in London played the last record and the News-beat jingle rang out and we were off the air, I thanked everyone involved in London and New York and meant it. We had a cup of coffee in the Deli and then headed back to the hotel. If that was the end of seventeen years on daytime radio, it did not feel like it, it didn't feel that special at all. The programme had been OK, nothing spectacular, though the live music had been superb and would event-ually be released on disc. But at least we hadn't allowed ourselves to roll about in nostalgia playing 'the best of' material, which would have been hideous. A good forty per cent of the music had been live and we had introduced two names who I believe in a few years' time will become substantial artists world-wide. We had all posed for the team photographs and later that night there would be a small dinner party at Cent' Anni in the Village, which would wrap things up nicely.

It felt very good, not to have to worry about what was planned for Monday's programme. I had signed a contract with Atlantic 252, so 'Our Tune' would live on and there would be an income which would leave me still able to afford the odd book from the Strand Book Store. Everything was complete, or almost.

It was a perfect, crisp day as we all left the Deli a little after seven o'clock in the morning. The traffic was just beginning to build up for the rush hour when, after we'd walked up to Columbus Circle and down Central Park to the Ritz Carlton, it struck me. After seventeen years and a final programme, I'd heard not a word from management in London. Not a phone call, not a message, nothing. An acknowl-edgement at the end of an Outside Broadcast is traditional, but on this occasion there had been silence. Even a handwritten note faxed to the hotel saying 'Now, fuck off' would have been an acknowl-edgement of some kind, but I guess I was expecting too much. The reality was that nobody in management felt that they could afford to be that generous. They had their futures to consider and paranoia was lying deeper than the carpet in the George Cinq in Paris. This pattern continued as other programmes came to an end and stole away.

My departure from Radio One was a contented business. I had been warned that times were changing and allowed by a comparatively amiable management to close down comparatively gracefully. It had been a pleasure to leave, not the station and the people I'd worked with, but what was becoming an increasingly tense and political atmosphere. Besides, I was knackered. I had never thought it would last this long, and there were other doors waiting to be opened.

To keep a radio station fresh, it is necessary to change personnel and formats. It is also true that Radio One had become less adventurous in the early nineties than it should have been. Heaven preserve me from the nostalgia buffs, but there is no such thing as a Golden Age for pop radio. It exists for the moment, just as its music does. The sheer joy of pop music is that it crystallises what it is, not what it was, and pop radio is exactly the same. So it is logical that there should be a high rate of turnover in music and on-air staff. But while I was treated well and considerately, for the others things were not to be so pleasant.

At a meeting of staff a few days before I left, Jackie Brambles asked Matthew Bannister if, now that Dave Lee Travis and I were going, that was the sum total of changes. He told her that he had no plans for any other alterations to the network. Jackie left two months later.

Gary Davis was told by Paul Robinson that his job was secure and that he was a highly valued member of the Radio One team. His contract was terminated a month later.

Bob Harris turned up for a meeting with Matthew Bannister to discuss his future. Matthew was at a showbiz lunch and didn't turn up for the meeting. Bob hung around for ninety minutes and then left Matthew's office and subsequently the network.

Adrian Juste was reassured that his future was safe and that he was part of the plans for the first quarter of 1994. Then, during a phone call from a junior executive, Adrian found he had been fired with only two weeks' notice. Matthew did not return his calls.

All this could be seen as part and parcel of life in an evolving radio station, and that's fine. My only reservation is to point out that people other than me were treated abominably and at best clumsily. There is always room for warning people that they may not be in place much longer. The kind of warning that I had.

In every radio and TV station that I have worked at it has been possible to strike a balance, where the pain of the departure of 'on air' or management personnel has been reduced.

It's an edgy little game of course, 'so and so is leaving to better his career', and inside the industry everyone is immediately aware of the truth behind the bland statement, but it helps the victims to keep their self-respect and that is a long-term investment, especially for the new management.

The next day, 23 October 1993, I flew to Pittsburgh to start work on the Christmas programme series about victims of the war in Bosnia. Simon Mayo took over the programme on Radio One the following Monday. Nothing much was changed, 'The Golden Hour' stayed in place and Simon's long-established shadow of 'Our Tune' occupied the same slot at eleven. The mix remained much as it had been, though two gagwriters were hired to sit in the reception area and write funnies for Simon. God, I wish I had had that luxury.

Following my long-held maxim that it really doesn't matter if you put a coffee cup on the radio at certain times of day, the same people will listen, more or less, nothing should have changed in audience terms. But something went wrong. Within three months, the audience for the show had tumbled by more than half a million. Mayo was a perfectly adequate broadcaster, so the explanation had to lie elsewhere.

Figures for the rest of the station's output also showed an increasing slide. As Matthew Bannister became more embattled and more heavily criticised for Radio One's sinking audience, instead of keeping out of the public eye and waiting for the audience to stabilise, he demonstrated his lack of experience as a Controller. With the help of his press officer, Jeff Simpson, he started to blame the outgoing management for the decrease in audience. However, a leak of the early 1994 ratings demonstrated that this was not the case and it seemed that the station might be in free fall.

Initially, Matthew made an uneasy appearance with Jonathon King on *The Late Show* on BBC2. I had been invited on to the show to debate with Matthew, but by this time I didn't feel like waving any more flags for Radio One as a music station, so JK was brought in.

It could well have been an uncomfortable experience for Matthew, but Jonathon, who is a generous soul, let him off very lightly. There was a *frisson* of excitement at the end of the segment when

Jonathon questioned Matthew about the inclusion of Shaggy as a nominee in the very British 'Brits' Awards. As an American, wasn't this a little odd? Matthew hadn't been briefed and knew nothing about it. It wasn't really worth fussing about, but on Monday morning the phones ran red hot from Matthew's office to anyone with any knowledge. Why hadn't Matthew been told and what were 'The Brits' going to do about it?

In truth, the days of Radio One having much influence over 'The Brits' were long gone. While the station was supporting and promoting the awards, it wasn't even broadcasting the ceremony – that commitment had been made by commercial television. Matthew was soothed and mollified by the awards committee. Shortly afterwards, a messenger from the committee arrived and asked for an assurance that Simon Mayo would not be involved in the station's coverage of the awards. It was felt that the aggression he had shown against artists in interviews on his programme since he'd assumed the job was less than constructive. Instead of Mayo, Radio One deputed Mark Goodier to do the job, one he did well.

A couple of weeks later the *Frost Programme* called and asked me to guest in a discussion on Radio One's future. Again I said, 'No thanks.' Matthew had also declined to appear when the researcher had called him. Later, Matthew made a surprisingly personal and petulant attack on me in the *News of the World*. But he and his adviser had not taken into account that old principle of having your cake and eating it. In a neat but rather unkind bit of footwork, the paper published his attacks on the old regime and simultaneously ran a long editorial criticising Matthew for dictating that 'listeners will get not what they want but what they ought to want'. It continued, 'If the long-term plan continues much longer, with its massive haemorrhage of talent, Mr Bannister will find himself presiding over Radio Zero.'

I was working in the south of France at the time and was sent a copy of both these articles in a fax sent from a Radio One machine. After this episode the drawbridge was well and truly pulled up and a rather obvious rethink went on.

At the end of February, Matthew asked Steve Wright for help and got it. Steve contributed a short article to the debate which appeared in *The Sunday Times*. Steve quite properly asked for time to be given to the new station to develop. Strangely, though perhaps with one eye on the future, Steve closed with the words 'we'll be right back', the line used at some stage or another by almost every broadcaster in commercial radio and television. *The Sunday Times* repeated the *News of the World*'s trick by running a cogently argued piece by Paul Donovan next to the one from Steve Wright. John Peel was wheeled out in the *Radio Times* to present the friendly corporate face of Radio One, but to me it was not terribly convincing.

Matthew then refused to appear on the Radio Four programme *Feedback* to answer criticisms and sent a statement instead. He began to rethink his strategy and rumour had him looking at the possibility of employing Jonathan Ross for a Sunday afternoon slot, as a method of pulling the figures up. Matthew attended the Radio Academy Conference in March, at which his decision-making and staffing attitudes were ferociously attacked by the previous Controller. He took this in comparatively good part though at the time, and given the bad press he was receiving, this must have been a Herculean task.

He also began to take a long-term interest in the playlist, which was being administered by his deputy Paul Robinson. This is the most important aspect of any radio station. The motivation to keep listening for anyone who may not like the DJ on duty, is the music the station plays.

Matthew's first query about the playlist was to ask why Richard Thompson didn't feature more heavily? Although the story whipped around the industry, no one present had the nerve to explain to Matthew's face. In an article written for the London *Evening Standard* he moaned about how tough things had been for him, though there was next to no comment on his changes and their effect on One FM.

He then took another, milder swing at me. At one internal meeting, he asked if there were any way of proving that 'Our Tune', which by this time was building an audience on one of his commercial rival stations, Atlantic 252, could be removed on the grounds that the copyright for the slot was owned by the BBC.

The problem for Matthew it seems to me has always been that he has never worked for a really accountable organisation as a really accountable broadcaster and that certainly is not the case now. When he was at London's Capital Radio, he had the commercially minded ex-BBC man Richard Park as his boss. He was significantly unsuccessful at improving the figures at Greater London Radio when he led that station, but of course he did not have to justify that issue to anyone but BBC management.

It seems to me that, had he made the inevitable and, for the most part, required changes with more tact and sympathy, or attempted in any way to garner the support of the staff and the audience in order to take them with him on his new philosophy, then perhaps he could have instituted exactly the same adjustments to the network that he did with a minimal loss of figures. I believe the unhappiness caused to the staff of Radio One at the time these changes were implemented was entirely unnecessary. Equally, there is an argument to be made for the idea that the public perception of management actions at the station contributed significantly to the collapse in figures, in that the audience saw the cracks in the façade of a united and user-friendly network.

However, things were settling down.

By March of 1994, the playlist had changed yet again, with a notably more commercial approach being taken. Bon Jovi broadcast from the Bahamas to One FM. This is what we call fun radio, and excellent stuff it was too. The station now seems to be going back to the job it does best, entertaining and innovating, in that order. As in all things, it is beginning to look as though the worst excesses are over, that someone, probably Liz Forgan, has had a severe word with Matthew and that things are sensibly returning to normal, with a perceptibly softer long-term view.

The next job for the management is to get back the audience that they have alienated. Even though there is a massive budget for advertising, and a considerable media propaganda machine within the BBC, I doubt, in these days of mass competition that an audience once lost will return easily, if at all. This is nothing to do with the competence or popularity of the current crop of broadcasters: most of them are excellent and present a fresh look. The problem is that audiences are promiscuous and any radio station relies on a bedrock of regulars, before being able to build on that with newcomers.

For many of the grass roots listeners, there is and will be for some time a nasty taste in the mouth at the mention of Radio One.

There is every reason for Radio One to exist, and this is all down to its programming. In that, I agree with John Birt utterly. One FM is less a jewel within the BBC than a rough diamond, but it has a place as important as any of the other radio networks. Radio One must innovate and bring its listeners the most eclectic mix of contemporary music, presented in as open and non-elitist a manner as possible. There can be no excuse for a bias towards metropolitan chic, and there can be no place for lame or badly researched attempts to outdo other networks in programming at which they are expert, and at which Radio One is plainly incompetent. These are just ego trips for immature management.

Radio One's job is music, the playing of it and the recording of it, much more than the spread of the already tarnished currency of political correctness or so-called youth culture. The nation needs Radio One and what it does best as much now as it ever did, if not more so. The crunch will come if audiences do not stabilise but continue to fall, and the station rejects so many of its listeners that it becomes difficult to justify as a frequency with a mass audience.

At that time, the question will be an economic one. Is it right to spend nearly £40 million per year – contributed as part of the licence fee by a complete cross section of the British public – on a station if it broadcasts only to an elite minority?

Oh, and the answer to the question, 'Have we just been through the Golden Age of broadcasting?' is 'No, Matilda, it never existed in the first place.'

Chapter 2

MY BIRTH CERTIFICATE says that I was born in Birmingham in 1946, but I only have a couple of memories of living there. I can just summon up an image of my leaning out of a second- or third-floor window and being mortified as the Rolo I was sucking fell from my mouth. And I can remember being surrounded by a group of women, all of them saying the kind of nice things you would say to a child of two or three. I hated it and them and hated the horrible feeling of claustrophobia and the carbolicky smell of them that went with the attention.

I am an only child and my parents were separated almost as soon as I was born. I was a bulge baby. Daddy came home from the war and I popped up to be greeted by the brave new world nine months later. God knows what makes two people come together in the first place and only they know the pressures that make them part, but at least I was proof of victory over the Germans in the Second World War.

If the omens were good then, along with the state of the country, I was sent to disprove them. I didn't have a particularly happy childhood. It wasn't my mother's fault, or my father's for that matter. Don't get the impression that I was badly treated, I certainly wasn't, I was just a crass failure at playing the part of being a child. Nearly all the males in my family are what is politely called 'late developers'. I would call us social and physical liabilities, unable to walk straight without falling over, unable to catch a ball or ride a bike, unable to lift a piece of cake from a plate without dropping it on someone's nice new carpet, unable to say the right thing at the right time. On top of all that, I did not look much. It was as though the Ministry of Health had a batch of reject bits and working on the basis of waste not want not, put them all together in as haphazard a way as possible.

The centrepiece of the family was undoubtedly my grandparents. Their nicknames, for which my uncle was responsible, were Chief and Queen – a perfect choice. They were essentially decent, good-humoured Edwardian people growing old in a pretty unattractive world. Both their families were made from strong, professional Manchester stock. If there was a middle of the middle class, we were there, bang in it.

My grandmother's ancestors, the Redfords, were always lawyers and civil servants. She claimed that it was the Redfords who spent their time in a tent just apart from the battlefield drawing up the peace treaty, while I suspect my grandfather's predecessors were out there getting their heads chopped off. I can claim that there was a Redford busy scribbling beside Wellington, and Queen always stoutly maintained that one of her forebears helped draw up the treaty at the Field of the Cloth of Gold. The Redfords were a respectable lot, and when there were no agreements to be drawn up on the battlefields, there was industry to be administered. For years, she got special treatment on British Rail, in part because she was old and they were tolerant, but also because she always reminded them loudly that her father had been chairman of the Great Western Railway. Once, when she was getting on in years and had come down to London for a weekend with me, I found my grandmother at Euston station talking very loudly and clearly to a young Ghanaian porter about her father and how well he always looked after his station staff during the Great War. The poor man was very gracious with her but highly relieved when I took her off his hands.

My grandfather's predecessors were a different kettle of fish. A ragtag army of gamekeepers and semi-villains in the eighteenth and early nineteenth century, they had eventually pulled themselves up by the bootstraps and become prosperous in the cotton trade during the last years of Victoria's reign. There was much bitterness as there always is in families. My grandfather never forgave his autocratic father for taking him away from school when he was twelve and forcing him to learn the business from the bottom up. My great-grandfather had a wicked temper, something that he handed on to his descendants. I never met him, of course, but my grandfather's description and obvious intense dislike of him make him as real to me as any Dickensian villain. He was the kind of man who would never evict anyone where pulling the house down around their ears was possible. If there are dark areas lurking about in the backs of our minds and if it is possible to summon them up as people, then my great-grandfather is a good prospect for exhumation as a spluttering, evil-tempered wraith. As a child, I read a good deal of the Victorian novels that lined his bookcase, Walter Scott, John Buchan and so on, and it may be that their dark and brooding villains affected my view of great-grandad.

All his life Chief felt undereducated, though he read widely, and his bitter disappointment at the loss of his education has affected the family down the years. At the age of twelve, Chief's first job of the day was to tack up the horse and cart for his father to drive to the office. Although he fought in the First World War, he never spoke about what he saw and that's a loss that I am only now beginning to grasp.

My grandmother lost a brother and never forgot the generation of young men who died. Neither did we, their photographs were on the radiogram in the corner of the living room. Carefully posed young men in Sam Brownes, expressionless members of the family lost in shadows, whom Queen would occasionally identify one by one.

Chief was a square peg in a round hole, and life on the Manchester Cotton Exchange with its top hats and post-war spivvery was almost unbearable to him. So, when he met my grandmother, he took his inheritance early and bought a farm. His timing was perfect for a man with no great financial sense, and he took to farming just before the crash of 1929.

They were an astonishing couple, as unalike as it is possible to be and yet somehow they survived together and made their relationship work. He was fascinated by the art of breeding Guernsey cattle, not particularly taken with 'abroad' and happy to live his life out on his own patch. An intelligent, endlessly polite man, he was physically large, though not tall, and had a light Lancashire accent which he kept all his life. She was thoroughly emancipated, and, I suspect, difficult and strong-minded before she met him. Part of her independence consisted of going to college in an age when this was not encouraged, and her parents would have been a good deal happier if she had waited for a suitable young man. She learned and then taught physical education, working 'for the good of her soul' in Liverpool in the early part of the century. She had lead a protected and secure middle-class life and she was appalled at the poverty that she saw. But she was always tougher than my grandfather, who had been equally horrified by unemployment lines and the miners' marches in the twenties and thirties and never failed to remind me about them. These were two remarkable people.

Early in their marriage, they realised that they didn't really share many interests. 'It was when we were in Rome in the Sistine Chapel,' Queen would tell me, 'and while I was admiring the ceiling. Your grandfather had managed to find a man who also bred Guernsey cattle and was discussing blood-lines with him behind a pillar. I realised then that he wouldn't be the perfect companion.' So for the rest of their lives they organised themselves around their differences. She would go on a holiday, preferably abroad with a friend, and when she returned, the two of them would disappear to Devon or somewhere equally safe in their little caravan.

They had three children, my uncle, my mother and a boy called Martin who died in childhood of diphtheria. There was always a photograph of Martin – a black and white one of a mischievous and beautiful-looking boy astride a bicycle wearing one of those white Christopher Robin suits – on the mantelpiece of the morning room. As a child, I knew that he had died in the early 1930s, but I also knew not to ask too much. It was only after Chief and Queen had both died that I heard the full story, of how the boy had become ill and then, suddenly during the night had become much, much worse. How my grandfather had driven off frantically into the night to find a doctor and how it had all been in vain. Queen never got over it and I doubt that my grandfather did. He never spoke about Martin. Occasionally she would, in no great detail but wistfully and sadly.

Following my grandfather's obsession with education, my mother Joan was sent to Badminton and learnt to be herself there. She went up to Newnham College, Cambridge during the war and remembers fire-watching over the Bristol Channel as a student evacuee. My uncle wasn't so lucky. The Second World War rolled along just in time for everyone to be too busy for him. Like most of the males in the family, he was a slow starter and his early life and lack of start-ling success, mirrored my later experience.

I was brought up after the war and lived in the shadow of it until I was twelve or thirteen years old. It affected everyone so deeply that the whole country was steeped in the Second World War until the sixties swept the obsession away. Everyone had their own memories of the war, and seemed to have been a part of it. My childhood was full of gossip about what so and so did during the war, or more ominously, what they didn't do. Time had warmed the memories, and all I heard was how everyone had pulled together and how good they had all been. The conversations were glowing and full of reminiscences about the good times, but they would always end with the more dreadful aspects. I found this very puzzling. There was a lady in the next village who had had a child by an American GI. Everyone knew and was sympathetic, they spoke about her behind her back almost as one would about a very dim child.

As kids we played in the backyard of the war. In Birmingham, I can just remember the ruins and the piles of broken bricks and tattered houses that were left-over bombsites. At home in Shropshire, the enormous drums of concrete that had been left by the side of the road ready to be heaved into the path of approaching German tanks, were still there, waiting for the brambles and greenery to grow over them and turn them into just another part of the countryside.

By the end of the thirties, the family had moved from a farm they owned in Moberley in Cheshire to become tenants of a three-hundred-acre farm in Shropshire. Home for them was a long, loping farmhouse that started in the thirteenth century as a chapel at one end and became a nineteenth-century house at the other. The farmhouse was in the centre of the village and therefore perfect as a local administration centre. My grandmother and grandfather both felt intensely that they were 'part of the war effort', as the whole village did. If the invasion came, then our farmhouse was critical to the defence of the realm! Up in the attic was enough dried food to keep the village fed for a few weeks, and my grandfather would presumably have taken to the nearest hills, which were a good few miles away, and fought a rearguard action with his shotgun.

In my childhood, the stories were retold every Sunday lunch-time. How once a German aircraft had frantically jettisoned a bomb, and it landed in the field behind the farmhouse but not exploded. My grandfather, the vicar and half the village had assembled around the crater to examine, poke and debate the bomb and its future. 'It's a dud' they all agreed. An hour later, at lunch-time, the bomb blew up and took all the windows in the village with it.

A number of prisoners of war worked on the farm in the forties. 'The Germans,' my grandmother would say with an element of surprise in her voice, 'were so rude and sulky, but the Italians were delightful.' There was a sense of bafflement that the Germans could be ungracious about being prisoners of war when they were being fed well. I remember my grandfather grumbling that, 'They never said thank you for anything!' There was always a feeling with my grandparents that there was never any need to be rude, even if you were a POW. They saw the Italians, though, as totally different and more socially acceptable. They were as popular as they could be under the circumstances. Several Italian POWs settled in the district and married local girls after the war. When children were born, the whole family would turn up at the farm and show off the new arrivals to my grandmother.

Thirty years after the end of the war and up in the attic where the emergency supplies of dried milk had been kept, I found a bundle of pouches and sealed envelopes with 'Secret. Only to be opened in case of invasion' stamped all over them. I was delighted, and couldn't wait to find out exactly what *had* been planned should the Hun knock on the back door of Church Farm. My grandmother was horrified at the idea of opening them, even thirty years on when their value would have been entirely historical. 'They were given to me in trust,' she said, and grabbing the papers she made a neat bonfire in the garden and burnt the lot. They were decent people, not the sort who would betray a trust. By the time I came along, they had settled into their lives and my grandfather's obsession with breeding had produced a milking herd of Guernsey cattle and an expensive interest in taking them to shows all over the country.

My mother and I lived at number 13 Church Street in Southwold in Suffolk. She taught at a girls' public school a mile or so outside the town, though she really wanted to go back to farming. The railway had been removed from Southwold years before, the town was splendid in its isolation, stuck at the end of the world. It had once been an extremely fashionable resort, a sort of reliable but upmarket alternative to Yarmouth. Getting there was a long hard haul, involving a train to Ipswich and then another slower train to Halesworth, where you waited and waited for the bus to Southwold.

Southwold was polite, discreet and quiet, with an air of gentility and a desire to keep the pre-war standards up. The beach huts at Eastern Bavants were rarely overbooked and neither was the Swan Hotel. Church Street, where we lived, runs off the main square. At one end, where there is now a supermarket, there used to be a fish and chip shop and a huge shed for smoking herring. At the other end, there was and still is a brewery and a fish shop. The combination of smells – fish and chips, burning oak chippings and hops being turned into real beer – reached from one end of the street to the other.

My mother and I lived in the middle of all this, in a tiny weaver's cottage, with gaps in the walls so huge that she used to stuff blankets in them to stop the wind howling up the little winding stairs. Life was pretty ordinary, with the occasional hiccup now and then. We didn't have a radio, and the idea of actually owning a television in those far-off days was not even worth considering.

My mother kept a horse for herself and a pony for me just across the river Blythe, and caused me endless embarrassment by insisting on turning up outside my school on her day off, riding her horse and leading my pony. It was a well-intentioned gesture, but it was the last thing I wanted. I desperately wanted to be ordinary and able to play football without making a total hash of it. The pony seemed to emphasise the distance between the other kids and me. Mind you, once I was up on his back and riding down the old disused railway lines by the sea, there was magic in the air. The horses were a major part of our lives.

One night both horses got out of their field and on to the road, causing panic and alarms in the next village. The constabulary were called and, confronted with a serious incident like this, had to act. A very embarrassed copper called at number 13 with a summons accusing my mother of 'not keeping animals in secure accommodation'. She was to appear before the magistrate. The lace curtains of Church Street were atwitch. On the day of the trial, there could be no question, she was as guilty as sin and was fined £2.10s. My mother nearly caused a riot by producing a five-pound note and asking for change. A court official had to be sent over to the Swan to get the cash.

My parents were still in contact at this time and making an effort to see if they had any future together. I remember my father as a very large, dark and frightening man when he first arrived. The poor fellow tried very hard, but being a timid child, I didn't care for him at all. I didn't understand what his role in my life was, so I had no idea how to react to him.

He took me out a couple of times. Once we went to Ipswich and I embarrassed him by refusing the offer of shrimps fresh off a little fishing trawler on the quayside. There was one of those family scenes that happen in every supermarket every Saturday, with him trying to be nice and tempt me with a bowl of shrimps and me rejecting the nasty pink things out of hand. We nearly missed the last train back to Halesworth and I remember him picking me up, flinging open the carriage door as the train began to move and hurling me bodily inside, before clambering in himself.

I fear I was a great disappointment to him. He probably visualised his offspring, like the son of some Greek god, running and laughing alongside him, the wind whistling through his golden locks. The reality was me and a pretty rotten reality it must have been. I wanted so much to be and do what was expected, but for the most part I wasn't quick enough or charming enough for him.

Like so many other families in the fifties, we never talked about problems, so I never discovered when the final split happened. He simply stopped coming and I knew better than to ask why. My mother was far too good a person to attack him after he had gone, she simply never mentioned him. Occasionally my grandparents would recall what he had been like when he had come to the farm, and their housekeeper would always say how my mannerisms were like his. I used to think quietly that he must be a rum sort of bloke if he walked around nervously twitching as I tended to. I didn't miss him, or create fantasies about him when I was a child. I grew to loathe him, because he was never there to talk to and I became convinced that he didn't give a damn. That at least gave me something to be miserable about whenever I was feeling self pitying.

They knew that there was going to be a hell of a gale a couple of days before the big one hit on 3 February 1953. Southwold was an old town and it had been around long enough to know exactly how to batten down its hatches and protect itself. For us kids it was seventh heaven watching the excitement as sandbags were put in place and windows boarded up. Along with my best friend, I clambered up to Eastern Bavants, past the flagpole where the Union Jack usually fluttered and the cannon stood, a hostage from an earlier battle and now used for fundraising for the Lifeboat Service. There, far below us, the men were emptying the beach huts and scrambling up the hill to dump their loads of deckchairs and knick-knacks on the pavement at the top. 'Out of the way, kids, out of the way.' Then we scampered back into the town, where serious-faced men were talking about what might happen that night.

My mother had made plans to go to the cinema with friends. One of her characteristics is an absolute firmness that if an arrangement has been made, then it should be followed through. While I was upstairs in bed that night, terrified at the noise, and the babysitter was downstairs, my mother was sitting in the local cinema, together with half the population of Southwold, unable to hear a word of the soundtrack. But those were the days when you did not complain, you sat there and convinced yourself and your friends that you were having a whale of a time. So, even though the wind was whipping up the sea and Southwold's defences were crumbling, nobody moved in the old cinema.

I will never forget the racket that the sea and the wind created that night. For a six-year-old child it was as though the world was coming to an end. The booming sound as the waves struck the sea wall and the scream of the wind grew louder and more insistent as the night wore on. The old house was shaking and every loose window or latch was rattling and banging as though hell was opening and letting up the Devil himself. In the morning all was chaos and water. There was water everywhere. Southwold was cut off from the outside world and several people had been drowned in the flimsy houses that had been built just behind the freshly breached sea wall.

'I've seen a body, I've seen a body,' my best friend called to me. He always managed to go one better than the rest of us.

It was much worse along the coast and over the sea in Holland, where the dykes had been breached and hundreds had been lost, but for us kids it was magical. There was *no school*. This was unheard of. Because my mother didn't have a radio, we had to go down to a friend's house and listen to the BBC news. 'Not much use,' my mother grumbled afterwards, and not for the last time.

After we had checked that everyone we knew was OK, there was the matter of the horses a couple of miles away. Were they all right? There was only one way to find out, and that was to go and see, but the floodwaters lay between us and them. At about midday, I was standing at the edge of the sea that was once the river Blythe, with Mrs Dawson holding my hand, and weeping as my mother was taken away from me in a huge American army six-wheeler that was ferrying essential civilians around. I never found out how she persuaded them that she was essential, but she can be very persuasive when she wants.

Things settled down over the next few days and gradually normality returned. A man came round to our school and told us all that we should not drink from the tap, and to only drink water that had been boiled. If we did not obey his instructions we would get a horrible disease. As soon as class was over, we all rushed out to the cloakrooms to try the tap water and then checked each other's tongues for spots. The people who had died were buried and the local families who had lost relatives up and down the coast slowly got back to normal as the summer arrived.

My mother and I went back to Shropshire. She had never cared greatly for teaching and had always wanted to work on the farm. Now she had persuaded her parents that this was a good idea, and we popped the two horses into an enormous horsebox and, with me sitting on the engine, we drove back to Shropshire. The street-lighting was pretty inadequate in the fifties and the drive was a real adventure. As we drove and I alternately dozed or watched villages picked out by the headlights disappearing into the shadows, this felt like a new start. For years as a child, the greatest thrill was to be allowed to travel in the horse or cattle box to and from shows. I would sit over the engine, or high up above the animals in the back on the ledge where the hay and the equipment was kept and watch the world roll by. If the show lasted for two or three days, there was always the joy of sleeping rough in the back of the box and eating baked beans in the stockmans' canteen.

I was seven years old when we moved back to Shropshire and almost at once I was sent to prep school as a boarder. It probably seemed a good idea at the time, but it was a disaster that took me years to recover from. I was a year younger than my schoolmates and unable to cope with this strange masculine world and all its rituals, so I tried to put up the shutters, but that didn't work. The staff encouraged a 'sense of community', which meant being part of every-thing. I was far too small, spindly and unco-ordinated to be a suc-cessful part of anything, and instead of being challenged by finding myself bottom of the heap, I gave up and stayed there.

What I needed was something to give me confidence, something I could be good at, but I didn't find it there. The boys all seemed much larger than me and much more able, and I felt like an undersized country bumpkin. I had been protected in Southwold by being just another kid from East Anglia who barely knew how to do up his shoe-laces. Now I was smaller and younger than the other children and I had a rough time. The school was run on traditional lines, which meant that anyone senior could thrash the living daylights out of the next tier down and there was no one more junior than me.

After two miserable years, I obtained my release papers, was taken away and sent to the local school to prepare for my eleven plus. It was here that God and I came to an agreement. Education was the focus of everything I knew. Back at home, my grandfather would remind me of the chances he had missed and my grandmother would encourage me as much as she could to do well. And then there was my mother. She is a strong and very logical woman and, all her life, when she has set her mind to anything, she has simply set about calmly achieving it. She's not ruthless in any way, just single-minded. Failure isn't part of her make-up and once she has worked out what she is going to do, or what her opinions are, she hangs on like a limpet, there's no moving her.

I rang her from Moscow the night that the Red Flag stopped fluttering over the Kremlin. Our relationship was much better by this time and I felt able to chuckle gently to a life-long socialist about the collapse of the Red Empire. She paused for a moment when I told her what was happening and then laughed. 'No, no, you can't blame the system, just because it fell into the wrong hands,' she said, and went about her business with her principles untouched by circumstance.

I really believe that when I was a child, she found it hard to accept that I simply wasn't as quick or determined as she was. Apart from a parental impatience, which anyone can understand, I think she couldn't grasp that, for example, I was virtually innumerate. And, to be fair, I wasn't the most persistent of children, I tended to work on the principle of 'if at first you don't succeed, give up, there's no point in continuing to make a fool of yourself'. It must be incredibly frustrating to have a child who looks at you with total bewilderment when you find whatever it is blindingly obvious. I'm still a bit careful with her about this. On the occasions when I have bought her a meal at the local restaurant, my hands have gone under the table as I've added up the bill on my fingers.

A childhood on a farm sounds like a blissful existence, and so it can be. In the fifties, almost nothing was a no go area. There was little or no consideration of what might be dangerous. 'Use your intelligence and don't get in the way of anything bigger and faster than you,' someone once told me. Certainly, the idea of a Health and Safety executive had not struck anybody as a good one.

As a kid I rocketed around driving a little Ferguson thirty-five tractor when I was allowed, delivering hay or moving equipment. I once made a serious and almost terminal misjudgement driving back under the arch into the farmyard with a front-end loader attached. When I had driven off earlier, the loader had fitted perfectly underneath the arch, which carried the main support beam for the whole house. What I hadn't allowed for on my return was the fact that the ground sloped upwards and therefore the clearance before that beam was a foot or so less. I careered through the arch at the intoxicating speed of about fifteen miles an hour and then BANG, the loader hit the main beam with enormous force. The whole house shook and the beam moved several feet outwards with a ghastly cracking sound, hanging over the edge of its supports. Silence. Then the sound of running feet, followed more ponderously by my grandfather's slow march. A small crowd of observers gathered. They all looked up at the beam hanging there and then at the rest of the house, hanging by the beam. My grandfather surveyed the surveyors and looked at me. He seemed to be about to say something, but went very red in the face instead and walked quietly away. I got off the tractor and knew better than to say a word. My uncle climbed into the seat and spent the next hour toing and froing with the front-end loader, banging the beam back into place. The subject was never mentioned again.

Today, the whole organisation of the farm would look prehistoric, like something out of Thomas Hardy. The emphasis was on my grandfather's beloved Guernseys, their welfare and success as breeding stock came first. All the cattle had their own names and most of them would come to call. One had cataracts and had become blind, but she'd adjusted perfectly. You could whistle to her and she would make her way carefully down the barbed-wire fence, walking just closely enough to it to feel the shards against her skin. Then she would walk down the farm alleyways in exactly the same way and into her stand, and chomp away at the grains that had been put in front of her, waiting patiently to be chained up.

For milking, each cow had its own stand and its own ration, carefully created in the meal house next to the cowsheds, with necessary vitamins added individually. The milk from each cow went into a bucket and was then laboriously poured through a sieve into a churn which stood at the corner of the milking shed. Then the churn would be rolled over the concrete ridges of the yard into the dairy for bottling by hand. Rolling that damned churn on an icy day was a skilled business, requiring great concentration. If you stopped thinking about what you were doing for an instant, the churn would slide through your fingers. It happened to me once and I have never forgotten the horror as I watched the lid come off and twelve gallons of fresh milk pour all over the yard.

By today's farming standards this was madness, but it was what

Chief adored and the legacy he left is not a bad one. He believed passionately in kindness to animals and he also believed in the debt that one owed to them. The responsibility for their welfare was totally ours, whether it was a house dog, a cat, a horse or a cow, they had priority and must be looked after before anything else was done. Coming back from a long day, soaking wet and tired, on a horse that had played up for the entire time, was unlikely to endear you to the animal, but woe betide you if that horse wasn't dried, fed and settled down in its stable before you came into the warmth of the kitchen.

Death, like life and sex, is omnipresent in the country. 'They're always shagging, ill, getting better or dying,' an old man in the village said to me once, and Chief's attitude to the treatment of animals covered death too. An animal that had given good service would never be sent away in the knacker's van for slaughter, but was put down at the farm. Totally unrealistic but it was part of his make-up and he was the boss.

At home I now had a radio in my bedroom. It was an old mottled brown Bakelite thing, with a dial full of mysterious names that meant nothing to me. It was decrepit enough to need a few minutes for the valves to warm up before you could expect much from it. The radio became a focus, only in the way that a child's bedroom is his territory. This was the much vaunted Golden Age of radio. Golden probably because of its rarity, there was so little of it. This was the era of the short radio drama aimed at a mass audience and most evenings it was possible to find something on the Light programme that involved blood-curdling screams and derring-do on the high seas.

Children's Hour was required listening in those days, when none of us realised quite how patronising the title was. The magic lay in being swept along by the broadcasters on the tide of their enthusiasm and immaculate production. Of course it was a one-eyed and middle class vision of Britain, but *Children's Hour* somehow worked a particular magic in placing me slap bang in the middle of the action.

I didn't notice that Hereward the Wake and Henry VIII, Bonnie Prince Charlie and Admiral Nelson all boasted the same actorish cut-glass accent, or that there was a certain simplification in the matter of who was right and who was wrong. I also didn't question for a moment the Admiral's motives in asking Hardy for a kiss, but wept along with, I assume, millions of others. When it came to the matter of values, *Children's Hour* had it down pat. Royalty was invariably right and peasants always wrong, though sometimes this was mitigated by the explanation of their being 'misguided'. But I was swept along by the scale and the excitement of what was offered to me at a time when Britain was bent on being as dull as possible.

Children's Hour also introduced me to poetry, which was not the most fashionable art form in the country at that time, and for that alone I owe David Davis a great deal. I once met him in the seventies, but as a fan I was too tongue-tied to say thank you.

Just occasionally there would be something that hypnotised me. Once, late on a winter's night, I was alone and a probably hammy dramatisation of the hoary old Agatha Christie story *Murder In Mesopotamia* was broadcast, in which the victim was dispatched by a stone dropped on his head, after his attention was drawn to the window by a tapping sound. Whoever produced the play had gone to a good deal of trouble to create a splendidly sickening squelch as the rock hit the victim's head. I was eight years old and transfixed with horror. My bedroom had brightly coloured curtains based on The Bayeux Tapestry, which would move slightly on windy, wintry nights. That night, the light stayed on way after the Home Service had closed down, and I sat hypnotised by fear as the curtains swung noisily this way and that. I survived, but it took years before I plucked up the courage to stick my head out of the window.

Certainly, there was just about the same proportion of dross on the radio then as there is now. No more, no less. Even as an eight-year-old I had the sense to sneer at 'The Chapel in the Valley', in which some old duffer – Sandy MacPherson – played the organ on a background of bird song on an effects disc. But kids are unique in their ability to absorb rubbish and not let it contaminate them.

As the family were not rich, an eleven plus pass was vital. If I did not get that, much like the doors of hell opening up for the good Catholics down the road who failed to make up some imagined sin for Confession, I would go straight from the village school to Hell, which was a secondary modern, and that would be the end of me. The message was drummed into me day and night, and finally I did a deal with God at St Bartholomew's Church, just over the road from the farm. I knew that I wouldn't be able to achieve on my own what was so important to my family. So, if God would get me a pass, then I would believe in Him, go to Africa as a missionary and save a lot of souls. God never actually signed a contract, of course, but from where I sat, in the front pew, I hoped that He'd honour the deal. I passed and thought a good deal about our agreement over the next six months. Pretty quickly I came to the conclusion that I had done all the work and that I didn't want to be a missionary anyway. So God and I parted company and we haven't spoken since, more's the pity.

Whether or not secondary modern school would have been any worse than what was to come I cannot tell. All I know is that one of my friends from the village school went to the local secondary modern and is now a happily married and highly successful accountant. He's worked hard and achieved a good deal in his life. I suspect that he is a great deal more at ease with himself than I am with myself.

I believe this idea of separating the so-called 'bright' and 'thick' into different schools was an appalling piece of social engineering. It left those of us in the grammar school, with our silly little betassled caps, being taught to feel wildly superior, and it quite properly drove the secondary modern kids to acts of mayhem and violence if we came within a hundred yards of their territory. It was a ludicrous policy, to have a grammar school with delusions of grandeur posing as a public school, but without the time, the cash or the committed staff to provide the background that would give us poor sad lumpkins protection when we stepped out into our own lives. We were being prepared for a world where the old-boy system supported you, just about as long as you supported it. But the fatal flaw was that we could never really be members of the system, we'd always just be jumped-up grammar-school boys struggling to make a crust. It was endlessly drummed into us how lucky we were to be there, and then, with a nod to the secondary modern school down the road, not there.

Teaching for the most part involved, for no apparent reason, learning by rote. We had to learn Latin and were never told why. There is every reason to be taught Latin and it can be an exciting and mysterious path to go down, but only if you are invited by someone who cares and is prepared to make the language intriguing. We simply had a blackboard and our verbs to decline.

There were some useful and creative people at school who were willing to try, even with a no-hoper like me. My English master introduced me to the cinema and suddenly a new world opened up. I had been before, of course, life wasn't that primitive, but I had never seen much more than the latest suitable release, accompanied by my mother or as part of a family visit. This was another world, and Saturday afternoons after rugby became a godsend. There were so many bonuses in going to the movies. For a start, I was no danger to anyone in the cinema, I couldn't trip up, spill or break anything, I was there in the secure warmth of the place and safe from myself for a couple of hours. I loved being there and like any healthy kid I was totally uncritical. I saw everything and anything and I began to learn from those old black and white films lessons that I wasn't getting at school.

With the help of one teacher I was seeing movies with a different point of view. Not just the thrillers and romances that I loved, but films from the Soviet Bloc – Eisenstein's *The Battleship Potemkin*, *Alexander Nevsky* and *Ivan the Terrible*. I saw films from India, such as *The World of Apu*, and old Italian movies like *Bicycle Thieves* and Jacques Tati's French comedies. They gave me a totally new outlook, because they were about people whose emotions I thought I understood but who looked and behaved differently. Their lives weren't as dogmatic as mine. They lived in a much more exciting world than mine or the world inhabited by Sandra Dee and Doris Day, which was supposed to be fun, exciting and desirable. These people lived edgily, their lives were really exciting, not like the Second World War heroics that dominated our lives at the local Clifton cinema, or those equivalent and endless two-page spreads in the *Sunday Express* commemorating some battle somewhere.

I started reading almost anything I could get my hands on about 'the other person's point of view' and slowly came to understand that although my teachers were well intentioned, they were unadventurous, tired and bored. They didn't want trouble and so it was easier for them to force the party line down our throats than challenge us in any way. The last thing they wanted was awkward questions, so they made life easy to digest and the past as well. I was a stupid country boy, but even I knew I was being fed a line of intellectual Mogadon. It was all so simplistic, like a Western, there were the bad guys and good guys. The British always wore the white hats, though sometimes even we threw up a bad penny. But he wouldn't last long and he'd be swallowed up in an orgy of niceness by the rest of us. Given half a chance and a decent crack of the whip we British could deal with any villainy in double-quick time. It was crazy, but we were taught that we were still the world's policemen and its conscience too. Viewed from this perspective, we were always seen to be the seventh cavalry riding to the rescue at the last minute. Sometimes we blundered a bit, but it was always heroic blundering and occasionally even amusing, so that took the sting out of the story. Officers were gentlemen and the troops were for the most part a decent bunch, even if young Attenborough needed a swift slap from his CO to bring him to his senses.

We didn't talk about the Irish question too much, we hurried over Israel. The Boer War was unmentionable, as were the Nazi concentration camps, and the slave trade was solved by comparing the Dutch and the Belgians' habits with those of William Wilberforce. I only learned, for example, of the true bitterness and sadness of Gallipoli years later from an old Australian I met in Brisbane in 1970. His friends had all been killed and he could never quite bring himself to forgive and forget. 'It's nothing personal against you, old son,' he would say, 'it's just that the bloody Brits turned us into cannon fodder and never said they were sorry.'

The view at school was the old Imperial one; we never actually wanted to hurt anyone, but sadly and from time to time it proved to be a bitter necessity. And that was the nub of it, history reduced to a fairy story. That way, everything that mattered, all the nastiness and horror, was diluted, which left understanding invalid. There were no thrills or heroes for us to latch on to, because they had nothing really to fight against. All these cardboard figures had to do was hang around and wait awhile until the British arrived and everything would be OK. Even to my pathetically inexperienced ears this was patent bullshit.

I had seen some form of reality up there on the big screen when the Polish patriots in *Kanal* had become trapped in the sewers and died. Their death hadn't been pretty and the British hadn't turned up on time. To an eleven-year-old boy there had been something contrarily proper in the fact that those patriots didn't do their Hollywood number and croak with not a smudge of make-up or a wisp of hair out of place. They were bloody angry about it.

Then there were books. Not just John Read, but O'Casey and Orwell, and everything they had to say conflicted with the assumptions I was stuck with at school. We couldn't be that good and in most cases the other guys couldn't be that bad. It was all such juvenile stuff, but while I was struggling with my lack of faith and trust in what I was being taught, first Profumo resigned and then Kennedy was shot.

Yes, I can remember exactly where I was when the announcement was made and no, I'm not going to bore you with it. Both events made me realise that there was more to life than was being even hinted at at my school.

In the wake of Profumo, along came *That Was The Week That Was*. This was the proof that we needed out there in the sticks, that we were right and they were wrong! We kids snuggled around our televisions, cosy in the accepted knowledge that it *was* all a plot and that the bastards *were* out to get us. But now at least we knew that other people knew, so maybe if we all got together . . . no, no, there was homework to do. But it was a start.

Both events and the sweet smell of decay around the government of the time proved to us that people with influence were usually liars. They had nothing more on their side than hot air, powerful corruption and the desire to stay where they were. This convenient revelation didn't stop the rot at school, and it certainly didn't induce rebellion.

Of course there was the radio and music. My family were never very keen on music of any kind; they simply didn't have time for it. Music was valid in ballet and tolerable in opera just so long as it did not obscure the words. So it was radio and one particular programme, probably forgotten now by most people, that opened the door for me.

Charles Parker developed an occasional series of programmes in the late fifties for the BBC called the *Radio Ballads* that moulded tapes of real, everyday people speaking about their life experiences with music composed by Ewan MacColl and Peggy Seeger into an hour long feature focusing on one subject. Its reality was brought home to me once when I was waiting for a train on New Street Station in Birmingham late one night in the early sixties and two policemen suddenly pushed through the crowd accompanying a boxer, still in his dressing gown with an overcoat thrown over the top, and helped him on to the Glasgow train. He was battered, bruised and bloody and the two men with the boxer were encouraging him as he clambered up into his seat. He had obviously lost his match and as the crowd moved back to let him on to the train, there wasn't so much a sigh of sympathy for him, as a murmur of horror at the state he was in. A few days later I heard Parker's programme *The Fight Game*, and for the first time I got a glimpse of how powerful words and music combined could be. It is just an old radio programme now which is occasionally dragged out of the archives on an anniversary or to celebrate radio's glory days. But even as an aged show from the days of wireless, it still packs a powerful punch. This was not an elitist, innaccessible series by the way. 'The First Time

Ever I Saw Your Face' was one of the songs MacColl and Seeger wrote for the Ballads.

The *Radio Ballads* were the motivation that took me off to see MacColl and so many other great folk and blues artists in Birmingham. That in turn gave me a taste for the stuff the charts were made of at that time, which led to listening to pirate radio, and a taste for Bob Dylan. And that is how I found myself learning my first big lesson about the rock business. Along with some friends, I somehow got tickets to see Dylan in concert on his first tour of Britain in 1965. This was to be the main event of the year and I settled into my seat high up in the corner of the auditorium virtually trembling with anticipation.

Yes, I enjoyed it and yes, Dylan was on superb form. I had a great time, but truth to tell, I was bored before the end of the two hours and in the years that have passed since, I have come to the conclusion that you really do have to be a huge fan of someone to sit through two and a half hours of their music without squirming occasionally. Rock concerts have become such a ritual in the last thirty years: dreadful journey to location, overpriced seat, getting ripped off at burger bar, lousy seating, disgusting sound. Then, band half an hour late on stage, with much fiddling about between numbers. Band disappears after an hour and a quarter whilst audience, fully aware that there *has* to be an encore applauds desultorily. Band returns and outstays its welcome by playing another hour-long set. The audience meanwhile is begging for mercy and wanting to catch the last bus home.

I have never fully understood the obsession some people have about all musicians having to sound and look great on stage. If it works on record, that's good enough for me and better for the millions who will buy the record, rather than the thousands who will see the artist live. I learned early on that I loved music, adored records and could only fully enjoy live bands when I was a total besotted fan. I finally came to this conclusion only a few years ago, when I was in Tokyo for a Phil Collins concert. Now he has always seemed a pleasant enough man to me, but sitting on seats premoulded to the Japanese idea of the size of a pair of human buttocks was agony for me and my team. Kenton Allan, my producer, who overflowed his seat in exactly the same way as me gave up and went out for a smoke. I sat in agony and held the flag for both of us. The concert was as good as you would expect from Collins, but by the end of it

I had a permanent reminder of the seat imprinted on my backside and a desperate longing to shout, 'No thanks,' when he asked the audience if they would like another number. But back to school.

For a while, to prevent joining the Cadet Corps, I toyed with the idea of being a conscientious objector and then rejected it. Although it meant that you spent Wednesday afternoons gardening, you were considered a pansy by the rest of the school if you made that choice. So I marched about in my ill-fitting uniform and lay in bushes pretending that I cared whether or not I was shot.

In time-honoured tradition, one of our PT masters was a crazed and frustrated youngish man. Years ago I would have generously said that he was trying to suppress latent homosexuality, but as time has passed I have changed my attitude, he was just a mindless Nazi. Every boys' school had one, it seemed to be a requirement of the Department of Education then and probably still is. Mr Hadley's idea of fun was to 'demonstrate' a protective move in boxing. For this, he would select one of the less able-bodied boys and instruct him to take a swing. When the hapless youth aimed a wild punch, our PT master would duck half-heartedly as the fist whistled a million miles from his head, land his own vicious low blow and walk away leaving the poor kid winded. 'There, boys, that's how you do it,' and he'd smile.

I was there when he got his comeuppance. Hadley had started to work on a tall, gangly, bespectacled lad. 'Right, boy, come on hit me, do your best. Come on, you little pansy, take a punch, you useless idiot.' Suddenly, and I suspect for the only time in his life, years of frustrated inadequacy boiled up inside him and the boy hauled off and bopped Hadley an almighty punch on the nose. The PT master collapsed in a heap, blood pouring from his nose. He lay on the gym floor for a moment, and then said rustily, 'Very good, boy, very good. Class dismissed.' It wasn't exactly the revolution but it was stirring stuff, marred only slightly by the hero of the hour bursting into tears. It was a rare triumph over the system, but it wasn't from me. I wasn't a very effective revolutionary, I never actually assassinated the headmaster, or waved a red flag during morning assembly. Though God knows, having suffered a beating after being found drunk in the bar of the theatre at Stratford-upon-Avon, I would have fire-bombed the school if I thought I could get away with it.

As a typically difficult, self-obsessed teenager, I sulked and grew increasingly to hate school and the idea that I was being moulded for a life that I wasn't certain I wanted to be involved in and, knowing the kind of teachers I was dealing with, a life that might have been extinct for ten years. It seems crazy now, but we had a thing called a careers officer who would talk to fifteen-year-olds about 'long-term plans'. Laugh if you will, but this was the early sixties. Admittedly these were different times and there was such a thing as a 'job for life', but we knew that this man was patently off his head. He would solemnly talk to us about pensions and marriage, when all we wanted to do was find out what the hell those bumps the girls on the high street had developed were really like when they took their clothes off.

Everything had a code linked to it – 'don't blot your copybook', 'don't rock the boat'. Even then I grew to recognise the type of authority who would use codes. They were always the people who were in awe of the outside world, or thinking they had got it sussed, were keeping it all to themselves and were trying to obscure the message. And of course some of them were too insecure to risk committing themselves to an explicable opinion. There was talk of university, of banks and maybe the civil service. I knew I was far too immature to think about all this, I wanted out.

I was endlessly absent for no reason and starting to slide into a vacuum. I wasn't embarking on a life of crime, I hadn't even broken a few windows or nicked a bike, but I was certainly thinking about it. A good deal of failure had left me not caring that much about what happened next. My family grew desperate. My grandfather once said to me, 'Unless you're careful, you're going to end up as an estate agent.' He paused dramatically before he said 'an estate agent', but even the thought of that horror didn't motivate me. So off I went to a crammer in Birmingham to do my A levels, which done and passed, what next?

There was nothing I wanted to do and, in my mind, nothing I could do. I felt that although I was still in my teens, I was already on the scrap-heap. I was just one of a million awkward, clumsy, stupid boys, I suppose. But when it's happening to you, there's a supremely satisfying self-obsessive feeling that you're the only one in the world who is suffering. Call me a victim, if you will, I was certainly revelling in it at the time.

However, just as the old devil did a couple of years later, fate took a hand. Although I had tossed aside the idea of being a missionary six years before, I still liked 'abroad' as a place that was probably better than here, and to irritate my already frustrated family, I talked about it a good deal. So one night I was waxing loquacious about getting the hell (I probably said 'Heck') out and going overseas, when my exasperated grandparents offered to match the cost of my fare. For every pound I raised, they would give me another. I was trapped, I would have to go somewhere. It was a pretty easy choice: New Zealand – cheap to get to, my farming background would virtually guarantee me work if the worst came to the worst, and my family had some friends there. So, that's where I would go.

A couple of months later, my uncle took me to the railway station to catch the night train to London. I hadn't wanted the whole family crowding round on the platform, so I had made my farewells in the morning room, with its open fire and huge supporting beam running across the ceiling and of course the picture of Martin. There was something terribly British about it all. Years later I learned that the family were terribly upset, but at the time we were all so jolly about saying goodbye that I thought they were quite pleased to see the back of me. That, oddly enough, was a bit of a comfort.

My uncle and I had never got on particularly well. He had always done his best, as had the entire family, and he was a kind man, so when we reached the station he was somewhat at a loss as to what to do. I just wanted to get the agony over, I stumbled into the carriage and waved a firm goodbye. In those days he was a lanky young man with a penchant for long overcoats and I can still see him, a little uncertain of how to say his farewells effectively, but far too inhibited to say anything that really mattered, waving and turning away to stump off to the station car park, his coat flapping around him.

Meanwhile I, ungrateful child that I was, settled down, a touch sad, but mostly thrilled to be getting away from duty and responsibility and above all the sense of total failure that I had about myself. Maybe starting again would work. If it didn't, who cared? At least life would be different.

Chapter 3

I FELL IN LOVE with New Zealand the moment I saw it. Then I fell in love in New Zealand and it drove me out again. There is rarely a day goes by that I don't feel in some way nostalgic for what the country was and still is to me. And for the life of me I cannot understand why New Zealand was so tolerant of my foolishness. By the rules of the game, I should have been taken out and shot as soon as I arrived.

The wharves in Wellington were exactly as wharves should be to my untrained eye, romantic and with a touch of derring-do about them. There are only a few harbours in the world that are near perfect – Sydney, and Hong Kong, and maybe Grenada, then there's Wellington, New Zealand. When the Maoris' god made Aotearoa and the volcanic agonies threw up what was to become Wellington, he must have known that he was making a Pacific paradise. In the sixties, the harbour's stone arms reached out into the bay, the bollards were built to restrain ocean-going liners, and shipping was still the lifeblood of the country. Cranes leaned into the open holds of the trading vessels that sailed around North and South islands and across the Tasman Sea to Australia.

When I arrived it was a particularly beautiful winter's morning in July 1966.

I'd read my Katherine Mansfield. As a teenage romantic I had become obsessed with the idea of a woman who shared her time between Europe and New Zealand, feeling perfectly at home in neither country and then dying of consumption at the early age of thirty-five. I was expecting the place to be the picture that Mansfield had painted and I wasn't disappointed: it was almost too perfect. Beyond the clutter of the harbour rose the hills, covered in the wooden colonial houses built at the end of the nineteenth century and the first years of the twentieth, which hung there with a sense of impermanence that always reminded me this was the other end of the San Andreas faultline. And the air: the air was so clean you could wipe your bottom on it.

If you asked about visas in those days, you would get an odd look and be marked down as a lunatic. We were all from England, weren't we? From the mother country, the place a good many New Zealanders who'd never been there called 'home'. We were white and reasonably healthy, so there weren't any embarrassing questions. We were just the new intake in a prosperous country, filling in the empty spaces and providing labour. The world was on the up and so were the opportunities for anyone who felt he could turn his hand to a bit of honest work in 'God's own Country'. As the last generation of Poms coming to help populate the islands, we were treated with faint contempt by the immigration officers and spoken to slowly and clearly. We'd had the misfortune to be born overseas, we probably kept coal in the bath at home and ate lard, but a few years in New Zealand would correct that. There was a slight *frisson* when I was told to hand over my clothing for fumigation. I wondered for a moment whether I should take offence, but it was a lovely day and there didn't seem much point. Besides, though the New Zealanders were obsessed about the importation of disease and I was confident that I wasn't carrying any, I did know what had been going on aboard ship and I thought that fumigation of my trousers at least would be a good move.

If there was a heaven, this was it. But when you're nineteen and all too aware of the limitations of the twelve pounds ten shillings in your pocket, there are likely to be other things on your mind. Trying to look as much of a New Zealander as I could muster, I stumbled over to a Maori who was sitting on a bale of wool almost as big as he was.

'Where's the work, mate?' I tried to lower my voice as much as I could and stuck my pigeon chest out.

The Maori eyed me with amusement. 'Oh, you want work, boy?' he said, both as a question and a statement.

He was an enormously fat middle-aged man who spoke English with the plosive breathiness of his generation, pronouncing the bs as ps. I waited.

'Well, if I were you, I'd head off to Hamilton, mate.'

I have often wondered what he told his family that night. 'Hey, I met this idiot pakeha fresh off the boat looking for work, so guess

what, I told him to go to Hamilton and, can you believe it, he did?'
How they must have laughed.

Clearly, the Maori thought I was a basket case. There I was unknowingly in a country that was giving jobs away, asking where they
could be found. But being innocent and naïve and above all British,
I did as I was told. I had come from a country where a sense of
humour was considered a liability, to one where to be humourless
was more or less a capital offence.

I found the railway station and took the overnight train to the
Waikato, to the rich dead centre of the North Island. In a country
with more sheep than people, the New Zealanders had designed their
railway system for the majority. I had a second-class ticket, and second class was hell in those days even for me and I wasn't expecting
too much. It was an era of 'do it yourself, otherwise some bastard
will do it to you'. Wellington railway station was chaos, people hurtling from one end of the platform to the other, doing their best to
recreate a scene from *Bowhani Junction*, which had been screened at
the Majestic in Wellington that night. Everything was an antipodean
copy of some Hollywood movie. The train was huffing and puffing,
doing its best to be worthy of *Anna Karenina*, the station was a
tribute to *Brief Encounter*, without the pervading presence of Trevor
Howard. Everyone looked mad and determined. These passengers
were not fools, they knew what they were in for and being hardy folk
they were going prepared.

I learned much later the rules of the game. First, remember that
the seats are made of wood and this is going to be one of the worst
journeys of your life. Second, remember that this train takes for ever
to get anywhere. Third, work in pairs. Find a corner seat, hang on
to it and get a 'mate' to rush off and hire pillows. Then lean out of
the window shouting 'hey, mate' at the top of your voices at no one
in particular until the incredibly old man pushing the catering cart
along the platform hears you and totters alongside the carriage.

I knew none of this, and wearing my Hush Puppies (which
marked me out as effectively as if I'd had green ears and a spacesuit
on), I wandered up and down the platform, looking lost. These were
real men when it came to overnight travel in New Zealand. They had
prepared themselves for the achingly slow journey ahead, and as I
tried to find myself somewhere to sit, they were snuggling down
comfortably amongst hired pillows, a bottle of beer close to hand
and a fund of rugby stories ready for the journey. As the train slowly

banged and rattled its way out of Wellington station, a few of them noticed the miserable bundle of spots wondering what to do next.

'Hey, mate, want a drop?' said one, leaning across the aisle.

It was my first experience of 'mateship'. In the New Zealand of the mid-sixties, mateship was the basis of civilisation, a kind of sexual masonry, only you didn't have to do anything silly like stand on one leg or be an accountant to join. You were automatically a mate by the simple virtue of being a 'bloke'. Whether or not you remained a mate for long depended on you. Mateship could carry you through the most appalling series of failures. Whenever you needed support all you had to do was call on your mates and there they would be, all concerned and supportive, brown paper bags under their arms full of grog, and big silly grins on their faces, ready to help see you through whatever horrors were threatening. Mateship extended to all parts of life and it wasn't entirely necessary to know the name of a bloke to become his mate. All you had to do was extend your right arm, grab a bottle or a jug of New Zealand breweries' finest, smile (but not too ingratiatingly) and you were a member of the club. Women were barred from membership for life.

Tom and Henry, my two new mates, were also my saviours. Through the night they talked and reminisced. As time went by and more beer was drunk, the talk became less coherent and more intimate. One worked on the docks in Auckland as a 'seagull', a casual labourer, the other was going to find work in a slaughterhouse. Both were immensely muscular, tanned and fit looking. They were also kindness itself and both would turn out to be extremely useful when hardship struck a year or so later.

After four hours rattling through the darkened countryside, the train stopped in what looked like the middle of nowhere and emptied. One minute the carriage was full of people talking and laughing, the next it was like a mausoleum. My two mates grabbed my arm and pulled me on to the unlit platform and into hell. Hell, was a small room with three unshaded bulbs hanging from the roof. It stank, and was packed with the train's passengers, first and second class all mixed in together, all shouting and trying to reach a counter behind which an exhausted-looking woman was handing out brown paper packages. By the time I reached the front of the queue, I had gathered there wasn't too much choice in what was obviously a canteen. There was to be no nonsense about what it was you were buying, the choice you were offered was what you had with 'it'. To retain the interest of the lacklustre lady behind the counter, you had to shout out loudly and immediately 'with' or 'without'. Anything else, like 'can I have a cheese sandwich?' would either get you knocked cold by the bloke standing next to you, or ignored by the lady. Like a child on his first trip to France, carefully memorising '*Une baguette, s'il vous plaît, madame*', I stepped up to the counter when it was my turn and spoke my carefully rehearsed line, 'With, please.' A grossly overweight man grabbed one of the brown paper packages in one hand and what looked like a syringe in the other, brought the two together and then handed me the bag.

My mates pulled me back to the train, which began a sort of to and fro banging process to announce its departure almost as soon as we had sat down. I took a look at what I had been given. It was an appalling, soggy meat pie, made of mince and tomatoes, crammed into a pie crust made of grease and cardboard. Only when I bit into it did I realise what the 'with' or 'without' ritual had been all about. The man with the syringe's job was to inject as much tomato ketchup under the gap in the crust as he could in one go. It was the most inedible object I have ever forced into my mouth, and ever since I have been unable to even look at tomato ketchup without my bile rising. But it was part of the university of life and I should have been more grateful. In a few hours, I had been introduced to the three staples of New Zealand culture: mateship, grog and the meat pie.

The train pulled into Hamilton station at about eight o'clock in the morning. It was chilly, with a light frost, and I walked over the criss-cross tracks of the terminus and into the town. Hamilton in the mid-sixties was like the Western town in *Shane*, without the mud and the gunfire. A prosperous place, it boasted a wide straight main street with shops on either side whose roofs bore down over the pavement and were supported by pillars at the street's edge. Down both sides of the street were parked the obligatory Holdens, which were the nearest thing to a national car. Actually, they came from Australia, but they were antipodean cars – massive and solid, with a fairly good reliability record and a bitch of a gear lever mounted on the steering-wheel – and they were the most desirable and unattainable thing on four wheels. It was every healthy male New Zealander's ambition to get his hands on one, and to get a healthy New Zealand girl in the passenger seat.

In the distance down at the end of the street, the greenest countryside imaginable stretched out to the mountains in the north. It was and is ludicrously beautiful, like some kind of private patch of perfection. This was one of the richest areas in New Zealand, confident, even a little smug maybe, but with good reason, the land was fertile and the farmers well-to-do.

There was no problem looking for work, it found me. I became a herd tester and occasional artificial inseminator. The matter of qualifications didn't seem to worry anyone too greatly, I was from a farming background in the old country and I should be able to handle the job. In so far as I could grasp what was required of me, the job entailed travelling around my allotted patch, visiting twenty-five farms a month, spending a day at each and staying overnight in the cockie's home. I was to attend an evening and morning milking, take a sample of milk from each cow in the herd and then, using a portable centrifuge, test each sample for butterfat content.

The first problem was that I had no transport. 'No worries, mate.' The local farm collective would lend me a horse and a two-wheel cart. Had I ever driven one? Well, yes, but . . . No buts were acceptable. I was introduced to Kit, a failed racehorse, given my equipment, shown how it all worked and sent off on my rounds. So there I was, on my own in the middle of nowhere, with a job to do. I quickly learned that the horse was to have the upper hand in our relationship. This was entirely fair, after all, without the horse I couldn't function, while the horse didn't give a damn whether I was there or not.

A brief career as an unsuccessful entrant in the local trotting races had left Kit with a few major hang-ups. First, there was the business of catching her each morning. She could be a trying old thing, but once you caught her eye, she would usually give up and stop trotting round the field just far enough out of reach to drive you crazy. But her biggest hang-up was about her purpose in life. She knew that she wasn't set upon this earth to lumber about the countryside pulling a cart with a Pom and a heap of aluminium on board for all the world like an old gypsy nag. The moment she felt my foot step on to the back of the little cart, she would go back to those glory days at the races, put her head down and accelerate off, usually leaving me in a crumpled heap in the road. By the time I was up on my feet all I could see was my horse and cart disappearing down the road at high speed, sometimes spraying the contents into the ditch if I hadn't lashed it down securely. She would stop all right, after the required half-mile. When I had wearily caught up with her, Kit would have her head firmly in the grass on the side of the verge and a look of sweet innocence on her face.

This sort of behaviour was tolerable on a sunny day, but when the clouds gathered and it began to rain, there was a kind of awful inevitability to the ritual that took place, and I grew to dread it. Once I was all packed up and ready to go, I would walk a few paces away from the cart, whistling as though I didn't have a care in the world. Then I would suddenly turn and run at the thing, as though all the hellhounds in the world were after me, and fling myself at the buckboard. If I had got the timing right, Kit would be taken unawares and by the time she had woken up to the subterfuge, I would be plumped in my corner seat, the reins in my hand, master of all I surveyed. If I got my footing wrong, or Kit sensed me coming, there were three alternatives. One had me flat on my face in the middle of the road, another left me lying in a storm drain, and the final and humiliating alternative was Kit trotting at high speed down a country lane with me hanging on to the buckboard with both hands, while running as fast as I could and making impotent little jumps at the cart. This would almost always end in failure and leave me spreadeagled on the tarmac. The one consolation was that my pathetic attempts to rule the animal kingdom brought immense happiness to the locals, who would often forgather as I tacked the wretched horse up, confident that they were in for some first-rate free entertainment. Kit rarely disappointed them.

Each day we set out on another of our little journeys together, another day, another farm. The idea was to surprise the farmer and thus prevent him making special arrangements to boost the butterfat content in his herd. The cockie could cook the books by putting his cattle on a particularly fertile field or by introducing his most splendid cow and quietly elbowing the useless one for the time I was there. The theory of surprise looked good on paper. Had I been cruising the district in a blacked-out limousine, I might have stood a chance of secrecy, but the reality was a horse and cart clattering around the district spraying buckets and test-tubes wherever it went, so any idea of the element of surprise went out of the window. I would arrive in the middle of the afternoon to be met by a farmer usually in a good humour because he had been warned for several days of my presence in the area. God knows, you only had to follow Kit's bowel movements to know where I was. Each turd could have boasted arrows pointing in the right direction and the message could not have been clearer.

These farmers were the heroes of New Zealand, they saw themselves as the cream of New Zealand's economy and that is what they produced. They were proud of themselves and their product. The cockies led good lives, and they revelled in it. In Waikato, at least, they didn't have to work that hard by comparison with their European counterparts. Those freezing cold mud-covered days back in England would have baffled them. In the sub-tropical climate of North Island, they tended to sit back and 'let things grow'. There were two milkings a day to be done, for sure, but after a good hot shower not much in between, maybe a visit to the pub, or a game of rugby or, joy unconfined, an international match. Red-letter days were when the Lions arrived, but in between, their priorities were pretty straightforward – their cows and their mates, or maybe the other way around, followed at a good distance by their wives and families. That was life and life was pretty good. Some, however, didn't see it that way, for some it was a lonely life.

Jamie Wilkinson had a small herd of about sixty cows and lived way off the beaten track. I dreaded going to his farm. It wasn't that the place was run-down, or that he rarely, if ever, showered, or that I slept in the chicken run when I stayed overnight, or even that in the ten months I had been visiting he had never changed the sheets. When you're nineteen you can handle that and come up smiling. It was an unaccountable, unreasoning fear of what he might do. He was a short, miserable-looking man with long sideburns, who rarely uttered more than a grunt, but there was a tension that meant I was always terrified of saying the wrong thing. We would sit together silently drinking soup after the evening milking, beneath the photograph of a woman I always assumed was his wife, whilst I would wrack my immature brain trying to think of something to say that would unlock the door and make him smile. After a while, he would get up and say, 'Right, mate, I'm for bed.' That was the cue to vanish to the chicken coop and I always took it. When I was there I never slept a wink. To this day I can't imagine what I was frightened of, he certainly wasn't the kind of man who would try crawling into bed with you. It was always the same with Jamie. His neighbours didn't care for him and he didn't mix with them, there was no particular antipathy, they just left each other alone.

One month he surprised me by saying a taciturn 'goodbye' as I turned Kit away and down his cart track. Nothing more than that. I thought that maybe he liked me. The next time I was in Hamilton, I took a call from the boss. 'Don't bother going to Jamie's place this month, you can go to so-and-sos.' No explanation at all. I found out what happened a long while later, during a whispered conversation in a pub. Apparently, about a week or so after I had been to his place, Jamie finished the morning milking, sat down outside the shed that housed his herringbone parlour and blew his head off with his shotgun. No one knew why he had done it, but most people accepted that it was inevitable and it was 'his business anyway'. I was stunned and for some reason felt terribly guilty. I found myself wondering if I should or could have done something, I still do.

My life as a herd tester and occasional artificial inseminator dragged on through the summer. The work itself was totally beyond me, I was a disaster. I had left England desperate to prove that I wasn't an utter fool, that I could do something right and here I was proving the exact opposite. The more I struggled with the primitive equipment, the more it defeated me. My legendary inability to subdue inanimate objects grew worse, I would drop and break almost anything it was possible to. I found I couldn't get the butterfat lists to add up properly. Every time I did a check on my own work, it came out twenty or even thirty per cent adrift. About the only time I felt at ease was with my hand up a cow's uterus. I have always adored animals and I think that I get on with them well. I liked being able to calm the cow down and keep her from getting upset. But then, after it was all over and I was washing up, I would find that I had delivered the wrong phial of semen into the wrong cow, and I would spend the next twenty-four hours agonising about how to tell the farmer, before agreeing with myself that it was too late and better to tell a fib than upset everyone.

The farmers were a mostly sympathetic bunch. They enjoyed my daily exhibitions with Kit, but when I was struggling red-faced with the hand-driven centrifuge, which must have been invented by the Inquisition, they would turn their backs and shrug their shoulders sadly. They did their best with me, introducing me around and taking me to their social evenings, but I was a hopelessly inadequate case socially and spent most evenings standing dumb with embarrassment or hypnotised by a silence, filling it with far too much talk, far too loudly. I desperately wanted to be what they wanted me to be, but it was a lost cause.

If life is a series of insights, I had a beauty around this time and I shudder when I remember it. A girlfriend and I decided to drive down to Rotorua. The town is full of the most beautiful hot springs you have ever seen and smells like the bottom of a birdcage. It's a suffocating, foul smell that gets to the back of your throat and ruins the contents of the average washing-line in short order. If you ask why the place stinks, the locals will tell you, 'It's the sulphur in the springs, mate.' That's all very well, but to New Zealanders this is one of their hot tourist spots. You would think they could use their ingenuity and chuck a can of Spray Fresh into the geysers once in a while.

We looked around for a time, sniffed the air, and caught the tang of the springs, mixed with the unforgettable smell of geyser burgers and decided it wasn't for us. So we returned to the pick-up truck for the drive to Auckland. In those days the road wasn't fully tarmacked and long stretches of it were finished in loose chippings. We were just unlucky. As we came round a bend, the truck slid to one side, hit the verge and flipped over twice, on to the driver's side, leaving the pair of us in a heap all tangled up with the steering-wheel. As the vehicle came to rest, there was a moment's silence before all my unnatural desire to save myself before anyone else surfaced. I charged upwards and out of the truck, and God help me, in my rush to get out of it, I stepped on the poor girl's head. I apologised afterwards, but we never really got beyond a nervous smile and a handshake after that. I had failed again. A decent bloke would have given the girl a hand out of the wreckage before even thinking of himself.

Amidst all the good-humoured mateship and back-slapping neigh-bourliness between the cockies, I have never known a group suffer from loneliness more than some of the people who lived on those isolated farms out in the back-blocks. For the women, it was infinitely worse. They often had few friends and relied on the telephone for contact. The problem was that most phones were shared lines, which meant that anyone could listen in to a private conversation.

New Zealand was the original country on the edge of the world. There was an extremely good radio system, with 'serious' networks based on the BBC model, and a couple of dozen local commercial radio stations. But there was only one TV channel broadcasting fitfully and, being pre-satellite, showing news bulletins from Europe that were up to a week old. So, for some out there in the middle of nowhere, the odd visitor became a highlight of their life and inevitably a regular visitor became a refuge for a woman who had little or no contact with anyone beyond the weekly demands of her husband back from the pub on a Saturday night. Even a skinny, spotty thing like me with absolutely no experience whatever, could sometimes grasp what was meant by a raised eyebrow and an invitation to visit again when the 'old man was away'.

I had been pondering the problem of my virginity for some time, and along with much thought went a real worry, I thought that I was deformed! I had spent most of my life on or around farms and I was perfectly used to the fact that animals were always mounting each other, or trying to mount each other. This I could accept, the problem was that, as an eleven-year-old, I had spent a long summer with a friend of the same age researching the business of mating cattle and a few years later, as puberty hit me, I had reeled back in horror. The problem was simple, I had observed that a bull's penis lies flat against his stomach, thus making entrance to the female a moderately easy business, and I knew that men and women made love, the one on top of the other, but I could not come to terms with my somewhat floppy erection. The damn thing refused to lie flat against my stomach! There was no way I could satisfactorily mate. I was deformed! I was doomed to a life as a virgin!

This was serious stuff and not to be shared with even the closest friend, so when I was staying with a well-to-do farmer one night and his extremely attractive daughter crept into my room intent on pleasurable evil, instead of welcoming the opportunity with open arms, I leapt to my feet clutching the sheets around me and with what must have been an expression of naked terror on my face.

'It's OK,' she said, and I think her name was Raelene. 'It's only me.'
'Me!'

My God, this was the moment of truth and here I was about to be unmasked as a total inadequate. Worse, they might burn me at the stake for being 'unlike others'. I held the sheet firmly around my loins, blushing furiously, until a rebuffed Raelene withdrew. Raelene was not a happy girl at being rejected in this way and made her displeasure known to all her girlfriends.

A few days later, Kit and I trotted through the village as the local girls sat in the sunlight on the porch of the local dairy giggling at us, or rather at me. I died a thousand deaths. I knew they were whispering, 'He can't do it, y'know.' I wanted to crawl away out of this life. Maybe I was a homosexual? God, even worse, maybe I was a pervert? What to do? I considered looking up 'pervert' in the local library, but I knew that the woman who ran it would faithfully report back to the Farmers' Wives Association that I had borrowed the medical dictionary and that could only mean one thing: the clap! It was getting worse. Here I was still a virgin confronted by the likelihood that if I tried to find out what was wrong with me, I'd be accused of having venereal disease. I spent a long time discussing this with Kit as we drove from farm to farm. But while she was as endlessly sympathetic as all horses are, she couldn't help much.

The next six months were hell on earth. It was the summer and the girls all looked so healthy and desirable, they wore shorts and tight shirts and seemed totally oblivious of the effect they were having on me. My hormones were doing somersaults and I spent a good deal of the time doubled up in agony. By this time I knew that I wasn't homosexual. A sprightly young vet had made an advance in a pub one night and I hadn't cottoned on to what he had in mind until he made a lunge at my trousers. My reaction had been to grab my honour and my zip and leg it out as fast as I could. So at least I knew that I wasn't 'one of them'. It only occurred to me a few years after the event that this might not be the truth I was searching for and that maybe my reaction simply meant that the vet wasn't Mr Right.

As autumn approached, my problem was solved by one of the kindest people I have ever met. By this time I had earned enough to give the horse a rest and buy a small Ford Thames van. Ungrateful callow youth that I was, when I took Kit to her field, I let her go without even a pat of thanks, I just walked away without a look backwards. Mind you, so did she. We had never got on that well and you could hardly have called it a marriage made in heaven, but you would have thought it was worth a wave from me or a glance from her. But that's men and horses for you.

Over the last year or so, and in the time I had to myself, I had taken to calling in at one of the smaller farms for a drink or a coffee and for endless soothing talk. The woman who kept the small herd of Jersey cows there was in her early thirties and had been on her own for some time. There was all sorts of gossip about her whys and wherefores, but no one really knew the truth and she never volunteered anything about the men in her life or indeed if there ever had been any. She was a strong woman, not pretty, but attractive. Working outside had left her with a deep tan but her skin wasn't leathery. She played the piano a little and had a great sense of self-assurance about her. She was also a good listener and I poured out my heart to her over the weeks. Incredibly, I thought of her as a much older woman, though I wasn't quite stupid enough to tell her that. Inevitably, one night the conversation and the drink combined and she quietly took me to bed and finally the deed was done. In the morning, being a selfish little bugger, I wasn't so much grateful as relieved that the whole system worked. I felt as though I had had every little bit of me checked out by a first-rate mechanic and been reassured that it was all systems go.

Of course, it got around. My little Ford Thames van had been spotted where I'd parked it all night, just outside her farm. A few nights later, I was in the local pub when someone slapped me on the back and told me I was 'a real sport for giving the old lady one.' To my eternal shame, I grinned and took the drink, enjoying the sense of being accepted as a 'real man'. Someone should have taken me outside and told me what a rotten piece of behaviour that was, but I suppose we were all caught up in the pathetic game of being young men. Equally, I guess, she knew what she was doing, I just hope she got some sort of pleasure from my sad little writhings.

Now, of course, I was Mister Confident. I had in my little world discovered what life was all about and I made another of those ridiculous mistakes. Instead of going back to the farm every now and then, I ignored the poor lady, became riddled with embarrassment at what had happened and started going to the pub far too often and for far too long. It wasn't so much demon liquor, as huge quantities of pale New Zealand beer which I pumped into myself. I drank morning, noon and night. When the pubs weren't open, I had a few bottles in the back of the van. Disaster was almost inevitable and not long coming.

Just after midnight one night I drove back to the farmhouse I was staying at, full of fizzy lager, and fell into bed. I awoke at five o'clock in the morning, just in time for milking, with a massive hangover and swimming in fluid. I had pissed myself during the night. Waking up in a swamp was the nail in my coffin. I was hideously embarrassed, of course, but that wasn't enough. There was no point in apologising, or even trying to make amends, it was impossible to carry on, I had to go. So I went.

To Auckland. To the big city, or the nearest thing to it that the North Island of New Zealand had to offer. I hadn't the faintest idea what to do, but I had a couple of mates. The old-boy system worked for me twice in my life and on each occasion in the most inverted way, it happened at this moment in Auckland, and it happened a few years later in Australia. I had kept in touch over the last year with Tom and Henry, my mates from my first day in the country, and, as the prophet says, 'When you're in deep shit, go to your mates'. I followed the sage's advice, took the bus to Auckland and tracked down Tom and Henry to their little wooden house in Ponsonby. At that time this was possibly the toughest area of the city, where the not-so-well-off Maoris lived and the incoming Islanders fetched up. The Islanders were primarily from Fiji, and like most immigrants across the ages, they were unwelcome in their search for a better life.

Most nights the knives would be flashing outside the house and on Friday nights when the boys had a few drinks inside them, there was every chance that someone would be daft enough to use theirs. You could tell what was going on by the shouts. If they turned into silence accompanied by moans and whimpers, you knew that someone had stabbed someone else. If it sounds like the Chicago of the Pacific, then I'm overdoing it. I never had any difficulties with anyone in the street, when I walked up to the bottle shop it was as though I was invisible, no one bothered the only pakeha in the district. For a while I drank in the local pub, until a policeman said it was extremely dangerous for a white man to go in there. I kept away for a week or so, then went back to my old habits. New Zealand was a multi-racial society, but that didn't mean that everything was perfect and that there was no racism.

A year or so later, I was going out with the daughter of a well-to-do farmer who was quite a catch – she had her own car. I noticed that a country cinema was showing Lewis Milestone's 1929 classic *All Quiet On The Western Front*. They probably thought that it was a first-run movie. I begged the farmer's daughter to take me to it and we drove off together one Friday night, down the country roads covered in loose chippings. When we arrived, I noticed that all the black faces were heading for the stairs, while the white ones were sitting in the stalls.

'Don't tell me there's segregation here,' I whispered to the girl-friend.

'Naah,' she said, eyes wide above her Orangina, 'but there used to be and these blokes know what's good for 'em.'

Back in Auckland, Sundays were rest days – rest from work and rest from whatever villainy the locals were up to. Sunday was also church day. Not for me, of course, but I was a direct beneficiary. There was a small Baptist church a few doors down from where we lived and on Sunday mornings it would be packed with Fijians keeping their peace with their god. I would go and lie in the grass outside and listen to them singing their heads off. It would bring back memories of church parade at school, of slow, chilly, unforgiving services presided over by the bony, sour-faced vicar, of sitting in lines, staring fixedly at the eagle on the lectern and praying that the pompous sanctimonious twaddle would end soon. All the memories faded at the straightforward good time these people were having. No one stopped them if they sang a bit too loudly or slightly off-key. Heaven help us, there was laughter during the sermon, and the tunes and harmonies were wonderful. I didn't want to be part of the church, I remembered the deal I had done with God over the eleven plus and still felt a little guilty about reneging on it. But I loved sprawling in the grass, letting the sheer enjoyment of the congregation and that wall of sound they produced when they sang, wash over me.

I felt that I was in a pretty good corner of heaven. Money didn't matter too much and I was sharing the little wooden house, perched up on its stilts to keep it away from the bugs, with two good mates. Tom and Henry were a pair of survivors. Whatever it was, just name it and they could do it; offer a price for it and they could get you one, or a pair if you had the ready cash. But both of them had the same weakness – women. Having ended the week with a pile of pound notes in their pockets, the two of them would arrive back at the little wooden house we shared on Sunday night with black eyes and no cash. But it was Tom and Henry who introduced me to the world of the seagull.

When I'd first arrived in Auckland, I had been determined to be as rugged an individual as I could and to make my own way. So, I worked at a slaughterhouse for a couple of weeks. The work wasn't hard, but it was soul-destroying. My job was to stand thirteenth in line beneath a system of conveyor belts and wait, a huge and frighteningly sharp knife in my hand. As the shift began, the belts would suddenly jerk into action and after a little while a sad row of naked dead sheep would appear from out of the mist of the freezer. Seconds before, these cadavers had been live sheep waiting their turn for their maker like, well, like lambs for the slaughter. A huge fellow with no teeth called Piri would select a sheep, pop it in a crate and pole-axe it. The poor sheep didn't know what had hit it, it just crumpled, or would have done if Piri's mate hadn't been quicker and hauled it up by its back legs on to a hook hanging from the conveyor system. By the time it got to me a couple of minutes later, its own mother wouldn't have recognised it. The sheep was just a skinless carcass with a slit down its middle. My job was to put my hand inside the slit and cut something off. I think it was the kidneys, but I didn't like to ask when I got the job and I was scared of making a fool of myself after I'd been there for a while. So, I stood there, day in, day out, plunging my hands into the warm insides of a lately expired sheep and cutting something off, and I might be there still if Piri hadn't made my mind up about my future for me.

We were sitting outside in the yard having our lunch-time sandwiches one day when he delivered himself of his opinion. It was slightly difficult to grasp the entirety of what Piri was trying to say because of his lack of teeth, but if you gave him the benefit of the doubt and smiled a lot, you could usually get the gist of it.

'Look, pakeha boy,' he said, 'you don't want to be staying here too long, it'll get to you.'

I nodded. It was getting to me already.

'You got education, so go work somewhere good.' At this, Piri took out the slaughtering knife he'd been using all morning and rubbed it along a carcass so that the blood flowed across it. 'You hear what I say?' And he wiped the blood on a thick piece of bread and handed it to me. 'You go look for a decent job.'

The idea of having to courteously swallow Piri's gifts for the rest of my life stuck in my throat, so I went back to Tom and Henry and begged them to get me a job anywhere but in a slaughterhouse. Which is how I found myself working as a seagull, a part-time docker. We stood, a little knot of work-hungry malcontents, for an hour or so at five o'clock in the morning, waiting for the allocation man to come. When he did, I always stood slightly behind Tom or Henry. They were huge and I was an eleven-stone weakling. Invariably they were picked for a day's heavy work and I went along almost as an afterthought.

These were the days before containerisation, so to empty the hold of a ship meant getting down in there and shifting the wheat or coal or whatever it was with your bare hands. Sometimes the cargo was in bags, sometimes it wasn't. There were those in the seagulling trade who drank a lot, and a close watch had to be kept on them in case they tumbled over and sank beneath a tide of loose wheat, never to be seen again. But there was an air of sophistication in the working arrangements for dockers. Depending on your cunning, your reaction time and your experience, it wasn't actually necessary to work more than two hours in every eight-hour shift. The trick was to keep working in the grimy hold of the ship with one eye on the hatch until you saw the shadow of the foreman appear. The moment this happened, you shouted 'yes', shinned up on to the deck and sat chewing gum or smoking for twenty minutes. I mastered this technique very quickly, but it took me some time to grasp exactly what was happening. The system was designed to give everyone on the shift a twenty-minute break. What should have happened when each man appeared was a shout from the foreman of 'Up' followed by a call of 'yes' from the next man eligible. I was unconsciously circumnavigating the system and unknowingly taking nearly everyone's breaks. The reason that the other men on the shift tolerated such appalling behaviour from me was quite simple: Tom and Henry were large and, unbeknownst to me, unforgiving men who ruled with fists of iron, and I was their friend. While they were present, I could nip nimbly from break to break and there wouldn't be a murmur of protest. Every night, as I got home with a nice fat pay cheque, I thought that seagulling was a marvellous career.

Until the day Tom and Henry were occupied in the local court over an embarrassing and trivial matter and I went alone to the docks. I came home a broken man. In one eight-hour shift I had suffered more back-breaking toil than any man in the history of the universe. There was no question of 'ups' for Bates on that day. To my credit, I took my punishment like a man, and to their credits, the other seagulls resisted what must have been an overwhelming urge to beat the seven bells out of me. But it was a final lesson for me that good honest toil was not what it was cracked up to be.

Although the countryside looks like heaven on earth, New Zealanders use their language like a sledgehammer. These were the days of 'the six-o'clock swill', a perfect description, but you'd have thought they would try to put a little charm into it. Ever since the First World War, the Scottish Puritan ethic in the New Zealand character had tried to limit his intake of alcohol by the simple expedient of closing the pubs at six o'clock in the evening. It's barely credible that the population stood for it, but they did and if nothing else it must have kept the numbers down with the heart attacks caused by frantic last-minute boozing before closing time. The ritual was horrific. Finish work, whatever you were doing, wherever you were doing it, by five fifteen and gallop to the pub. Fight your way to the bar and order a couple of schooners or a jug of beer. Force the lot down in time to fill 'em up before being chucked out as the clock struck the hour. Accept the risk of throwing up or having a coronary when you left the pub as one of those chances you take in life. It was a tribute of a kind that so many could get so drunk so quickly. By eight o'clock in the evening, the streets were empty, hence the old joke about arriving in New Zealand to find that it was closed!

It was, however, at one of these six-o'clock swills, at an appropriately titled pub in Ponsonby called the Gluepot, that I met my mentor in showbiz. Tom, Henry and I were leaning up against the bar when a slightly theatrical figure forced his way through the crowd. They knew him, I didn't. It turned out that he was a drama producer for NZBC radio and in Tom's terms 'a bit of a left footer, if you get my drift!' But he was buying and a man can tolerate most company when someone else's wallet is on the bar.

Keith was getting on a bit, but he was a flatterer and a name-dropper. That's how he got what he wanted and he started to flatter me. Tom and Henry were faintly amused by what was going on and I of course didn't have a clue as to what lay at the back of Keith's shabby old mind. When he handed me his card and said, 'You have a pleasant voice, come on up to the office, I think I might be able to find some work for you,' I believed him. Tom and Henry just laughed.

I phoned Keith the following day from the box on the corner and when I had reminded him where we'd met, he invited me down to the studios for an audition. I hauled out the Hush Puppies, put on a collar and tie, walked up to the top of the road and caught the trolley bus down into the city. Keith wasn't entirely single-minded. He did as he promised and coaxed me through an audition. I hadn't the faintest idea what was going on, but he was patience itself and a day or so later called me with the offer of a small part in a radio drama series. An actor, eh! There was no apprenticeship required and they paid you for it. Even Tom and Henry were impressed. It sounded pretty good to me, and for a while I was in and out of the studios, playing boy heroes in some pretty basic radio serials.

We 'actors' were paid for each twenty minutes we spent recording. The trick was to stretch out a recording as long as we could and then, just as the twenty minutes was up, fluff a take and say, 'Ah, Jeez, sorry about that!' Then we were into another twenty minutes' pay. These serials were always atrociously written, wildly overacted and always seemed to be sponsored by the most ludicrous organisations.

Cue deep reassuring voice ... 'The New Zealand Broadcasting Corporation presents an epic of our nation's early days.' (pause for effect) '*The Boy Jack*' (cue organ music from slightly scratchy record played in the control room by elderly lady with a taste for prurient novels) 'brought to you by Heavenly Nightware. Ladies, remember the man in your life and soar heavenwards in some Heavenly Nightware. Come and see Mr Jerald, he'll accommodate you in every way. And now, here's episode three hundred of *The Boy Jack*'. At which point, the little red light on the end of the microphone would wink, and I would step smartly forward and read my script. ('Far too fast, dear boy,' Keith would mutter afterwards, 'but infinitely better than last time.')

The extraordinary thing, looking back, is that I was never nervous. Excited yes, but never intimidated by what I was doing. The nerves, the insecurity were all to come much, much later. Right now it was all too ridiculous and funny to take seriously. A whopping error had been made by the heavenly clerk of the scheme of things and I was the beneficiary, until some celestial being checked the books. Then I'd be back on the docks. But life as a young actor went on in a pleasant enough haze. I even bought myself a green suede jacket and learned to hold my beer glass in a slightly affected way. There was money in this and people called you 'lovey'. Mind you, I also learned not to get into the lift with the wrong kind of people.

Inevitably, after six months it was pay-back time. Keith asked me to dinner! Both Tom and Henry said that I shouldn't go. 'He'll be in yer pants quicker than a ferret up a drainpipe unless you watch the old bugger.' But I thought I knew better, until I got to the house. I was pretty thick, but even I could grasp that the evening was set for seduction. The lights were low, music was playing on the radiogram and there was a lot of expensive booze around. More to the point, the table was set for two and the bedroom door was half-open. I tried to be as polite as I could while working out rejection lines. I sat miserably through dinner, picturing the scenario planned for after dinner. Me pinned to the sofa, Keith a roaring mass of perversion, poised breathily above me ready to have his evil way.

How was I going to get out of this? What should I say? 'No thanks, Keith. Mummy says I shouldn't.' Pathetic. A firm handshake perhaps and a 'Now look here, Keith, let's talk about this man to man'? No one could possibly take that one seriously. 'Get off me, you foul-breathed evil pervert.' I'd never work again and I was pretty certain that I wouldn't get my old job down at the docks back.

In the end, and as he or she so rarely does in real life, fate took a hand. As we munched through our meal, Keith was silkily prising all the information he could out of me in what I imagine he considered a reassuring sort of way. After a while, we got on to the subject of my family.

'And tell me what your father does, old thing,' purred the over-dressed predator.

Haltingly I told him that my parents were separated and what little I knew about my father. Suddenly the atmosphere changed and became distinctly cold. Keith went a little grey, stood up and switched on all the lights until the room looked like a fully lit Wembley Stadium. Then he muttered something to himself, and seemed to make an effort to pull himself together and become much more businesslike and brisk. He smiled a thin smile and urged me to eat up quickly. Obviously he had changed his mind and wanted to get rid of the situation as quickly as possible. The evening was almost over.

Within ten minutes, I was standing at the doorway and Keith was shaking my hand in a slightly embarrassed way. Just before I left, he said, 'Don't worry, I think there'll be a good chance for you coming up in a new TV series a friend of mine is doing. And if you ever hear from your father, give him my best wishes. We were at university together. No need to mention that you came round for dinner, is there, dear boy?'

I didn't have the fare for the trolley bus home, so I had to walk the three miles, but I didn't give a damn. I looked up at the Southern Cross and thought about my father. The old sod had never done me any favours before, but maybe he had done me the best turn in my life when he'd hatched some kind of friendship with Keith before I was even born.

I learned a good deal from this episode and from Keith. First, that a person's sexuality doesn't matter a damn. Second, that being alone and vulnerable with a rampant homosexual never hurt anyone. Just so long as he/she went to university with your parent. I didn't tell Tom or Henry about Keith's pursuit or his revelation, they knew that nothing had happened simply because I got home before they did. I put the whole thing to the back of my mind and began a single-minded pursuit of an extremely attractive girl I had met at a university party.

Chapter 4

ER NAME WAS MAIRI, she had the most beautiful long black hair and an enchanting smile. I had a sneaking suspicion that she knew more about life than I did. I was totally obsessed with her and determined not to make a mess of my chances. Her father was a distinguished man, a European academic, which meant that people stopped and pointed him out in the street, rather as one would a conquering general. 'He's from Europe, you know,' the old ladies would say, adding, 'I'm sure he suffered dreadfully during the war,' and, pursing their lips in agreement, they would pass on. He was also President of the Goethe Society and I'd been invited to one of their evenings. This made things easy.

I began to take Mairi to Auckland's only arts cinema. If there was a Czech, Russian or German film on . . . Correction, if it had subtitles, we were there in the front of the queue. I also frantically set about improving my German.

Mairi was what New Zealand matrons called 'a nice girl', that is, she was no use to anyone in the back seat of a Holden. Coincidentally, Mairi's niceness didn't render her stupefyingly boring. She was fun to be with and extremely bright. God knows what she saw in me . . . my brain was firmly fixed in my loins, and that must have been all too obvious. But she persevered and accepted that my shortcomings – no money, no car and no prospects – were part and parcel of life. We enjoyed the movies, days out at the beach and just wandering around in the sunshine.

While I was chasing after some kind of love life, show business was chasing me – in the short, fat shape of Michael J. Devine. Michael was a television producer. In New Zealand that meant something, but in television terms it meant very little. New Zealand TV was so primitive that virtually anyone could say that they were a television producer and no one else could deny it, they lacked the basic knowledge to contradict the claimant. Michael J. Devine had it in his head to produce 'the best children's TV series in the world' and his attempt to do it nearly finished me off. Ever since getting to know Michael, I have always mistrusted men who put an initial in between their surname and their Christian names.

Other lessons I've learned include never believing that any American is president of anything until you've sat in his office, and never to take seriously the additions 'Jr', or 'the third' to anyone's moniker unless they are American politicians. Oh yes, and if someone is Dave one day and then becomes David on promotion, stick his card in the bin where it belongs.

My failed paramour Keith had done the decent thing and presented my name to Michael, who called me into his office. Calling me wasn't easy, a message had to be left by his secretary at the Gluepot. If I was drinking somewhere else that week, some good soul would stagger out of the pub and leave a garbled message with Tom or Henry. They were usually too busy with their women or legal problems to take an accurate note of who the message was from or what it was about, so by the time any message filtered through to our house a good deal of guesswork was involved in my daily trysts with the phone box on the corner.

Michael sat in his office and fired questions at me. Could I ski, play the guitar, do handstands? Did I know John Lennon personally? Had I appeared on the stage before? I couldn't do any of these things and I had never been closer to John Lennon than a Beatles concert at the Gaumont in the early sixties. But Michael made it clear that if I said yes to all these questions, I would face six months' continuous employment with no heavy lifting involved. Privately I was ecstatic, not only would I have an income for six months and not have to rely on Tom and Henry, but I would also become respectable and socially desirable through being on television and I would get to sleep with Mairi. Things were working out well. I said 'yes' to every question Mike asked me and stepped out into the sunshine with a contract in my hand. That night I borrowed some cash from Tom and Henry and we went on a serious celebratory bender.

A week or so later, I was called for the first programme. There was to be no pilot programme, pilots were for cissies, we were blokes and we didn't do all that piloting stuff. I have since learned that 'no pilot' is usually a synonym for 'disastrous show'.

A couple of days later I got an elaborate script from Mike and

discovered one of my greatest shortcomings: I find it almost impossible to learn anything word for word. I walked around half the parks
in Auckland trying to learn the bloody thing, but each time I hid the
script and started declaiming my lines, my brain would reject what I
had learned and come up with what it claimed was 'a much better
version'. It was when I met the two actors with whom I would be
working over the next six months and tried desperately and pathetically to bluff my way through the rehearsal, that I learned a basic
truth: actors don't like surprises, they like to know what's coming,
who's going to say it and when.

The following day we were scheduled to record the show in the
studio. There would be no second chances and I was on pain of death
to be word perfect. Tomorrow was also the evening of the Goethe
Society meeting, the night when Mairi would be mine. I took the bus
home in a sweat.

I begged Tom and Henry for help and they did their best. But
when they read the script, their brains reacted in the same way, and
eventually, exasperated with my incompetence, they both reached for
the same panacea and said simultaneously, 'Fuck this, let's go to the
pub for a quick one.'

Six hours later, at one o'clock in the morning, I crawled into my
sleeping bag, supremely unconcerned about the recording the following day, and woke seven hours later with a monumental hangover
and a deep-rooted desire to kill myself. The other passengers on the
trolley bus must have thought I was insane. I hung on to the strap
mouthing, 'Hello, everyone, in our first programme I'm going to be
playing the guitar and we'll be talking about our upcoming skiing
special,' frantically and breathing fire all over the conductor. Even
with my limited experience, I knew this wasn't going to be my day.
It wasn't.

I tried, I really tried. But my old cack-handedness returned. Everything I picked up, I dropped, everything I walked past somehow
became entangled in my clothing and smashed. My tongue, which
was furry enough already after a heavy night out, grew arms which
clung firmly to the roof of my mouth. I could remember most of the
lines by this time, but I couldn't speak them! The other two, profes-
sionals to their socks, stood aghast at this floundering wild-eyed mess
that was sinking in front of them. They did their best, laughing nervously when I bumped into something, and trying to intervene when
I stood in front of them spluttering, my mouth opening and shutting

like a goldfish, but it, or rather I, was truly dr~ ~ful. The problem
was that not only did *they* not know what I was going to do next, *I*
didn't know. I was inside this mass of flesh trying to control everything and all the systems had shut down. My body was totally out
of control, about the only things I managed to suppress were my
bladder and my bowels, and at one point when Michael was screaming at me, I had my doubts about them.

After eight searing hours it was all over, thank God. Michael
stayed up in the gallery, his head slumped over the desk, moaning
something about his career and how it was finished. The two profes-
sionals sidled out of the studio trying not to meet my gaze. I didn't
care about anything any more. As I left the studio, a sympathetic
floor manager put his arm on my shoulder and said, 'Wasn't that
bad, mate', but I knew it was and my mind was working on how I
would get my old job back with Piri at the slaughterhouse. And there
was Mairi. There was no way she would get into bed with a bloke
who ate blood sandwiches.

I sat in the park for a while with passers-by staring at me in an
odd sort of way. I considered getting aggressive with them, until it
occurred to me that I hadn't taken off my make-up and that the
reason for the stares was that only a very specific kind of male wore
make-up in the park during the day. I went to the public lavatory,
brushed myself up a bit and tried to pull myself together before the
Goethe Society meeting. Out came the Hush Puppies from the carrier
bag and on went the size fourteen and a half pin-stripe shirt with the
button-down collar that I'd been saving for this moment. I pulled on
the size thirty-two corduroy trousers and the size forty matching
jacket with real leather buttons and took a look. Hmm. Why did
nothing ever look as good on me as it did in the shop? Pity about the
pimples and the bit of hair that always stood up at the back like a
startled cockatoo, but it was too late for the Clearasil and Brylcreem.
Time to go.

You have to remember that there are excuses for my subsequent
behaviour. I had just had TV stardom snatched from my grasp by an
unforgiving God. As I walked up the drive, I went over the little
speech in German that I had prepared for Mairi's father and gave
myself a final check-over. Everything seemed to be operating fairly
well and my tongue had regained its former elasticity. The door
opened and there stood Mairi's father in the porchlight. I smiled, not
too effusively, and began my little speech, '*Guten Abend*', when a

huge dog appeared from behind him. My little grey cells spotted a chance. 'Their dog, eh? Of course, their favourite pet. I'm good with animals. Ha, my chance to totally and completely ingratiate myself with the family.' Mairi was as good as mine. I stopped my speech for a moment and bent forward to pat the enormous mutt, which grunted very slightly and bit me quite hard in the balls. Although my corduroy trousers protected me from permanent damage, it hurt. It hurt a lot and without thinking I reacted.

'Oh fuck,' I wailed, my eyes starting to water, and then without thinking I took aim and kicked the dog hard in the jaw. The dog howled as I had done a moment before and after a split second's satisfaction, I took a look at the expression on the face of the President of the Goethe Society and father of all that I desired. It had hardened. I didn't bother with the speech. I never even crossed the threshold. I turned, and trying to keep my dignity while hanging on to my bruised manhood, tottered off down their drive. I never bothered calling Mairi again.

She was far too nice for me anyway and now she's probably married to an equally nice academic with nice academic children. I hope so. Every now and then, though, I think about that dog. I wonder if it got blood poisoning as a result of biting me. I hope so.

I spent the next couple of days in pubs. There was no point in calling Mairi or the television station. In the space of eight hours I had managed to do just about as much damage as I'd ever done before. We didn't have a television, so I didn't watch the first and what undoubtedly would be my last show, and I turned down Tom and Henry's offer to go round to a mate's to watch it. They came back and were kind. 'It wasn't that bad, not when you think that all kids' shows are fucking horrible.' They did their best, but I was not to be consoled.

Then something strange happened. Out of the blue, the television critic of the *Auckland Star* wrote a complimentary review of the programme and singled me out as 'fresh and innovative'. Of course the poor man was a fool or a drunk and he certainly didn't know what he was talking about, but suddenly that one review gave me not just a second chance, but a whole career. The office left a message and I called them ready for the blast, only to hear a sympathetic Mike on the other end positively cooing down the phone. If I was not totally rehabilitated, at least they were going to keep me around and give me a second chance. I never met the critic who did me such a huge favour. I thought that he must be mad to write such stuff and I didn't want to be personally responsible for pulling the scales from his eyes by meeting him face to face. Wherever he is, I owe him a beer.

And so we continued churning out our little show. Michael had to fire someone to make his point, but as my sentence had been commuted, he sacked the girl in the team. One moment she was there and the next she was replaced by a splendidly experienced and theatrical old hand who terrified me when she arrived and still terrified me at the end of the series. Carol was the first pro I had ever worked with, and her judgement of me was that I was not a pro and she was right. Not being a pro meant that Carol would take her time when she spoke to me and make sure that I understood every word she said. Hence, I was addressed, with some reason it has to be said, rather as the village idiot, loudly and clearly. In the studio that was bearable, but in the canteen, it was a toe-curler.

Nothing much changed over the six months of the series, except that Mike got pretty bored with the programme when it became obvious that, try as he might, it wasn't going to become the best kids' show ever made. The last time I met him was in Australia a few years ago. Still the same dapper little man with the bow-tie and the middle initial, he was working on a TV station in one of the feeder towns around Sydney and getting ready to make 'the best bloody TV show about Australia ever made'. I never heard what happened to it, if it was made, or if it was a success or a failure.

As Mike became more disillusioned, so the opportunities increased. I took to making little five-minute films, which was fun, and spending a good deal of time in the shadow of the other frontman, Rhys Jones. Rhys was ten years older than me and infinitely more mature. He was what I ached to be, sophisticated. He never spilt things or dribbled, he never talked too loudly or left a guilty stain on his trousers after going to the loo. Women found him devastatingly good-looking and he usually found an excuse to give them whatever it was they were after. I, meantime, was still licking my wounds, both physical and emotional, after the non-existent affair with Mairi. But Rhys was patient and inevitably I would tag along, like some sad younger brother, when he went pubbing and sometimes I got lucky when his sexual bookings became too much for him to honour.

Rhys was one of those men who appeared laid-back, but always became deeply involved with women who subsequently went mad.

Whether they were that way when he met them, or whether he drove them over the brink, I don't know. After a particularly heavy night, I woke on the settee in his living room to hear knocking. I staggered to my feet, stubbing my foot on an ashtray full of half-smoked hash. I was experienced enough in the ways of beer to know that the knocking sounds might not be real, but then I heard a female voice outside the living room.

'Jones, you bastard. I know you're in there with a woman, let me in.'

Of course he was in the bedroom with his latest flame, but I wasn't too worried. There was a picture window the length of the living room between me and the inflamed ex. Then I heard a sort of female roar and a crashing of glass, and saw the rejected one smash through the window and, ignoring me and the broken glass, stride into Jones's bedroom bearing a rather large object in her hand that made her look like an inflamed Britannia. I scarpered, as a true friend would under such circumstances, and saw Rhys a couple of days later, with the same smile, same head of hair, but an enormous black eye.

'How's Sheila?'

'Oh, she's fine.'

'Nuff said.

It was a pleasant summer. The money kept coming in and there was a little coterie of entertaining people working in television at that time. One was Ray Samuels. As camp as a row of tents with not an ounce of venom in him, it was impossible to ignore his sexuality, he wore it with great pride. Ray, who was then in his forties, had worked as a steward on the big liners doing the great circle from Southampton to Sydney and back, but had taken enough time to fall in love with a younger disc jockey in Auckland. They had set up home on the North Shore, and in a country that was ostensibly wildly homophobic had been almost totally accepted as a couple.

It was Ray who introduced me to The Musical. Sometimes on Friday evenings we would drive over the harbour bridge and end our evenings at Ray's place. Ray had two obsessions, apart from his partner. The first was his appearance, which was always immaculate, though there were the first signs of a receding hairline, and the second was his piano. He played fairly well and sang passably, but he performed superbly. For someone like me, born after the great era of musicals and who had never had a chance to see them performed on stage, Ray was the perfect discovery. Given a few drinks and a receptive audience, Ray would launch into a concert version of one of the great Broadway musicals, complete with narration to cover the lack of cast.

Over the months, he gave me a taste of what was so magical about musicals and an understanding of the difference between crap lyrics and creative ones. Ray's income came mostly from the odd bit of TV he did, but every now and then he would do some cabaret and I have a feeling that his heart lay there. He once took me to an Australian touring production of *The Pyjama Game*. It was appalling, but I couldn't be rude to my host, so when he asked me if I'd enjoyed it I said 'yes'. Quite properly, Ray didn't believe me and pushed for some criticism. For want of something uncontroversial to criticise, I commented on the way the male chorus line never looked directly at the audience.

'Yes,' muttered Ray, his lips narrowing, 'the problem is, darlin', they're all in love with the fucking drummer.'

Everytime I see a slightly overweight or faintly fey male chorus singing 'Steam Heat', I remember Ray's grim disapproval of that bunch of Australian fairies and I crack up.

Around about this time, in midsummer, Auckland became gripped by pirate radio fever. Well, gripped is a bit of an overstatement. It's hard to think of Auckland being gripped by anything stronger in the summer than the desire to go to the beach. Tall stories of the pirate radio stations out in the English Channel and around the North Sea had filtered back; tales of disc jockeys with buckets between their knees as they broadcast and opposing operators boarding their ships bent on violence.

I was approached one night by a man who asked me if I would like to work for an outfit called Radio Hauraki. In an age of carefully administered radio, this was to be New Zealand's first pirate ship and was to be moored just outside New Zealand waters. There were three objects, depending on which of the organisers you spoke to – a mighty profit, a long-term aim of forcing the authorities to grant them a shore licence, or a bit of a laugh. I said an immediate 'no thanks'. I had no idea of what was required in being a disc jockey and my sense-of-adventure tastebuds were not stimulated by the idea of sitting out in the middle of the ocean for weeks on end. But I went down one dark Saturday night to take a look at the vessel being fitted out and wasn't entirely surprised to see a couple of familiar engineering faces and quite a bit of equipment marked 'NZBC – Do not remove' being slung aboard.

The good ship Hauraki slipped its moorings one night and slid off into the harbour. A day or so later the test transmissions started and a week later they were on air, using 'Born Free' as their signature tune and I found myself regretting not joining them. I changed my mind on that score a year or so later.

When the children's series was grinding to a halt, I got a telephone call in the studio from Wellington.

'Would you like to work in radio for a bit?'

My days of saying 'yes' instantly were well and truly over, so I said cautiously, 'Sounds OK. For a bit.'

The voice at the other end said, 'We're short of announcers. You'll have to go on a course for a couple of weeks, but if you get through that you've got a job for life here, mate. We'll send your ticket.'

So I packed my one respectable shirt, the matching trousers and jacket and said goodbye to anyone and everyone.

Rhys was staying on in Auckland. In the future he would become a sort of Michael Aspel figure professionally and, apart from a tendency for continually getting married to the wrong women, he seemed set for life. But it wasn't to be quite so rosy. He spent a while working at BBC television in London and then disappeared back to New Zealand. I bumped into him in 1988, crossing a road in Sydney. Time hadn't taken its toll and I recognised him immediately. He was running a video company. We talked briefly and he laughed when he said he was on his umpteenth marriage and living in Brisbane. I asked him if he was happy and he smiled a weak smile, shrugged his shoulders and said, 'Oh, it's OK, you know.' That was the last time I saw him.

Tom and Henry were a different kettle of fish. They weren't an emotional pair, so they just said, 'See you around, mate', and went back to worrying about their women and their beer. I never saw them again.

The winter was on its way and my impression of Wellington this time around was a sombre one. Compared with Auckland it seemed a blisteringly cold and unwelcoming place. The streets were narrow, the buildings either early colonial or loose attempts to follow the Frank Lloyd Wright formula. And they had earthquakes there. There'd been a lot of laughter about that at the airport in Auckland when I left.

Perhaps the harshest reality that I now had to confront was something I'd managed to avoid all my working life – the nine-to-five day and the collar and tie. It came as a brutal shock to have to turn up for work on time and to have to dress decently, but the NZBC was paying, it was quite fun and it couldn't last for ever, could it? I knew that I was living on borrowed time and it wouldn't be long before they caught me out.

The course was hardly challenging, but it was an effective introduction to radio. First, we were shown how to work the equipment. Then a little bit of additional work on languages to get you used to pronouncing French and German proper names and a hasty introduction to Maori for obvious reasons. I'd done a basic Maori course while I'd been in Auckland, God knows why, so I was able to enjoy it all. The joy was Bob White, the course instructor. A big, bluff no-nonsense man with a great sense of humour, he was able to communicate the most important aspects of addressing the microphone in one sentence.

'No bullshit, do it straight, and if you don't know what the fuck you're talking about, speak loudly and with great conviction.'

In the last twenty-five years, I've examined Bob's philosophy minutely and I cannot for the life of me see any weaknesses in it. Almost everyone I know who's adopted it and refused to compromise has gone on to greater things.

Bob had one pet loathing: anything that got in the way of the meaning of a sentence. Meaning was the most important thing in the broadcaster's list of skills. He was obsessed with the idea of the broadcaster as a conduit for the message, and equally determined that the broadcaster should not dilute or distort the meaning of what he had to say, whether they were his or her own words or someone else's. Accordingly, he would roar at anyone who adopted the sing-song style. He couldn't stand anyone who read their script or spoke their piece with that classic decaying emphasis on the last word. He would splutter at any woman who cosied up to the microphone, or any man who suddenly adopted an accent or approach that wasn't his own. Anything folksy or tricksy in presentation would see him flinging his arms out, shouting, 'But it's so bloody simple. If you don't fuck about with it, it'll sound fine.' And it usually did.

Bob was an 'attitude' man. Get the attitude right, then get lots of experience and everything would be hunky-dory. I learned more from Bob in two weeks about the nuts and bolts of broadcasting than from anyone else I've ever met. If subsequently I've got it wrong, it's probably because I didn't follow his basic tenet.

'Keep it simple, fer Chrissake, Simon, and don't try so bloody hard. It isn't brain surgery, you know, it's only bloody radio!'

After a couple of weeks of doing very little on the course, Bob called me into his office. 'You're off, mate.'

'Off where?'

'To work, you start over the road on Wednesday.'

'Over the road' was Broadcasting House, Wellington, New Zealand. The head office of the New Zealand Broadcasting Corporation, sometimes known as 'Toshiba Palace'. The title was perfectly valid, because some crackpot engineer, forgetting that nasty business in the 1940s, had rushed off to Tokyo and agreed a contract with the Japanese for them to completely fit out the technical side of Broadcasting House. This caused a certain amount of antipathy with those who had been in the Commonwealth forces, but the contract had gone through. As a result, the self-operated and commercial studios were dominated by desks made of metal. Everything was made of metal and, as an ominous afterthought, someone from the health and safety executive had decreed that a wooden broom handle should be slung somewhere obvious in the studio. There were written instructions to the effect that should anyone be electrocuted, 'The power MUST BE SWITCHED OFF before removing the person concerned. The wooden handle may help in this.' By the time the wooden handle was brought into use, whoever had plugged himself into the mains would have been nicely broiled. As far as I can remember, no one actually died as a result of the equipment. But if you really concentrated you could give yourself a hell of a belt if you touched the wrong bit of exposed metal at the wrong time.

One deeply gloomy broadcaster, a skinny bloke, Hubert by name and Woody Allen by appearance, became convinced that some people were more likely to be electrocuted than others. 'Y'see, I'm more sensitive than you, I've always been sensitive and that's got to make me a better electrical conductor.'

Hubert took to wearing wellington boots in the studio for a while. Then he started refusing to press any buttons, so they gently pensioned him off by asking him to do clerical work in the administration block opposite. His weight bloomed instantly.

The night before I was due to turn up at Broadcasting House, I found myself wondering what a new recruit should wear and then I stopped bothering. Wearing my trusty Hush Puppies and the whole corduroy ensemble, I reported for work the next day and was escorted along the corridor to 'the announcers' common room'. It was a room with no personality and smelled slightly of stale underwear. I stood, cack-handed as ever, uncertain what to do, while a succession of tall, short, thin and fat people were introduced to me as some of my colleagues. Each in turn grinned wolfishly at me, sizing me up. I suspect they weren't very impressed with the gangly, bumbling thing that stood in front of them. They were polite enough, all saying the right thing, until the door opened and a cloud of old shag walked in.

Old Shag was about five feet four inches tall and had the worst smoker's cough I have ever heard. He had the look of a bedraggled school caretaker, but the eyes were the giveaway. They weren't ungenerous, but they were sharp and under massive eyebrows they darted all over the room.

'This is Morris King,' said someone. 'Morris, this is, er, Simon, er, um, the new bloke.'

King stared at me. 'New, are you? Well, don't make the mistake of hanging round here, get out while you've got the chance and your mind's still your own.'

There was a moment's silence and then a little nervous laughter as Morris retraced his steps to the door.

'Don't forget what I told you, get out before it's too late,' and he was gone.

Morris King was a legend. In the next couple of years I got to know him quite well. He was a one-man Luddite movement and disapproved of any new technical gismo. When a 'cough' button was introduced into his studio, he refused to master it, claiming that it was too complex. So, most nights he would press 'on' when he meant 'off' and vice versa. As a result, the nation would hear a racking, rasping series of coughs, followed by dead silence as Morris pressed the 'cough' button down and cut himself off the air for his next announcement. It was part of his attraction and a tribute to his ability to charm the birds off the trees in a gruff sort of way that his audience adored him and would put up with almost anything from him.

Morris didn't care greatly for producers, and if there was a complex programme going on around him he liked to run it himself. This meant confrontation and Morris was a master at winning. Sometimes during a programme, he would put his script down, glare over his spectacles through the glass at the hapless, gesticulating figure trying to attract his attention from behind the glass and, with the listeners hanging on his every word, he'd snort, 'There's a man next door waving his hand at me, I can't imagine why. Fool.' And he would carry on as though nothing had happened.

On one occasion, he made a slight blunder on a time check, announcing the hour as five o'clock when it should have been six. An overenthusiastic producer leapt to the talk-back and whispered in Morris's ear while he was talking, 'You got it wrong, Morris, it's six o'clock.' Without pausing for breath, without looking up from his script and without turning the microphone off, the dark-brown voice said, 'If I say it's five o'clock, it's five o'clock and that's final.'

Once when I was in deep trouble for some major sin, it was Morris who gave me the King guidelines for sidestepping the management. 'If you're in the shit, old son,' he told me, 'just walk around the offices looking mad as hell and muttering, "those bastards, those bastards," loud enough for everyone to hear. If you do the job well enough, everyone will think you've gone off your rocker temporarily and chances are they'll keep out of your way until the crisis has blown over.'

Morris and his kind were people who knew radio backwards and while they loved it, it didn't frighten them. They weren't impressed by its mechanics or intimidated by it. They all had their egos, or at least the good ones did, as well as a few of the bad ones. But going to do a radio programme was a job of work to them and they didn't like anyone to imagine they thought it was a big deal.

My first programme was on the following Saturday, a six-hour shift, playing records and commercials from midday until six o'clock. Nothing special, but for me the run-up to it was like being tied to the tracks waiting for an oncoming train. I tried not to think about it too much and spent the next couple of days finding somewhere to live. On Saturday, I was in the building by eleven. By eleven thirty, far too early by the standards of the time, I was standing outside the studio door twittering quietly to myself.

The disc jockey on duty grinned through the glass and waved me in, shook my hand and introduced himself. 'Look, mate, I've got a game to go to this afternoon, so d'you mind if I shag off at twelve. You'll be OK, the gear's dead easy.' He waved a vague hand at the knobs and dials that seemed to stretch forever. 'This is yer mike, these are yer grams, commercials on disc over there, schedule up on the clipboard and if you're really in the shit there's a phone somewhere with the chief engineer's number on it. Look,' he glanced up at the studio clock, 'I'd be really grateful if you'd step in a bit early, mate, I've got the kids to pick up as well.'

I gave him a look of blank terror.

'You will, oh, that's great, I owe you one.'

And he was gone. I stood there looking at the seat he'd been occupying a moment earlier as the imprint of his bottom in the cushion slowly disappeared. Something truly dreadful by Ray Conniff was warbling away in the background and I was totally on my own. I sat down and counted the faders from the left until I found the third one, which I knew was the microphone. 'Hello Dolly' was about half-way through. My confidence started to blossom a bit as I identified what piece of machinery performed which function. I put a record on to the turntable, lowered the arm, opened the mike and tentatively announced it, pressed the button and bugger me, it worked! I could hear the bloody thing going out. Bob was right, it wasn't brain surgery, it was only radio.

A few minutes later the phone rang. I tracked it down under a pile of wood at the back of the studio. A female voice asked if Mike was there. I said he had just gone to collect his kids before he took them to the rugby match and she left a message confirming a meeting they'd planned. I asked who I should say had called and she became very coy.

'Oh, don't worry about that, he'll know who it is,' she said.

Then I understood. This was radio, of course. Even then I didn't kid myself. The NZBC employed me because of my potential not because of any ability they might have spotted. But they gave me plenty of chances, and I started learning more about myself and building up my confidence as a result.

The first thing I discovered was that I wasn't that talented. Still, nothing came very easily to me. I was disappointed, but not that surprised. To achieve anything I seemed to have to work a little harder than the next man. But at last I didn't feel entirely clumsy, I found that in a radio studio I felt almost totally at ease for the first time ever. And there were no lines to learn. For the first time in my life I enjoyed nearly everything I did, however trivial, and I was quite happy to put more work in than most to learn to do it properly. There was always someone around who was prepared to show you how to edit, or how to dub and once you had learned the basics, step by step it was moderately easy to develop your own style. The joy was that no one said, 'You can't do that, mate,' when I asked for something that seemed to be unattainable. People tended to scratch their heads for a while and come up with a simple way of achieving whatever it was I was after.

I used to lie in the bath sometimes at night and listen to Keith Richardson and Paddy O'Donnell, as I would Wogan and Imus, Laws and Humphries, The Grease Man and Keillor over the years and wonder 'How the hell do they do that?' I wasn't jealous, jealousy isn't one of my sins, just delighted and amazed to listen to these people, as I still am. Whatever they were like as people didn't matter when they were on the radio. They could be intellectual midgets, up to their ears in marital problems, just been busted, broke and pathetic in private life, but when they operated that microphone there was and is a magic that has nothing to do with ego and everything to do with being great communicators. The point is that if they're any good, *they* don't know how they do it. It is a gift that is above criticism. It's a secret that you share with the broadcaster and you only hear it when you're alone with your radio.

I had discovered sound, noise and the infinite variety of ways you could use it. Sometimes I was so excited, I could hug myself with the sheer joy of it. I was lucky, because of the bureaucracy, I wasn't simply left doing record programmes or pop shows, and because of the shortage of staff I seemed to do everything and anything. I didn't care, it was all fun and I was being paid.

The major problem in the first six months was a show that went out in the early hours called 'Rural Report'. I dreaded being rostered on to it, and if you try saying 'Rural Report' a few times when you're hungover, you'll understand why, it's almost impossible to avoid dribbling.

For the most part, the staff were tolerant of me as a Pommy upstart and indulgent of my wild overenthusiasm. Occasionally they would get niggly and tell me to slow down a bit, but generally they sat back and waited for me to run out of steam.

One night shift, as I sat gossiping with an engineer, the talk-back burst into life. 'Go to channel eight, fucking Hauraki's sinking.' The pirate station only had a signal strong enough to serve the Auckland area, so we tended to forget that it was still out there in the Gulf pumping away, playing the latest waxings. I rotated the knob and there, mixed in with the static, was Hauraki's signal. It was always distinctive, as it was overcompressed and made a sucking sound if for any reason there was a pause in the flow of noise. It was being monitored by the NZBC and we were listening to a fully fledged nutter who was apparently close to meeting his maker.

'Hey, everyone, this is Radio Hauraki,' said the voice, Australian with a tang of American and that bright artificial smile added to the mix, 'and this is a mayday call. We're sinking. Yes, this is Radio Hauraki sinking right now and calling for *your* help. But let's get back to the music and see if we can stay afloat.'

Then the nutter put a record on. This extraordinary mix of a man, virtually alone on a vessel that had slipped its sea anchors and was close to sinking, making the necessary distress call for help and trying simultaneously to keep a DJ show going was one of the most bizarre broadcasts I've ever heard. This mix started by being fifty per cent music, fifty per cent distress call and a hundred per cent entertaining, but gradually the proportions changed and the music became less and less important as the situation became more serious. Eventually, the authorities told the DJ not to be a bloody fool and got on with the business of rescuing him.

This broadcast was only capped a few years later by the very final show that Hauraki transmitted before the station was given its land licence. One larger-than-life figure, considerably the worse for wear, announced on air that he was going to celebrate by walking on the waters of the Gulf. He proceeded to try to, unsuccessfully. It was the only truly tragic event that took place during New Zealand's flirtation with alternative radio.

Meantime, I had met the older woman. I encountered Rachel at a Saturday afternoon party. She had introduced herself to me, and while I stood in front of her, my toes curling with embarrassment, she had chatted to me and put me at my ease. She was in her late thirties and to me was wildly sophisticated. Rachel knew who Joan Miro was, she drank filtered coffee and had met Jack Kennedy. Rachel was American and a divorcée, which made her even more mysteriously attractive, of course.

I imposed a kind of exotic character on her. She was no more of a mystery woman than anybody, but that's how I liked to think of her. She was comparatively tall and certainly not beautiful, but to say that she was striking would be to do her an injustice. She was a confident woman who wore her clothes well and she had a wonderful, long sweeping back that seemed to go on forever. Her voice was strong and the timbre owed a lot to the unfiltered cigarettes she smoked. She laughed a lot and knew what she was talking about, but was prepared to let me in on her conversation and to take what I had to say seriously.

The daughter of a small Boston publisher, Rachel was deeply antagonistic to the American government's stance on Vietnam, and had made her views known by leaving her country and settling in Wellington. Her family had been furious and felt let down, and they let her know how they felt once a month, regular as clockwork, in long and vituperative letters that arrived at her little house with American air mail stamps on them. Only now that I am older and Rachel is long gone, do I begin to realise the pain those letters must have caused her. When she got them, she would laugh and dismiss them as rubbish and laugh again, but she would always push them deep into her jacket. I never saw her throw any of them away.

Rachel was great fun to be with. She talked well and entertainingly and she seemed to like sharing her knowledge with me. I suppose she must have been flattered by having me around like a hyperactive puppy. Sex was only part of it, though there was a warm glow to finishing a late-night radio shift, then walking in the rain to her house and being discreetly let in by what Tom and Henry used to call 'a real experienced woman'. I felt completely welcome for the first time in my life. There was a sense of confident calm that she exuded and that I fed off.

I had read enough Hemingway and Lillian Hellman to get to grips with the kind of woman I thought Rachel was and I wasn't that surprised at the drinking problem I discovered she had. Discovery is too big a term. It was obvious and unmanageable but she kept it a secret by keeping it for the weekends. It usually started on Saturday mornings and ended in tears on Sunday nights. But it was a vicious and demanding addiction only just obscuring enormous pain. I simply didn't have the skills to cope with the maudlin sad heap that I would find on occasion. I hated the way she smelt when she'd been at the whisky and I didn't know whether to be reassuring or stern when she wept with self-pity or when she chucked the contents of the living room at me. All my experience of how to handle drunks came from movies and it didn't take long to discover that people don't follow Dalton Trumbo's scripts when they're pissed and unhappy. Whatever demons Rachel had tucked away in that quicksilver mind of hers, ruled her when she was drunk. And when she was drunk, I was a baffled and incompetent liability.

Of course the affair didn't last long. I didn't really have that much to offer and Rachel needed someone with much greater depth than I. She was sober when she very gently asked me not to come around again and I surprised myself by not being that surprised. I'd begun to dread the scenes, the unpredictability and the smell of it all, and I suppose I was selfishly relieved that it was over and that she'd been the one issuing the marching orders. But I was also terribly and unnecessarily embarrassed when the brief affair was over. I would do anything to avoid seeing or being seen by Rachel. If I saw her in the street, I would hide in an alley, and if I was at the same party, I'd vanish as quickly as I could, or stand scarlet-faced, tongue-tied and hypnotised with embarrassment.

A few months later, she went back to the States, I'm not sure why. Maybe those letters had something to do with it. But years later, when I was in Australia, her name came up in conversation. I was in a group discussing the anti-Vietnam War movement, and a visiting American mentioned her and said that she had died in 1970. I was transfixed for a moment, and then that old unwelcome embarrassment roared into my mind and I became tongue-tied at all the memories that came flooding back. So, by the time I'd pulled myself together, the conversation had moved on. I never found out what had happened and why she died so young. Now it's too late to start asking those sorts of questions.

Meanwhile, back at Broadcasting House, I had discovered a woeful deficiency on my part. I had not had my sense of humour removed, the problem was that almost anything would set me giggling, I was and still am the world's worst corpser. I was doing a good deal of newsreading at this time and I'll put my hand up to agreeing with Michael Aspel when he advocated a good newsreading technique as 'in through the eyes, out through the mouth and bypass the brain'. I'll add to that, the ideal newsreader is humourless, unimaginative and self-important.

My problem with news begins and ends with the writing of it. The style that the worst of broadcast news is still written in around the world is so patently absurd. It assumes a deep knowledge of what is being talked about and it talks in a code only known to a regular audience. What's more, the code is changed whenever the writer feels like it. Today's insurgent is tomorrow's friendly government. Come in as a stranger, or abandon your fix for a few days, and you'll find yourself being addressed by someone who could be an alien from outer space. Going back to Aspel's remarks, God help an intelligent or thinking broadcaster if he sits there with the bulletin he is reading and actually hears what he's saying. Prime ministers and members of the Royal Family land at airports. When this sort of thing was given to me, I pictured them crumpled on the tarmac. 'Three armed guerrillas.' Say it out loud and you'll understand what I mean.

The very nature of working in 'serious' radio, which I was doing a good deal of the time, meant that there weren't many laughs. So if something was funny, it tended to hit you like a thunderbolt. And if it was unintentionally funny, it could leave you like a stranded whale, gasping for air. At this time, the Vietnam war was on everybody's mind and in nearly all news bulletins. To keep President Johnson sweet, the New Zealand Prime Minister had bought him off by sending young Kiwis to the battle zones. There was nothing funny about this at all, but when it came to the Vietnamese politicians' names, it wasn't xenophobia that reduced me to a quivering hulk every time I had to pronounce them.

One fateful night, I was doing a two-hander with a first-rate and much more senior broadcaster than I. The programme was a hard-hitting thirty-minute read and disaster struck in the opening story. Lee Phuoc Yu and An Phuoc Me were the two South Vietnamese names. I did everything I could to underplay them and not to sink into the trap of overpronouncing them, but the moment I uttered those infernal words, I looked up and saw Mark's eyebrows shoot up and his hand make an obscene gesture. Fatally, I hesitated for a second and was lost. I started to giggle, stifled it and then began to feel the restriction in my chest that meant I would have to gasp for air. I just finished the story and waited for Mark to pick up with his. I looked at him again, and his face was a picture, having cracked me up, he'd corpsed himself. His face was bright red and he managed to deliver the story in a sort of strangled falsetto. This was serious. We still had twenty-seven minutes to go and if we kept on laughing we probably wouldn't last five.

The trouble was that the ricochet effect had taken over. Every effort made by one of us to stop laughing, reduced the other to a whimpering heap. Mark was a desperate man and prepared to resort to desperate measures. While I choked through yet another atrocious display of total lack of self-control, he slipped quietly out of the studio, found a fire bucket of water somewhere, emptied it over his head and returned. I saw him come back in, hair plastered to his forehead, suit drenched, shoes beginning to curl up and was completely destroyed. For the remaining ten minutes, I did everything I could to keep breathing as I shook with laughter. Well, of course, it was the end.

I knew I would have to go and I took the initiative. I called the boss's secretary, who would barely speak to me and asked to see him.

'Come right up,' she snarled.

So I went in and humiliated myself. I told him that I was resigning and apologised, but despite that I would never be able to hold my head up again. I told the poor bemused man repeatedly how sorry I was and after five minutes of this, just as I was about to do it all over again, there was a knock on the door.

'Come in,' said the Lord High Executioner.

The door slowly opened, and Mark crawled in and across the office on his hands and knees, grabbed the boss's leg and held it close to his chest. 'For Christ's sake, don't fire me, I've got a wife and kids to support.'

I broke down in tears of laughter and, thank God, even the boss smiled, though wanly.

Years later, when a particularly nasty British murderer nicknamed 'The Black Panther' was arrested, the Radio Four newsreader proved my point about the ideal qualifications for the job. As the sound of Big Ben faded into the background and using his best 'I've got something terribly important to impart' voice, the poor man uttered the immortal opening lines: 'The Pink Panther has been arrested.'

The newsroom erupted with delight. For some of them, this was what they'd been waiting for for years. A little light in an endless darkness. The reader was baffled and annoyed when he saw through the glass, the entire newsroom en fête. It was as though General MacArthur had suddenly come back from the dead. He finished the bulletin and came out, a mass of hurt pride, to ask what the hell was going on. When he was told what he had said, he refused to believe it. When they played him the tape recording of the bulletin he claimed that they'd cut it round to make a fool of him. He still believes that and why shouldn't he? It eases the pain.

Newsreaders are a weird mob. Eventually they all crack under the strain of being so relentlessly po-faced. I'm faintly proud that I was there one day to see one fall off his perch. There was in the NZBC an astonishing man in mid-life called Roy Serent. Roy rated himself just alongside God in the broadcasters' almanac and he certainly wouldn't waste time acknowledging the likes of me. He was one of the most dignified and unbending of men, and that's how he read his news, straight and unbending. But Roy had a couple of weaknesses – he was screwing one of the cleaning ladies on a regular basis (after ten o'clock most nights you'd hear the cry, 'Oh, come on, love, just a quick one' ring out down the darkened corridors), and he couldn't hold his drink.

I was standing in the lavatory one morning doing up my zip, when Roy tottered in. He looked dreadful and stank of last night's de-bauchery. He scowled at me and then lifted himself up on to the stand and reached inside his zip. His face went pale.

'Jesus Christ, it's gone.' He fumbled for a moment and then re-peated himself. 'Jesus Christ, there's nothing there.' And, going white as a sheet, he crumpled on to the floor, his trousers hanging at half-mast.

I was no fool and I certainly wasn't going to check him out, so I went to get the receptionist, who collapsed in giggles and called an ambulance. They took Roy to the hospital and discovered on the way that, after whatever nasty business he'd been up to the night before, he had put his old-fashioned underpants on back to front, leaving the access point for his willy somewhere around his backside. No won-der he couldn't find the offending member.

Roy came back to work and continued to stalk haughtily past me, but it was never the same again. He knew that I knew, and he must have known that I had told everybody. He stopped screwing the cleaning lady, got religious and left the NZBC to preach. A few years later, he was killed when his car stalled going over a level crossing and an unscheduled train appeared from nowhere.

We kept our jobs, Mark and I, but the incident didn't slow Mark down. He was an unpredictable bloke and he held the management in healthy disdain. Once when we were both being carpeted for some offence or other, he listened while the list of his supposed crimes was read out to him. Normally, Mark would erupt and shout back, but on this occasion he played the part of the pussy-cat.

When the boss had finished, Mark smiled and said, 'Look, mate, I realise the situation. You're the boss, you're paid to stop me doing my job. I'm the broadcaster, my job is to push the boundaries that little bit further. You're the boss and you're paid to try and stop me doing anything creative. Now we both understand each other, can we call it a day?'

Mark smiled, stood up and left the office with me sitting there lost in admiration for such a splendidly delivered load of hogwash and wishing I'd thought of the line.

His finest hour, though, was when the NZBC hosted the Commonwealth Director General's conference. Mark laid his plans and waited until the flock of VIPs was shown into the studio he was occupying. The NZBC Director General flung the door open with some pride and there, spreadeagled across the desk and fettered to it with heavy chains was Mark. He looked up with a pathetic expression. 'For God's sake, feed me,' he cried.

Shortly after that exploit, Mark disappeared to work on a country station that no one had ever heard of.

Apart from the professional and personal crises, life went on, until my body abruptly let me down one day. I'd been having tummy-aches, but I'd put them down to the chemicals the filthy beer I was drinking probably contained, and took no notice until I found myself doubled up with pain and walked down Lambton Quay to the doctors.

'Right, mate, you've got a swollen appendix and the little bugger's got to come out,' he said, after almost kneading me to death.

'When?'

'Well,' and now he suddenly adopted the expression of a concerned medical expert, 'I'd like to get you in today.'

'I can't. I'm working and I'm taking a girl out tonight.'

'All right, if you want to kill yourself, but no beer and go easy on the girl, right?'

I said yes, but then I would have promised anything. I was taking a spectacularly stupid girl engineer from Invercargill out that night and I'd borrowed a car. Even I couldn't fail with that combination. Back to Broadcasting House I went, feeling bruised and sore and took the lift down to the studio area. As soon as I opened the studio door, I blacked out.

I woke in hospital a few hours later, in pain, minus an appendix and with a nurse leaning over me slapping my face. 'Give us yer autograph, love.' It was my first experience of fan worship.

I was put on to the early morning network news bulletins not long after and almost immediately learned an enormous lesson: check that your voice is still there. I had got myself a little flat in Parliament

Street, on a hill about a quarter of a mile from work. Once the area had been pretty grand, now it had become dilapidated. But the house I lived in had the most perfect view overlooking the harbour and Broadcasting House. It was also perfect for work. I could slide out of bed at 5.50 a.m., be in the newsroom to pick up the bulletin by 5.55 a.m. and in my little booth ready to say 'NZBC Network News at six, this is Simon Bates' in plenty of time for the pips.

This became a pleasant ritual until one lovely sunny morning, I fell out of bed as usual and gambolled down the hill doing up my flies as I went through the double doors, grabbed the bulletin, sat down in my little chair, opened the mike and my mouth and said . . . nothing! All that came out of my throat was a breathy gargling sound. I hadn't cleared my throat before I went on air and a little phlegm had wrapped itself thoughtfully around my vocal chords. Being a fool I tried to carry on and nearly throttled myself, but by that time the studio downstairs, aware that they were dealing with a fool, had taken over. From then and ever afterwards I have always said two words to myself before going on air, 'just checking'. It's good to know when the system is working.

Of course, as one lesson is learned, God sends another rap on the knuckles. A month or so later, I forgot my name. God knows why. I said 'NZBC Network News at six' OK, then my mind went blank and I blundered into 'this is, er' and sort of faded off into the next story.

As I walked back into the newsroom with my tail between my legs, Ron Jones said, 'Personality crisis, eh?'

Ron was my hero. He was the news organiser on the early shift and managed to get through a bottle of whisky and cream on most days. He had a face like the surface of the moon, and every line that had been added as time went on mirrored the amount of alcohol he'd sunk and the number of wives he'd had. Although he had plenty of wives to deal with, his liver had disappeared years before. Ron's system had found a way to make the liver superfluous, but he was living on borrowed time. Ron was an immensely kind, tolerant and patient man. He was also very good at what he did. But it was the wives who finally did for him.

Every year he hosted a reunion of all of them in Dunedin, on the tip of South Island. These were invariably hugely successful events and resulted in Ron doing his best to drink the town dry. On his last trip there he almost succeeded and was taken to hospital with severe pneumonia. When they heard the news, the powers that be sent a young journalist to Dunedin to see if there was anything Ron needed.

The boy was shocked at the sight of Ron, pale, skeletal and even more deeply lined, lying in a hospital bed. 'Is there anything you need, Ron?'

Ron's beady little eyes shot fire. A skinny hand snaked from under the sheets and grabbed the lad's arm. 'Get me a bottle of whisky.'

'I can't do that, the nurses won't let me.'

The whisper became extremely firm. 'If you don't, boy, you can kiss your future goodbye and that's a promise.'

The next day, the whisky was smuggled in and Ron drank the lot while no one was looking. He died a few hours later, but as someone said at his wake, 'He died with a grin on his face.'

By the time all this happened I had left New Zealand and had been living in Australia for quite a while. A year or so before his death, I got a letter out of the blue from Ron. I opened it on a glorious sunny morning, sitting on the small terrace of my house in Sydney. Inside the envelope was an extremely generous reference typed on NZBC paper and accompanying it a handwritten note: 'This may come in handy one day. Best wishes and good luck. Ron.' I have them both still.

Chapter 5

THINGS WERE CHANGING IN NEW ZEALAND. The times were catching up with her; a new currency called the dollar and new drinking laws were on their way. The end of 'the six o'clock swill' and the arrival of civilised drinking hours in New Zealand's pubs was scheduled for two weeks after I was sent to Greymouth.

Greymouth is a small enclave on the west coast of South Island. Its population is surrounded by the sea on one side and a range of mountains separating it from the Canterbury plain on the other. The jokes about this small community and its isolation were endless and usually focused on incest and intermarriage between families. Certainly, when I was sent there, it had an ingrown feel about it.

The senior announcer at the small radio station in the town had met with disaster. One night, not long after the pubs had shut, he was tottering home in the darkness when an earthquake struck. It wasn't a major one and he was a philosophical chap, so he stood under a door frame, as the authorities recommended, and waited for the ground to stop shaking. The earth had stopped moving, and our friend had stepped out into the street to continue his faltering way home when a tile loosened by the quake slid down the roof and plopped on to his head. He died instantly and, so rumour has it, happily. 'He knew he'd never have to go home to the wife again,' someone told me.

As a result, there was a job vacancy in the radio station and a gap to be filled until the arrival of the lucky applicant. I was sent there for a couple of weeks to be the infill. I flew down to Christchurch and caught a Cessna over the mountains to the little town. The centre of life was still the mining community and it was a barren place, but I was warmly welcomed and taken to the local hotel where I'd be staying.

'See youse fer a drink tonight,' said the engineer, and I agreed to meet him at eight o'clock. Drinking for hotel residents was OK, but the bar would be off limits to the locals at this time because of that infernal six o'clock rule. At least he could be my guest. I felt thirsty so I went to the bar at about 5.30 p.m. and, as I had expected, it was packed. At five forty-five the cry of 'Time, gentlemen, please' was ignored in traditional style. At six o'clock, two policemen came in and gently reminded the lingering hordes that it was time to go. Five minutes later, the bar was empty. Then a door at the back opened and the two policemen came in, followed by the masses they had just thrown out. It was like an Ealing comedy, all these people had done was walk out through the front door, which was then locked behind them, pause for a moment and re-enter the bar from the rear. There was method in their madness. The same ritual was performed at the same time every night, and while the law was satisfied that the bar was emptied on time, the miners got their late-night drinking as 'residents' in the tiny four-bedroomed hotel. All two hundred of them.

The Greymouth radio station wasn't a twenty-four-hour-a-day business. Neither was it a high-tech establishment – just two rooms above a fish and chip shop. It provided a breakfast show, a lunch show and an evening news service to the town and the countryside around. The bits in between were relayed programmes from the radio station over the mountains in Christchurch. The late senior announcer's job had been to do the breakfast show, so that was where I was filling in. It wasn't a particularly onerous task, just a few records, some news and those perennial advertisements typed on pink sheets with 'Simon, can you do this at 7.45 please. Thanks, Naomi' handwritten on the border.

Every radio station had a Naomi (pronounced NaoOmi). Her kind was always of an uncertain age, wore blouses that buttoned up to the throat and wrote little notes in spidery handwriting. She was also, along with the chief engineer, the only person who knew where the bodies were buried and wild horses wouldn't drag the information out of her. She would write the copy for any local commercials:

'Ladies. Did you know that Wilsons on the main street have just received a delivery of new autumn frocks from England? They're in startling colours and they'll have the man in your life smiling all over his face when you wear one of these new frocks from Wilsons. Don't forget, Wilsons, where the newest always arrives firstest. Oh, and for the kiddies, Wilsons have the finest Aertex shirts just for you.'

But this Naomi in Greymouth had a dark secret. For twenty years she'd had an arrangement with the chief engineer, who was married to a frightful woman who screamed at him constantly. Once a week the pair would stay late at the station 'doing an inventory' or having 'staff meetings'. They would lock the door of his technical store, get down to business and emerge a little flushed and breathless about half an hour later. Everyone in the town knew about this and accepted it. The two protagonists, on the other hand, believed that their discretion had kept their secret. The chief engineer would arrive at the pub, looking very chipper after his staff meeting, at about eight thirty on Wednesday evenings, and sink a couple before allowing his head to droop and heading for home and a rollicking from his wife. This was all explained to me by the publican on the night I arrived.

'Why are you telling me this?' I said in my naîvety. 'It's none of my business, I don't want to know.'

The barman eyed me contemptuously. 'I am telling you, yer bloody fool, just so youse don't get any ideas about working late up there on Wednesday evenings.' Greymouth looked after its own.

Then there was the 'school bell'. This was a part of New Zealand life that had been broadcast at eight o'clock since the dawn of radio time. It had always been sponsored by the Apple and Pear Board, and consisted of a racket from a handbell that hung in every studio in the land, a few unscripted dedications, a homily about the weather or anything the announcer could think of and a reminder, 'Don't forget your New Zealand apple, girls and boys.' On most stations, the job was done by the announcer, in Greymouth, they had a much-loved local personality do it. I had never heard of him, of course, but I was only going to be there for a couple of weeks.

On my first day, at 7.50 a.m., an enormous man, the spitting image of Piri, squeezed through the door.

'Hey, boy, how ya doin'?'

His name was Sam and while he was quite a modest quiet sort of bloke off the air, he changed magically when the microphone was on. His arms flailed as he rang that damned handbell in my face. As a Maori, it was impossible for him to go pink with effort, but he would have done if he could as he fairly roared his head off shouting, 'Gooood Morning, Boys and Girls.'

On the first day I was there, sitting opposite him, aghast at all the effort he put into this, his false teeth gave up the attempt to stay glued to his gums when he said the word 'Girls' and, as his mouth was wide open, both sets flew out. But Sam was accustomed to this local difficulty, caught them mid-flight and scooped them back into his mouth. This happened two or three times during the five minutes he was on air and it happened regularly each day I worked with him over the next couple of weeks. I never heard him falter in his speech and I never saw him miss those teeth as they whizzed past his nose. The man should have had an Olympic sport designed for him.

It was in Greymouth that I saw my first earthquake. After the big one, there are usually a series of aftershocks. On the day I arrived, I was standing in a field somewhere near the town, when one hit. There was almost no noise, no rumbling, but as I looked across the field, the energy created by the plates moving in the San Andreas faultline out under the sea was visible. Like a tiny series of ripples in the air, they bounced across the field at me. I saw them for a split second as they came towards me before the shock struck, the ground heaved and I fell over.

I have never been too concerned at earthquakes when I'm out in the open. The worst that can happen is the sudden appearance of a chasm at my feet and I have always assumed that, as in the best Hollywood movies, I'd be one of the heroes who survived. It's when I'm in an enclosed space that starts shifting from side to side that I get a little nervous.

It was in my second week that, somewhere out in the Pacific, one plate started grinding against another and caused more than a ripple. The aftershock hit Greymouth with a strength of about six on the Richter scale, just as I was about to launch into a commercial for the local coalman. The room heaved and strained, the windows buckled and one caved in. I looked up, and saw the engineer calmly get up from the bench where he'd been soldering something and stand in what we were always told was the safest place, under the door frame. He just leaned against the frame and calmly continued to smoke a roll-up. He was used to this, I wasn't. The earthquake seemed to go on for ever, rumbling and swaying. 'Oh, fuck,' I said with great presence of mind, and then, as I realised the microphone was still on, 'Oh, FUCK' again. The engineer roared with laughter.

A week or two later, when I got back to Wellington, Morris King told me not to worry about the gaffe. 'They're used to worse than that on the east coast,' he said. 'Besides, anyone who hasn't said the magic four-letter word on air at least once in their career has got to be a ratbag.'

Back in Wellington, life was pretty good and the audience more tolerant than we had the right to expect. You could get away with most things, just so long as you took rugby seriously. All that sweaty stuff that men were supposed to revel in was sacrosanct, but there were plenty of other things to do.

I had discovered Blue Note records and the fact that if you reviewed them on air, you got to keep the records. So I invented a weekly blues programme and began my authoritative collection of John Mayall albums. I had the strong conviction that I was a major force in innovative radio when I did these programmes and that one day everybody would realise just how important this sort of broadcasting was. I even debated changing my name to something more suitable, like Chuck, or Waylon. Almost nobody listened, either to my agonising over my name, or to the programmes. Eventually I was overcome with lust one night and failed to turn up for the show. Some bright spark filled the gap by playing a selection of 'Music From the Shows'. No one complained at the absence of my ground-breaking programme.

The only major bugbear with day-to-day life, as with all broadcasting outfits, was the politician. There was an added complication in this case because we had a herd of the things next door. The Beehive, Parliament itself, was just a hop, skip and a jump from Broadcasting House, and if any politico felt like it he could virtually lob a brick through our windows.

I came unstuck with a particularly unsavoury character called Muldoon. Piggy Muldoon was nicknamed such because he was an overweight, reactionary slob. He was no fool, however, and although he could do nothing about it, he was well aware of his nickname. About this time Peter Cook and Dudley Moore made a record called 'Spotty Muldoon', and though it wasn't really that applicable, I pounced on it and childishly played it to death on whatever show it was that I was doing at the time. There was an instant howl of delight from the audience. Piggy erupted. This would not do, the honour of the House was being besmirched, there was a lack of respect being shown to him personally, so get the fucking thing off, right? Piggy was not a man to be argued with. The record was duly banned and I was hauled over the coals.

Piggy became Prime Minister a few years later but I got my own back. After his inevitable fall from grace, he became a talk-show host and when I met him at the Sydney Opera House in the late eighties, he invited me to join him on his show in Auckland. I did. He was crap. I loved every minute of it.

Simon Bates

On the morning of 10 March 1968, I woke early and alone, to find no roof on my bedroom and the earth moving. I had been on a bit of a bender the previous evening, so I didn't react straight away, but lay there going through the usual checks. Was I awake and was everything in place? All the proper confirmations came back, but my face reported that it was covered in rain. The roof had vanished. The earth was still moving, it was time for me to do the same thing. I got up and looked outside. A tree, complete with roots, flew past the bedroom window and I was on the second floor. Whatever was going on, I didn't want to be part of it. By the time I got outside, I found myself clinging to the front gate, more than slightly worried that the howling gale that was blowing would whisk me down the hill in pursuit of the tree I'd seen blown thataway and the others that were now following it. Something was dreadfully wrong and I had the feeling it might be 'The Big One', the ultimate earthquake that every-body had said would happen one day. We had been used to little shocks, sometimes bad enough to break a few window-panes. After all, Wellington was at the end of the San Andreas faultline and we were as vulnerable as Los Angeles on the other side of the Pacific.

The safest place to be under such circumstances was Broadcasting House, it had been built a couple of years before on a central core, rather like a set of gimbals, that allowed it to remain static while the shock moved around it. It had been a strange feeling during the previous small shocks, to look through the window and watch the street move up and down as the studio stayed in place, rather like being on board a ship. By the time I had crawled into Broadcasting House, all the other cowards had had the same idea and the place had the look of a refugee camp. Only one station was still on the air and the engineers were struggling to keep that transmitter going. It became pretty obvious that this wasn't an earthquake but a very severe hurricane. Even so, nearly all basic services had been knocked out and in the harbour there was a story that was growing in import-ance.

The inter-island ferries were huge things, built along the lines of the cross-channel ferries in Europe, and one of the newest, *The Wahine*, had been standing off the harbour riding out the dreadful conditions since the previous night. No one had thought much about it, but as the morning wore on, so more people took it seriously. Along with a few others, I drove out to the harbour. By peering into the howling gale and the rain, you could just make out the shape of

The Wahine, swaying horribly from side to side. She was too far away to see clearly or to see any of the passengers and crew on deck, but there was no mistaking her. There was no hearing her either, if her crew had been sounding her horn, it would have been impossible to hear because of the fearful screeching of the hurricane.

It was while I watched that I saw *The Wahine* disappear, or rather I thought I saw her disappear. One minute I could just make her out and then there was nothing there, just the rain. I wiped my glasses, but it only served to smear them and I could see even less. I looked around and shouted at the people I was with, but it was impossible to hear their replies. Judging by their faces, they thought the same as me. Two hundred people died that morning when *The Wahine* sank. There was a commission of enquiry, of course, and it's too late to dig over old bones now. Suffice it to say that some of the crew of *The Wahine* didn't seem to me to cover themselves in glory.

After a while, the police moved us on. The survivors and the bodies were being brought ashore. Most of us went back to Broadcasting House. Things had improved slightly and now both commercial stations were back on the air. One bright spark in management had realised that the commercial schedule was falling behind, so in order to keep the money rolling in, he had two announcers sitting opposite each other reading commercials, one after the other. Later that evening, someone punched him in the face, as much for his sense of priorities as for his decision-making abilities.

The summer came and I fell hopelessly and pathetically in love. This was the real thing and not lust, though lust had a tendency to rear its head when I was with Chris and a good deal of rushing to the bedroom went on when we were together. Chris was a delight. In her mid-twenties, she was desperately attractive, with dark, generous eyes and a wide perfect smile. The fact that she paid the attention she did to me was staggering. Here was a genuinely gorgeous girl who seemed to be able to tolerate my social and physical clumsiness.

There were drawbacks and complications, of course. For a start, she was a good Catholic and when we were in friends' houses that meant turning the Virgin Mary's face to the wall before we made love. And then there was her indecisiveness. She had been going out with a chinless wonder, a member of one of New Zealand's better and more established families. I could be accused of bias, but I thought the man a fool then and I still do. He was my immediate opposite – quite good-looking, mature, well connected and full of money-making ideas, a civilised man with a well-planned future. I, on the other hand, was a hopeless case in all those respects. I never actually got round to hating him because he made such an effort to be nice to me, damn him!

Chris was going through a phase of making up her mind, or so she said. The truth was that she was young, it was a particularly lovely summer and she was quite enjoying being pursued and why not? The fact that the good-looking mature one and I were both on the point of suicide didn't quite enter into Chris's thinking. She was probably agonising as well. You see, we all suffered a great deal that summer.

About this time, I had started working for TV again. I was a success doing terrible light-entertainment shows. I got good seats in restaurants and people said 'hello' in the street. So, as a member of the *nouveau riche*, I got a telephone. One of the first calls I got on it was from a man who introduced himself as Derek Morton and said, 'I want to make a kids' TV series and I want you to front it.'

Horrific memories of Michael J. Devine and unsuccessfully learning lines flooded back, and I told him so.

'No, no, no,' said the voice impatiently as though speaking to a very dim child, 'I don't work with scripts, for heaven's sake.'

We met for a coffee and I was captivated. Derek was apparently mad. A pair of twinkling, amused eyes were tucked away in there somewhere in a face that was trying to get out from behind a huge shock of ginger hair, with a beard to match. Derek seemed to live in a chaotic house full of kids up in the hills. Sometimes he lived there and sometimes he didn't. His relationships fluctuated wildly and I was never quite certain whose children they were, who he was married to or if he was married at all. He also smoked a good deal of high-quality dope and seemed prepared to cut me in on his supply. That sealed it really and we made our series.

Derek had that kind of magic that made normally sane and demanding engineers work happily for him, no matter how infuriating he was. He always refused to prepare, there was never a lighting design for any programme I worked with him on and rarely a script of any kind. And people put up with this! Derek's trick was to put in a lot of ingredients, let them simmer a bit and see what happened. Because he was genuinely creative and not in the least pompous, he would usually win through and something good would come out of it all. Editing, though, was hellish.

Days spent in the studio with Derek were always stressful, but the consolation was location filming. Derek had a complete understanding of magazine programmes and what they required, as well as a healthy contempt for them, so he would sit and plot a filming excursion in his office. In those days, to keep costs down and the audience hooked, it was traditional to go to a location for a few days and make a series of five films about the same subject. The idea was five for the price of one. These films were universally deathly dull, they would start with a stand-up piece from me introducing the subject, then there would be cutaways illustrating what I was talking about, maybe an interview and a final wrap from me. The sort of stuff you still see on news magazines all over the world to this day.

Derek's principle wasn't to challenge the established order of things and try to make art, but to go along with what the management expected, and have a bloody good time while you were doing it. A lesson I learned well. Hence, half a dozen of us would go skiing on Mount Ruapehu for a week. For six days the Arriflexes and the sound gear would be locked away and we'd concentrate on having a good time. On the seventh, we would labour. And how we'd labour. Derek's eye for camera angles was astonishing. Having made up his mind what each of the five vignettes would be about, he would have the five interviewees lined up and bang off each film in double-quick time. By changing the camera angles imperceptibly and moving each of my stand-ups a few feet, he would manage to make a series of films that looked as though they'd been shot at locations miles apart. Thus did we justify our weeks away from base.

To our surprise, the first series was a critical success and won a couple of American awards. Doesn't time fly when you're having a good career? We became socially acceptable and the management developed an alarming tolerance of our activities. At times, it verged on indulgence. We, ungrateful things, immediately set about taking advantage of them and planning bigger and better scams for the second series. We overreached ourselves, of course.

For the next series, Derek wrote a children's serial, involving a white and a Maori boy's adventures. For the time, it looked and still looks quite effective. The problem was that the villain was played by an ex-schoolteacher friend of Derek's. This man has subsequently become a well-known actor, so I'll protect his anonymity. He gave a superb and prize-winning performance and, come the annual awards bash, was to be presented with his gong by a member of the Royal

Family specially freighted in for the event. The day before the ceremony, he broke his leg. Even though he was in plaster up to his waist and half-wrecked by the pain-killers he was taking, he insisted on accepting his award personally. Much debate went on about how this was to be achieved, and finally it was agreed that he would be placed behind some tabs, that his award would be announced along with an explanation for his lack of mobility, and that Her Royal Highness would graciously walk across the stage and present him with his prize.

Come the night, with the great and the good present and up to their ears in imitation jewellery, the moment arrived and the announcement was made. The curtains slid open and there he stood, or rather leant, on his crutches. He looked irresistibly like an overweight Fred Astaire waiting for Judy Garland to join him for 'We're a Couple of Swells'. He was wearing an evening suit with one leg slit nearly to the waist to allow room for the plaster and was glassy-eyed. The drugs had got to him. At the end of the announcement and before Royalty had a chance to do anything, he fixed the audience with a crazed stare and cried, 'Ladies and gentlemen, I have an announcement to make. I can walk!' To a stunned silence from the audience, he threw away the crutches and fell flat on his face, before being dragged off stage by two burly men hauling on his arms.

The atmosphere at work the next day was not good. Chris and I were going through the bad patch before the split, only I was too thick to understand it, so I was drinking and smoking quite a lot. Derek had gone off his rocker. During one of our forays on to Mount Ruapehu, he had decided that he wanted to be a cameraman again and make the ultimate film about snow. Rather than bother management with this idea, he had nicked a couple of cameras and a good deal of film stock, and taken himself and one of his ladies into one of the huts high up on the mountain. Everyone knew he was there and everyone knew that he had finally signed his death warrant with the NZBC.

A few weeks after all this became common knowledge, I was sitting in Wellington in one of the offices on the fourth floor. Downstairs, unbeknownst to me, Derek was trying to get past the commissionaire and reclaim some graphics he claimed he'd left in what used to be his office.

'I'm sorry, mate, but they won't even let you darken their toilet paper, let alone their doorstep. You'll have to bugger off and use the phone.'

But Derek was made of stronger stuff and he asked where I was. A few minutes later, there was a knock on the outside window of the office and I looked up to see the familiar beard hanging on to the drainpipe with one hand and banging on the window with the other. I've lost touch with him since and I wish I hadn't. At least he got his graphics.

My reward was to get the heave-ho from Chris. It was a painful time, but the omens were there and I booked a flight to Sydney.

Looking back, I wonder about the person I was then. Maybe I was lucky, or maybe I was just too immature to understand how dumb I really was. If that is true, then I couldn't have landed in a more tolerant and generous country at a more appropriate time. I've been back to New Zealand on occasion and of course I've been disappointed. The countryside is still breathtaking, that never changes, and whenever I've been out in the countryside I can hear the echo of what I had. I have stupidly tried to recapture a little of what there once was, I've been back to the long narrow country lanes around Hamilton, and clambered up and down the still winding streets in Wellington, but my old house in Parliament Street has been swept away. I've wandered around Auckland and Christchurch, but now they're just cities.

What became of all those people? Some like Ron drank themselves to death happily; some like Rachel died alone, I suspect, and embittered. But there must be so many of them around still. And yet the faces in the streets are like the streets themselves, impersonal, blank, like a million faces and streets in any city you'd care to name anywhere in the world. There is nothing left in them of what I knew and had. And whatever happened to that damned horse? Kit must be long dead.

Last year I walked past what used to be the old theatre in Auckland. It had been a small but perfect Victorian theatre, the pride of Auckland at the turn of the century and almost impeccably preserved until its demolition in the eighties. I saw *The Pyjama Game* there.

I saw Micheál Mac Liammóir do his one-man Oscar Wilde there, and afterwards let him pat my bottom playfully in the bar up the road. He was just a harmless old actor with an eye for an easy conquest. When he walked up Auckland's main street he stopped the traffic. His top-hat and cane was enough, but what really staggered the citizens was the idea of a man wearing a carnation in his buttonhole and in broad daylight at that! I suspect that the only reason he wasn't arrested and carted off was because he was an artist and New Zealanders at the time accepted that 'artists are different'. Mac Liam-móir was surely that.

The theatre has gone now. Like their cousins across the seas, the worthy burghers knew the value of the land, knocked the theatre down and had it redeveloped. Maybe that's what happened while I was away, they just redeveloped the country.

To take a shower, or even bathe in nostalgia is fine, but when you let it take over your life, then you're in the kind of trouble that has you agreeing with taxi-drivers who say 'they don't write 'em like that any more'. So, I'm not saying that New Zealand isn't a beautiful and madly delightful country any more, of course it is. It has just lost its infernally irritating and wonderful uniqueness. It's been internationalised. Somewhere along the line, Trusthouse Forte got involved and it's now just another package.

I'm not part of New Zealand any more, and neither should I be, I made my choice. The friends there who welcome me know that when I come, I'll be around for only a short while and they make too much of an effort to fill my time. They welcome me as a stranger. Whatever I had, vanished years ago. I suspect that it was lost the moment I got on that Air New Zealand Electra and flew across the Tasman to Sydney. Now New Zealand has poverty, racism and an armed police force, all the trappings of the new society. I don't think that I'll go back. But now and then I bump into my past coming around again.

Last year in Los Angeles, I had a meeting with a particularly loathsome record company executive. He'd arranged to meet in one of those vast and interminable Californian hotels. I was early and dreading seeing the man, so as I had nothing better to do, I was wandering around taking in the sheer awfulness of the architecture when I thought I heard a familiar voice, or rather I heard a familiar piano accompanying a familiar cackle. The huge door was ..ightly ajar, so I peered into what was one of the many function rooms and beheld a vision. Row on row of those particularly ferocious Californian ladies 'of an age', each with the same tinted hair, substantial bosom and cruel glasses, were sitting with their backs to me. Endless nipping and tucking had gone on here for the approval of friends, but friends were forgotten at this moment. Hands were clasped in rapture at the figure on the stage. Impeccably dressed and with a suspiciously majestic head of grey hair, it was Ray Samuels, doing his time-honoured Liberace impersonation. When I arrived, he was half-way through 'Mammy' and would segue effortlessly into 'Born Free'.

By my calculations, he was at least seventy, but nothing had changed, he was immaculate. He must have been wearing the most severe corset imaginable, not a spare pound was showing. The teeth were twinkling, the eyes were a bright blue and a tribute to the drops he must have popped in them before going on stage. Ray had triumphed, he'd survived the lot of us, he was in that time warp. Almost the only thing that had changed was his mane of grey hair, it was too thick and luxuriant to be true. But then this was California, so why not? The ladies loved him. Correction, they adored him.

I watched as for twenty minutes he cosseted and flirted with them, flattered them and then with a last flourish of 'The Wind Beneath My Wings', stood at the piano, bowed low and left the stage. I couldn't resist going back and saying hello. I wasn't even certain that he would remember me, but he clearly did.

He flung his arms around me as he used to in the Vic and chortled, 'Darlin', how are ya?' Then looking me up and down and with no venom whatever said, 'My God, you've let yourself go. Have a drink.'

We sat down, me with a Corona, 'How can you drink that piss, love?' and Ray with a gin and tonic. His fingernails were a tribute to the manicurist's art. His legs neatly crossed. 'It's the only time they stay that way, dear!'

We talked and reminisced. Yes, he was still with the same partner and yes he came over from Wellington once a year to do these lunchtime concerts for little old ladies, 'bank raids' he called them.

'Aaw, you know, love,' he said, 'it isn't the same now back home. I mean, we all had such a good time, didn't we?'

I agreed and we talked some more about people we had known, and then it was time to go. I left Ray smiling and signing autographs for the little old ladies who had been waiting so patiently for him.

As I slipped away he winked at me. 'Bloody stupid, isn't it,' he whispered, 'an old New Zealand queen and I've still managed to find a bunch of people who think I'm God? Fuckin' stupid, but that's life. Cheero, darlin', see you again.'

New Zealand was a topsy-turvy country. Flying out of Wellington, the capital city, the home of the government, meant taking a propeller-driven aircraft – the runway was too short for anything else. If you wanted to fly by jet, you had to commute to Christchurch or Auckland.

The fact that I was going and not coming back was accepted. All I was doing, in an odd sort of way, was following the first steps that thousands of New Zealanders took every year as they started the 'grand tour'. This was and still is a required tradition, or maybe it's something to do with their hormones. Between the ages of eighteen and twenty-three, all New Zealanders and Australians migrate following one of two routes. The first takes them straight to Britain and then has them wandering through Europe, India and South-East Asia until they get back home a few years later. The other sends them to Singapore and a long journey on foot, by bike, bus and rail to London. In the years they're away, and to qualify as a successful traveller, it is necessary for them to sleep around an awful lot, drink even more and smoke vast quantities of hash. Some of them never make it back and stay in Britain to run the National Health Service or the current affairs end of British broadcasting. Others shack up with unsuitable partners for a while and talk a good deal of amiable nonsense about writing the novel or catching the ultimate wave. They are usually amongst the nicest people you'll meet travelling anywhere in the world. They almost always have a low expectation of people and a high appreciation of life, and they're rarely disappointed.

There was a small contingent at the airport to wave me goodbye and a bunch of flowers to remember them by. Then it was off across the Tasman Sea, with a shoulderbag and not much else. But there wasn't that much to worry about. After all, I had a couple of hundred dollars and the address of a friend I could stay with in Double Bay. Apart from the lack of Chris, life looked pretty good.

Chapter 6

THE OLD JET PROP ELECTRA wheeled across the red roofs of Sydney's suburbs and into Kingsford Smith airport. When the steward finally unjammed it and opened the door, a blast of hot air hit me. To avoid putting anything in the hold, an obsession I still cling to, I was wearing two sets of clothes and my body immediately came to the boil. Everyone else was wearing shorts and crisp white shirts and by the time I got to the front of the immigration queue, sweat was pouring down my face and on to the first of the two jackets I had on and they still let me into Australia.

I was staying with friends in Double Bay, which was then and still is one of the most expensive areas in the city. You could tell it was wall to wall wealth by the way the women walked, with that special disinterest in what surrounds them that only money can buy. Even though I had a couple of hundred dollars and I didn't really need to earn immediately, the work ethic started rattling at my conscience. One of my weaknesses is a tendency to feel guilty if I'm not working, or about to work, even if it's not necessary.

I had only the vaguest idea how Australian broadcasting worked, but a few long boring nights sitting in a warm studio in Wellington gossiping down the line with an engineer doing the same thing in Sydney had left me aware of the ABC as the national broadcaster. So, out with the Yellow Pages and call them. I chatted with the operator for a while, explained that I was after a job and that I thought that talking might be appropriate. She said that she was putting me through 'to Michael. He'll know what to do.'

Over the last couple of days, I had got used to the easy flow of the Australian accent and for a moment I was lost at the next voice I heard.

'Hello, what's your name, dear boy?'

It was a distinctively masculine sound, nothing faintly fey about it, but it was so British. More than that, it was an accent I hadn't heard since leaving the UK four years ago. It was like stepping back into a world I'd never known. Crisp and with a touch of the thirties about it, it was the sort of voice that would have done some movie matinée idol proud.

A couple of questions and then, 'Well, look old boy, you'd better come in and have a chat.'

'Yes, sir,' I said nervously. 'When would suit you?'

'Well, I have tea at about three thirty, so come and join me then, would you.' This was Michael Eisdell, head of presentation.

It was a humid summer's day, and I made the mistake of changing into my trusty corduroys and a tie before taking the bus from Double Bay to Michael's office in George Street. Everyone else on the bus was sensibly wearing shorts and open-necked shirts and keeping an eye on the raving maniac in the back who had burst. I was pouring with sweat by the time I got to the ABC and was sent to Michael's office. Behind the desk in an office with three fans whirring away, sat a small man who looked as though he had been designed by Fortnum & Mason. He was impeccably dressed in rat-catcher and was pouring the tea.

After the courtesies, he looked at me sharply and said, 'You're not a public-school boy, are you?'

I looked at him, tried to guess at the right reaction and plumped for a democratic stance. 'Heavens no. I'm state educated.'

'Bloody good thing too. Can't stand those bloody remittance men. Well, look, I think we can probably find you something for a month or two, I'll give you a call.'

And that was that. No audition, no demand for a c.v.

Michael was one of the most extraordinary men I have ever met. He was that rarity, a man who had healthily disgraced himself when he was young and had never forgotten it. In fact, I suspect he was mildly proud of it. He retained an adoration for anything to do with cricket, until his dying day he was a member of Lords. But he was simultaneously deeply suspicious of what he referred to in his clipped accent as 'The British' and believed that anyone who had escaped the system should be helped. As a result, he had a tendency to be far too generous to any lame duck he came upon. In the twenties, by his own admission, he'd been a 'bit of a bad lot', and to spare his family any more embarrassment after being slung through a plate-glass window in Piccadilly Circus, he had legged it off to the colonies, where he'd stayed.

He loved Australia dearly, but he'd clung to his accent like a limpet and that had finally been his downfall. During the Second World War he had served as an Australian in the desert campaign against Rommel and had once found himself lost and quite badly injured in his right leg. 'Shot in the arse retreating,' he would always say. Somehow he managed to crawl back to the Australian lines and was challenged. 'Who goes there?' a young Australian from Tasmania shouted. Quick as a flash ('After all, I *was* bleeding to death, for God's sake') came the reply, 'Eisdell. M. old chap, and I'm bleeding to death. Can I come in, there's a good fellow?' The suspicious Tasmanian heard a cut-glass English accent ringing out in the darkness and putting two and two together immediately jumped to the conclusion that he was dealing with an overeducated German spy.

So Michael lay there for about an hour while the Tasmanian questioned him about the make-up of the pre-war Australian cricket team. Once he had satisfied the examiner on that, there was another hurdle to overcome when a Sydneysider arrived. He questioned Michael minutely about tram routes in the city and then pronounced himself satisfied. Forget the accent, this bastard knew what he was talking about. He couldn't possibly be a Kraut. Michael was dragged in from the desert and treated as effectively as possible, but he was left with a limp, which would in later years cause his death.

His PA was a lovely girl called Diana who I found terribly attractive. She was more intelligent than I was and had a very sensible set of priorities. On one occasion when we'd decided to take off somewhere, she called into Michael's office and told him that she wouldn't be in the following day.

'Oh, really,' he said, half-interested. 'Why?'

'I've got to go and get my wound dressed.'

Michael's head shot up and he blushed to the roots, 'Yes of course, er right, yes, er fine, good.'

We spent a day in the garden, drinking cheap wine and sleeping off the after effects. He was a terribly jolly and deeply sensible man who simply refused to let corporate life get him down. I'm afraid I lead him a pretty miserable dance. I still hadn't got used to the idea that this was a real job, for which you got paid rather well. The ABC wasn't a demanding employer, but they did expect you to offer some sort of return and their primary requirement was that you turn up for work and on time. I persistently overslept and was late for the morning news shift, which initially caused raised eyebrows. When it happened on a regular basis, it ceased to be funny for anyone. Insensitive to the last, I didn't notice the chaos my bad time-keeping was causing.

On the last occasion I was late, Michael crawled out of bed, drove round to my house in Paddington, stood underneath the balcony that led into my bedroom and called up from the street in his cut-glass English accent, like some caricature of Colonel Blimp: 'Bates, get up, you bounder, you're late and if you do it again I'm going to have to fire you.'

It was a beautiful sunny day and I ran downstairs naked to let him in. I opened the front door and before I could say anything Michael got the wrong end of the stick. 'For God's sake Bates, you can't go to work like that.'

I wasn't late again.

Most of my mistakes were based on the fact that I didn't understand this new culture. I had come from a sleepy, amiable country with not much to get upset about. Australia, in general, and Sydney, in particular, was flexing its muscles and doing its damnedest to become a major force in the Pacific, and if it could, in the world.

The old days of Empire when an Australian Prime Minister could get away with quoting poetry at the Queen, were gone. This was a country going its own way and building a future for itself. Inevitably, it had a thin skin and could prove oversensitive about the little things. Consequently, when I made a facile remark about a debate in the House of Representatives sounding like a bunch of underwater wrestlers, the shit hit the fan. My head on a plate, with the giblets on the side, was the least of the demands and I thought the game was up.

Eisdell – who enjoyed plotting – called me at home. 'I'm calling from someone else's phone,' he whispered. 'I think I've got you off the hook, but you're going to have to write a grovelling reply to my note.' The note arrived later that day, I have it still.

Dear Simon.

As a result of your stupid remarks on the air yesterday afternoon, I have been swamped with complaints and have had to reply to them all. This has meant that I have not been able to attend the Test Match. Please don't let this happen again.

Best wishes, Eisdell.

I wrote and I grovelled.

I was sharing a small but beautiful house in one of the older parts of the city with James, another ex-Englishman. God had put James in entirely the wrong place at the right time. We shared our opinions about the British education system, although James was a former public-school boy and knew a darned sight more about it than I did. He was the product of moderately well-to-do Lloyds brokers and it had always been assumed that he would follow in the family footsteps. He did and loathed every moment of it, he hated the formality and the inevitability of it all. But he was made of stronger stuff than most of the moaners who complain endlessly but do nothing about it. James hated working indoors and loved practical things. He was actually good at making things, not money.

So one day James tossed his topper in the air and didn't catch it when it fell. He took a boat to Sydney and when I met him had just finished working as a jackaroo on a ranch in the west. It was something he admitted he wasn't very good at, but he stuck it for a while and quite liked it. Next he decided to be an odd-job man and do anything and everything. So he placed an advertisement in the local paper and the next night, a man dripping in jewellery called. This master of appalling taste and sickly aftershave wanted the first floor of his house ripping out and the walls replacing with Spanish arches and he was prepared to pay well. James and I sat at the table in the garden, listening as this tribute to gold-plated taps and genuine wood veneer warbled on about how he wanted it to look 'really, really elegant', before agreeing a price with James, shaking hands and leaving. Ever since meeting Mister Gold Plate, the word 'elegant' has been anathema to me.

I knew perfectly well that James was entirely unqualified and had never laid his hands on so much as a trowel, never mind built a Spanish arch. When I tackled him about this and the likelihood of total failure, followed by the collapse of a substantial home on the North Shore, he scowled.

'There is such a thing as the public library, you know.' He became more aggressive and poked his chin out. 'I'm going to look up how you build Spanish arches, aren't I?'

And he did. It took him four months but eventually he completed the job. The arches were built by this almost entirely self-taught ex-Lloyds broker and are still there, glinting in the sun on the North Shore. Or they were when I was last in Sydney. Those arches are a tribute to the public library system and the Australian principle that anything is possible, just so long as you take your time.

Simon Bates

The best way to describe the Australian attitude is to compare it with the aggressive American 'can do' stance. Australians are a little less aggressive and a lot more cynical. They're less likely to jump to attention and more likely to check out if it's entirely necessary to salute in order to achieve the object. My deeply healthy mistrust of my betters was almost entirely learnt in Australia and I'm grateful to the country for it.

We lived in Paddington, just behind the Greek fruiterer's, opposite the Barracks and up the road from the Yugoslav, who sold tinned goods from a shop that was called 'The Blunderer' because it was so ill-lit that you had to plan for your shopping to take an extra five minutes simply to let your eyes become accustomed to the darkness. Further down the street were the shops that sold imported joss sticks and Indian bangles in the front and more specific smoking items in the back. Then there was the independent cinema where you could catch movies like *Zacharia* which you knew were lousy even before you went in, but as you were stoned out of your mind the film being screened didn't matter that much.

Paddington was a British enclave for a while, a home for the last of the remittance men – failed sons of the gentry who had made such a cock-up of their lives at home in Britain that they were sent regular funds by their families just to keep away. They were an unattractive, overdressed lot, drinking in a pub at the bottom of the road and talking in that strange way that British middle-class people do when they're abroad, braying accents and far too loud, as though they were trying to scare off the bogey man before making their way home. Most of them were filling in time before they went back to Britain, or waiting for permission to re-enter their homeland after doing something so awful that their parents had bought them a ticket and checked that they were on the first plane to Sydney. However, the women used to freelance for a while when they were between one Brit and another, and if someone wanted me to be their bit of rough every now and then, well, it kept me off the streets and their flats were better than the places I usually ended up.

Although this round of hopping into different beds sounds like a wonderful lifestyle, it wasn't. The hopping was OK I guess; it was the waking up that left me wondering where I was and who was this person next to me anyway? For the person next to me, the shock could at times be close to terminal. On one occasion the poor woman was so shocked that she gave me a cup of coffee and my bus fare home.

The issue of whether or not this sort of thing could go on was solved by the arrival in my life of Diana, who was one of the few genuinely good people I have ever known. She was slim and charming and had a great sense of style, so I suppose you could say that it was a classic case of opposites attracting. I was far too selfish and stupid to behave correctly, but I was aware in the dim recesses of my mind that she was a particularly special person. Before she left Australia and I moved to Bondi, we lived together for a while and I would love to report that we were in perfect harmony, but I did not behave well enough for that to be the case. I was not so much badly behaved as selfish, always away doing something else, and my relationship with Diana always came second to what I was doing next.

Sundays were the best days. Winter or summer, the paper boy arrived between 7.30 and 8 a.m. Like all Australian youngsters, these kids were built on a vast scale. Often, if I walked home and a knot of schoolboys were on their way to the bus stop, I would cower in a shop window while these monsters elbowed their way through the streets. I came to the conclusion that there are no weedy Australian children. I reasoned that in the Antipodes, weediness was an affliction of the mature, it happened later in life, maybe at about thirty. Their size and strength meant that the paper boy or girl – who was probably eight or nine years old – had usually developed the art of chucking a bundle of newspapers up on to the balcony of my bedroom and catching my payment hurled down on them in half a dozen coins in one graceful movement. And all this while riding a bike at moderate speed. Why these kids were never taken up by a European circus baffles me.

So, Sunday meant the papers, of course, and then a drive up into the Blue Mountains a couple of hours away from Sydney, with flagons of cheap wine and bread and cheese in the back. Or maybe it meant people dropping round.

It was also a time when first rate hash was readily and cheaply available. For a while I bought my own and then I realised that nearly everybody on our street was smoking the stuff like chimneys, so all you had to do to benefit was sit on the step and breath in to get a first rate, though second hand intake. Which is what happened when I nearly became the Mr Big of international drug-running.

I had got to know a splendid hippie called Albie. Albie was British, had hitch-hiked across India and South-East Asia and had arrived glassy-eyed one afternoon at Kingsford Smith airport. In those days, the police were extremely sensitive to what was beginning to be called the 'drug culture' and were likely to haul you away if your window-box so much as wheezed. The likelihood of ending up a bruised accused by the time you got into court was very high. New South Wales policemen at that time were an unrewarding lot to get involved with.

So, when a call from his family in London asked me to meet Albie, I drove to the airport to pick him up in my little Mini. Gradually the passengers filtered through immigration, mostly respectable besuited Australians coming home from business trips or being reunited with their families. Then a riot of colour appeared, a visibly stoned hippie standing alone, and sticking out like a sore thumb in his sandals, Indian shirt, leather trousers and beads, with his hair cascading down his back. I panicked, into the back of the car he went, burbling pleasantly, and I drove home, keeping just under the speed limit all the way, looking nervously in my rear-view mirror and telling Albie to shut up.

There was worse to come. As I showed him his bedroom, Albie tapped the side of his nose and said in a confidential whisper, 'Got a present for you, man.' Yes, people did talk like that in those days. He produced a painted bauble and cracked it open. There, under the paint, was a ball of first-rate black hash. At first, I was horrified and then, as I began to consider where to hide it, grateful.

Albie stayed in Sydney and took up with a very upper-class lady. But he never forgot his roots, and one day about a year later he knocked on the door. 'Got a suggestion, man,' said Albie.

We sat down over a glass of cheap red wine and he sketched out the idea. Albie's ideas were always ridiculous and sometimes when he became enormously amibitious, they were mad. This one was insane. Albie had met an elderly American hippie a year or so before who had sworn that he was going to get his family out of the rat race. This one, unlike so many others, had done as he'd promised and ended up in Papua New Guinea, where he'd set about building a two-masted schooner, as you would. Sadly, as he'd been putting a bolt into the concrete hull, our hero had electrocuted himself and gone to the hippies' happy hunting ground where the grass is free and so is the sex.

Now Albie's eyes grew cunning, always a danger sign. His idea was to buy the boat as a co-operative of ten and fit it out. Then ten of us would sail it up to the Pacific islands, where we would invest in an oil drum full of hash each. So far so good, then came the madness. We would sail the schooner off the heads at Darwin and, each pushing an oildrum, swim ashore, having scuttled the boat. There we would be met by accomplices, drive the hash to a safe house, sell it and become millionaires.

'Easy, eh?' said Albie.

I was appalled. 'Albie, it'll never work. For starters, you'll get nabbed by customs, and if that doesn't happen you'll drown, and if that doesn't happen the sharks will get you. Don't do it.'

But Albie was insistent and over the next six months he recruited a motley crew of co-investors and against my pleadings vanished one day in the direction of Papua New Guinea. He reappeared six months later driving his own car, wearing a huge grin and bearing another present. It was similar to the first he'd given me only much much larger. He had achieved the impossible, for which I unstint-ingly condemn him. This was an illegal act against the welfare of the Commonwealth and I hope he's thoroughly ashamed of himself. Mind you, I know he isn't. He now commutes between his two homes, one in Australia and one in the UK, enjoying two summers a year. He is a happy and satisfied man, with a delightful family, who hasn't done another dishonest day's work since, although he hasn't exactly worked for a living either. And they say crime doesn't pay.

Dealing with the police in any country is a good subject for a twenty-four-hour debate. In Sydney at that time, you tangled with the long arm of the law, one on one, at your peril. I once found myself trudging dispiritedly along Sydney's main streets as one of a million marchers on Vietnam Moratorium Day. It wasn't that I really wanted to be there or to be warbling 'Hey, Hey, USA, How Many Kids Did You Kill Today', it was just that I had no choice. I had just come back from South-East Asia and, like most of my generation, I felt that the blasted war was so dreadfully and cynically wrong that the least one could do was trudge and warble, however silly it felt. I can't remember exactly what happened, but while I was t'ing and w'ing, something large threw me on to the pavement and that pave-ment hurt. I made my only radical move of the day and the crucial mistake of trying to look round to see what the something large had been, and was immediately arrested for assaulting an officer and chucked in the back of a police wagon. This all happened so quickly that all these years on I can't remember how I assaulted this helpless sixteen-stone, six-foot-one-inch gorilla while on my face in the gut-ter. But if they said it was true, then it must be so.

To say that we, my fellow arrestees and I, were unwelcome in the truck is an understatement. It was very clear to us that our arresting officers represented a diametrically opposed political view and that if we so much as said 'hello, pig', we could expect long and intimate discussions after being processed. So we all behaved like mice, much to the chagrin of the police charged with our welfare.

As we drove to the station, I had a chat with myself. 'This is great. Here you are, an employee of the state broadcasting organisation arrested and about to be charged with beating up a policeman. That's going to do you and your career an awful lot of good. But, ho hum, isn't this what keeps life interesting?'

Although I knew that Michael would be furious, my first concern was whether or not we were all going to be roundly thrashed by the selection of thugs responsible for our welfare. The truck arrived and we all piled out and waited to be dealt with. I had reconciled myself to brain damage, instant dismissal from the ABC and then the Australian equivalent of Devil's Island. In we went and stood in a neat line waiting for whatever happens to you when there are a lot of people waiting in line at a police station. Bless him or her, fate turned up again in the considerable shape of a very large policeman I couldn't remember having seen before. If this was fate, then he scared the seven bells out of me. He walked up and down eyeing our miserable little bunch and when he came to me, took a second look and had a word with a colleague.

A moment's pause and then he walked over to me and said, 'You, fuck off.'

I fucked off, sharpish. And before you claim that you would have stood on your dignity and demanded an enquiry into false arrest, I can assure you that faced with any other option you would have fucked off too. But ever since then I've wondered why they let me go? The policeman didn't look like the sort of chap who watched 'cultured' Channel 2 or listened to the river reports for New South Wales. But you never know and maybe he was just feeling generous that day. My fellow sinners, of course, must have all assumed that I was in the CIA, or a government agitator. Why else would I have been allowed out? Maybe the copper thought I was in the CIA? Maybe I was in the CIA and no one had got round to telling me.

Although life was good, there was plenty of work and the music suited both the weather and the times, there was always that damned war. It wasn't a matter of being politically correct. The results were on the doorstep. Even those who had no connection with the war and hadn't been near it had their noses rubbed in it. Living in Sydney meant that there was a constant reminder of what was going on a few hours away. The American forces used the city for Rest and Recreation. At first there was a good deal of hostility to the idea and to the presence of US soldiers with cash to spend and a limited amount of time to do it in. And then you'd see these poor kids – hopeless cases who couldn't get their draft deferred, get themselves declared unfit or join the National Guard. They would pour into Sydney for a few days, spotty-faced ghosts, and then, after they'd drunk too much, maybe fought a little or cried a bit, they'd be off on the plane 'back to 'Nam'. Some of them used the opportunity of being in Australia and legged it out of the army and the war. There was a fairly well-organised escape route for the few who took that option. From Australia some would be taken by sea to New Zealand. Then with the help of private individuals and the Seaman's Union amongst others, some made their way to Scandinavia. Some stayed in New Zealand and Australia and some ended up scattered all over Europe. Most, of course, ended up climbing aboard the jets that waited at Kingsford Smith airport ready to whisk them back to the business of destruction.

For Australians, there were the terrible, irreplaceable deaths of Australian servicemen, and then the ones who came home with bits of themselves missing. I watched one Anzac Day march, with all the old soldiers marching past in their respectable suits and their bits of brass. There were bands and there was cheering. Bringing up the end of the procession were a hundred or so yellow taxi-cabs provided free for the old and the infirm who couldn't march. As I watched the cabs drive past, I waited for the grizzled faces I expected – the old boys, the First World War veterans – but what I saw were the grey faces of young lads, none of whom seemed over twenty years old. Bound up in all this were the memories of other wars and other losses, of Gallipoli and the campaigns in the Second World War and the Korean War. It was too much for a young, sparsely populated country. If the Vietnam War itself was a cynical thing, the commitment of Australian forces to it was a deep and purposeless offence to a country with an optimistic future.

Making some film or other, we flew to a settlement in the middle of nowhere. It looked like mile upon mile of scrub and desert to me, but people were making a fair enough living to justify a school and a pub. The arrival of a film crew was the big event and the entire population of fifty or sixty people turned out to meet the aircraft on the grass strip. Not only did they turn out, but they dressed for the occasion . . . ladies in summer dresses and the men in white shirts and pressed shorts. We had barely got off the plane when we were whisked a few yards to a barbecue, again to welcome us. Although the event was in our honour, it was also a great excuse to get together and gossip, to do nothing for a while and to do it honourably.

Bob O'Neal, our host, in his seventies and probably the healthiest looking man I have ever met in my life, made a welcoming speech, which was dry and laced with a pleasant xenophobia which was not only aimed at foreigners, but also the Australian Broadcasting Commission and pooftahs from Canberra. This latter category seemed to combine all politicians by inference if not by sexual preference. It was O'Neal sitting on his porch that evening, who made me remember the awful inadequacy of my education. We talked about the difference between the Poms and the Aussies, and for him it had nothing to do with beer and skittles and everything to do with class and the past.

'You blokes think Churchill was quite a fella, right?'

I suppose I must have nodded.

'Well, to me, he was the ratbag who sacrificed most of the men in this town, me grandad and me uncles included. They never tell you that at your schools in England, do they? The way the bastard just said, that lot can go and get their balls blown off. The Aussies and the Kiwis, no one'll miss *them.*'

He talked on and on into the evening, never raising his voice but always so definite in his loathing of what he saw as the British upper class and what he felt it had done to his family and to his home and all through snobbery. For Bob, anyone who regarded anybody else as inferior and therefore dispensable were 'no-hopers', 'shitbags' and he had no time for them. Everyone was entitled to 'a fair go' and no one should be condemned out of hand. He was an old-fashioned man with old-fashioned Australian values and he taught me a good deal in the couple of hours I spent with him.

A few weeks later, I found myself in Canberra covering the Prime Ministers' Commonwealth Conference. The Prime Minister of Australia at that time was a garrulous ex-World War Two fighter pilot called John Gorton. Aside from being a hero, he struck me as being a bit grumpy when I met him, but it was a lovely sunny day and the job would be finished after lunch, so who cared?

We crept into one of the larger reception rooms as the PM rose to welcome the delegates and it was obvious that something was wrong. Gorton was on his feet having trouble speaking. It occurred to me that he might have been badly shot up and that this might explain the slurring that was going on, but then his head went down and his long body began to follow suit as he started to slide inexorably downwards. Quick as a flash, an assistant appeared from behind and in one sweeping movement, while looking in the opposite direction, he grabbed Gorton by the scruff of the neck and levered him back into position. The manoeuvre was carried out with such expertise that almost no one in the hall noticed or appeared to notice.

'Christ,' said the engineer next to me with a defeated shrug of the shoulders, 'he's pissed again.'

Travelling around the country was a joy. Australia is a lot of desert surrounded by green bits on the outside where the people live. In one small town I ended up at the local radio station asking for directions and was immediately taken across the road for a drink by the station manager who was also the breakfast DJ. The low, one-storey building consisted of a front door, an office, a dunny and the studio. That was the sum total of the facilities, but the view out across the Pacific Ocean made the lifestyle. The manager/DJ reckoned that given a record or a news bulletin longer than four minutes, he could run across the road, dive into the sea, swim a couple of strokes and be back in his seat ready for the next item.

The announcer on another station in the far west of New South Wales was only just coming out of a period of self-imposed purdah. One morning, after a pretty heavy night on the booze, he'd staggered out of his bed and followed his daily routine. He'd let himself into the station, switched on the transmitter and started up with the breakfast show. It was only when he'd opened the fader an hour later and taken in the news from Sydney that he realised he had kicked off everything an hour early. The whole town lived by their radio station and if Harry told them it was six o'clock, then that's what it was. So when he realised that he'd started the town's day at five o'clock rather than six, Harry left and went to Melbourne for a few days. When I arrived people were just starting to talk to him again.

We moved on and found the ultimate pub – this was a really *Australian* pub. It was built of corrugated iron, and inside there was a circular bar with a foot-rail running right around it, and in the corner a spittoon and that was it. None of your Sydney frills here. If it was hot outside (and it was), inside, even with the fans in the ceiling whirring, it was a functional hell-hole for the consumption of beer. Behind the bar there was virtually nothing except a row of glasses, six or seven taps for the beer and a largish man with the most dreadful breath I have ever encountered.

We had ordered a beer each and were trying to lean against the bar, one foot on the rail in a 'non-pansy bloody broadcasting bastard' sort of a way, when there was a shout. 'Everyone out.' I had almost got my Jack Palance look perfected, but when I got a whiff of the man behind the bar as he shouted, I knew better than to argue. So we got out along with the other drinkers and stood in the blazing sunshine wondering what this was all about.

'Aaw, they clean the place everyday come rain or shine,' said a local, looking in the direction of a pitiless sun.

I peered through the door. Old dreadful breath stepped lazily from behind the bar, picked up a hosepipe and drenched the entire place – spittoons, foot-rests, taps, the lot. He must have worked in a livery stables in a previous life. The water went everywhere, before dribbling away into drains in each corner.

'Youse can come back in now.'

We all trooped back in and by the time I'd resumed my Jack Palance impersonation, a glass of beer was in front of me and the place was beginning to dry out.

A little while later, Her Majesty The Queen came out for a State visit to Australia and nearly got me killed and then bankrupted in the process. I was scheduled to fly to Darwin to do some pre-Royal tour razzmatazz. In the end, the only way that this was economic was for me to hitch a lift with the representatives of NHK Japan. I was quite happy about this, though there were some in Sydney who warned me and muttered darkly about the 'Japs meaning trouble'.

During the summer, I had got to know a couple of Japanese girls who were spending some time in Sydney learning English. I had been determined to learn Japanese and had got as far as '*Ohoyo Gezoimas*', before giving up. But they were pleasant girls, given to giggling a lot and offering whisky with warm water, so I thought that I knew the Japanese. As I got on board the fixed-wing aircraft, I was greeted warmly and much slapping on the back went on from my new colleagues from the Land of the Rising Sun. It turned out that these three young blokes were Anglophiles and had just discovered *The Goon Show*. Whether they had fully grasped the subtlety of

Spike Milligan's scripts I doubt, but they did Eccles impersonations, said 'Ah, so' a lot and fell about laughing at their own good humour.

The arrival of HM The Queen coincided with an explosion of interest in the Australian Stock Exchange. Every secretary had a portfolio and every messenger boy spent his waking hours on the phone to his broker. I had jumped on the bandwagon and was busy buying and selling like a good 'un. I had made a little cash and had invested all my worldly wealth in a mineral stock called Amsil, which had then soared after sensational reports. As we flew over the desert and since we were all getting on so well, I pointed down at the Nullabor Plain and allowed myself to exaggerate a little to the Japanese. 'I own that.' I grinned. They were suitably impressed.

We touched down at Darwin in the middle of the night. I was boiling hot as we stepped on to the tarmac and we made our way to the bar for a long cool one. My mistake was to go into a bar at night, when the heat was suffocating and no one could sleep, with three Japanese men giggling and saying 'Ah, so'. The silence as we opened the door gave me the message, but I chose to ignore it and stepped smartly up to the bar with my new friends. The barman, being a generous soul, pretended to ignore me, but I knew better than that. 'Scuse me, mate.'

He turned and without a hint of anger looked me straight in the face. 'Look, mate, these blokes,' he gestured towards about two hundred extremely sweaty and very large men gently coming to the boil, 'have been drinking for ten hours and you've just walked in with three Nippos. I would call that a recipe for suicide meself. If I were you, I'd just piss off and save your skin.'

I saw his point and we left. The three Japanese hadn't got the point and were all for staying and making friends, so I had to be rather firm. I had always sneered at the *High Noon* situation where the populace form a sort of avenue as the hero walks slowly to the door of the bar-room. Will he make it or won't he? I will never sneer again. Getting out of the bar was a complete re-run of any Western you care to name and, in the finest tradition, we only just made it. The first bottle followed in a gentle curve as we legged it back to the plane.

By this time, the Japanese understood that the principle of the brotherhood of man wasn't always practical. We waited for the transport to arrive and went about our business in a more sensible way from then on.

We were in Darwin for about thirty-six hours before flying back to Sydney. Just time enough for my shares to be suspended on the Stock Exchange and for me to lose my million and a bit more. Instead of arriving in triumph and buying Double Bay, I came out of that trip owing a year's salary. The lesson was well learned and when, fifteen years later, I was invited to join Lloyds of London as a 'name', I had no qualms in refusing.

The Queen and half the Royal Family arrived in Australia and while the populace seemed to have a fine time waving flags and cheering, the ABC went crazy. You have to remember that these were the days when there were gongs aplenty for those who successfully organised the broadcast coverage. So if Royalty breathed, we were down on them like a ton of bricks, describing the breath, dissecting it, discussing it and speculating about the next one. I spent half my time wandering about like a lost soul being a roving on-the-spot commentator.

This sounds good and for the most part it was good. Don't get the idea, though, that I was up in some custom-built eyrie being ministered to by a bevy of assistant make-up and catering people – that's American TV and we'll come to that later. Get real, this is Australian TV in 1970 and in those days you walked or rather plodded after people. And there is worse to come. You carried your own backpack, the ultimate technically approved torture device. This backpack was a fairly heavy knapsack weighing in at about forty kilos and filled with bits of wire and batteries. But the real difficulty sprouted from it – a huge, and I mean huge, whip aerial. It was about twelve feet high, but when you were walking around with this damned thing swaying over you, you felt like a triffid. At best, you were a target for little boys who'd screech, 'You an alien, mister?' as you burbled into your lip mike. Not only were the damn things top-heavy, which left your centre of gravity somewhere about two feet above your head, but they were impossible to deal with when it came to going through doors. Can you imagine how humiliating it is to try and appear as though you're in control of the situation when that aerial gets caught in the hinges of a revolving door?

'No, no, it's OK really, don't worry about me, I'll be fine once I stop looking like a milkshake.'

Even when you were in the clean and fresh God-given air, that aerial had a life of its own. If you moved too fast in one direction, it would bend in the other, nearly forcing you on to your back. If there was a high wind, you could easily find yourself turning into a human kite. On one occasion, I ended up being plucked from my commentator's spot and forced in the opposite direction down a hill at high speed by a light wind that had got into my aerial. To my credit, I kept talking, though the voice went up an octave. The worst thing about these monsters was feeling so totally conspicuous. No one could possibly miss you as you moved sedately through the crowd swaying gently with your aerial.

Towards the end of this Royal tour, I was beginning to hate my aerial and so was Princess Anne, I suspect. Bear in mind that temperatures were in the high nineties and it wasn't the done thing to carry a six pack of beer around as part of your technical equipment, so there was no form of refreshment. HRH saw me sweating away under my aerial and my knapsack and my lip mike for the umpteenth time on a walkabout in a country school in the far west of New South Wales. As she walked past, she very quietly whispered as I struggled with my commentary, 'You do look silly.' Thanks. I didn't need her in her crisp summer dress to tell me that, I knew.

This blanket coverage was as nothing, though, when the Pope decided to make a visit. Obviously, the pontiff's first journey to Australia was a significant event and so that not a papal second would be missed, the ABC organised pool coverage with their own commentators sharing the job with those of the commercial stations. The problem was the age-old difficulty of combining two totally separate cultures, neither of which had much time for the other. Each of the commercial stations contributed a commentator who was to join a colleague from the ABC, most of whom saw themselves as being in the fine tradition of the BBC. The commercial boys, on the other hand, were used to hyping an event up a bit, making it more exciting if you will, and there were endless clashes between the two traditions, as the dark-brown voiced ABC men tried to silence their squeaking excitable commercial brothers with sheer *gravitas*.

It all came to a grinding halt at the airport farewell as His Holiness walked up the steps of the aircraft, where the ABC commentator, having performed with impeccable taste, handed over to the next commercial voice. This man it transpired later was a lapsed Catholic, for whom the papal visit had been something of a revelation.

There was a pause, before a slightly shaky voice said, 'Thank you, Martin, yes, I can see the Pope and His Holiness looks lovely, just lovely and, God, I know you're listening and I do believe.'

At least he had his religion to console him when he got his marching orders the next day.

The ABC was a pretty gentlemanly organisation in those days. There was always the feeling that if you really screwed up in one department, they would do their level best to find you work in another.

The announcers were an odd lot. One suffered dreadfully from a psychological problem that had him falling asleep at the most inappropriate moments, like when he was on air. Once a week or so, you'd hear someone sigh, 'Oh, Jesus, Terry's nodded off again', and, looking through the glass at the studio, sure enough, Terry would be leaning back in his chair, eyes closed, mouth wide open, with a record just about to run out.

There was another bloke who was a bit odd, he used to hear voices. These were voices that told him there was an Asiatic plot against Australia and that one day the Chinese would sail into Sydney harbour and the game would be up! He knew that he was in the minority but, taking the Vietnam War as his model, he would spout on for hours to anyone willing to listen about how the danger was imminent. This was regarded as being tolerable until one day, during a recording, he began to spout the theory in fine detail, adding a little speech begging Australia to 'wake up before it's too late'. He worked in the music library after that and seemed very happy sitting in the sunshine outside the studio with older messengers, drawing maps in the gravel of the forthcoming campaign.

Then there was Charles, a perfectly good radio man who hated television. He didn't hate watching it, just being on it. But there was a shortage of staff and for a while he read the weekend news bulletins. Charles wasn't a great technician, when he was doing a radio shift an engineer always had to remind him to switch on his microphone before he spoke. So for him, sitting behind a desk, reading a bulletin to a pair of cameraman's legs, with a small panel of instructions in front of him was agony. These instructions were on an illuminated panel obscured from the viewer behind his name-plate. Nearly all broadcasters wear an earpiece now, but in those more primitive days 'faster, slower and phone' were the basic demands from the gallery. On the night of Charles's undoing, he was half-way through a bulletin when the phone sign lit up. The directors and secretaries in the gallery could be a wicked lot. When I was reading the news, there would often be a phone call during the bulletin and

I'd pick up the receiver, with a nod in the direction of the camera, to hear heavy breathing or a voice saying, 'God, you look really stupid tonight'. But with Charles, they were merciful. So when the phone rang for him, it must have been important. But the moment the light flashed, Charles went into a coma. His eyes glazed over when he saw the words, sweat broke out on his forehead, he grabbed for the receiver and clamped it to his ear shouting 'Hello, hello' as though he was the wireless operator on the *Titanic*. His eyes had that mad look that you only get from real fear. The problem was that he had somehow got the mouthpiece clamped to his ear and the earpiece directly in line with the microphone on the desk. As Charles babbled 'Hello, hello', the clear and concise tones of the Australian director boomed into a million homes.

'Jesus Christ, look at the stupid fucker, he's making a prat of himself again.'

Charles dropped the phone and burst into tears. The presentation department mercifully went to black. Charles was around for a few more days and then went to Adelaide.

In the late sixties and early seventies, Sydney was a radio town and Australia was radio country. There was a tradition dating from the twenties that had kept radio as important in people's lives as it had been in the USA and for similar reasons. Australia is also vast and so far from anywhere else that radio was almost the only way of giving the country a sense of national identity.

Until the late 1960s there was no such thing as a national newspaper, so radio provided news. But it also provided culture with a capital K on the commercial stations as well as the state-owned system. In the thirties, forties and fifties, live concerts and live plays were recorded in Sydney on great drums of wire so tightly wound that if it snapped 'it would take yer fuckin' head off'. The drums would then laboriously be ferried round the country for broadcast on Sunday nights, sponsored by some large corporation keen on prestige. These were big events. The best of the local talent, people like Peter Finch, were regular stars and any visiting troupe would have seduced their top names into playing the role of guest star by offering large sums of money.

By the time I'd arrived this particular Golden Age was well and truly over, though soap operas were still being produced in a small way and the country was loaded with people like Algie who worked in radio in the days when each breakfast show had its own live band. 'And a bunch of drunken tossers they were too,' Algie would reminisce. 'Trouble was they were always changing vocalists. Two of them were poofs and wanted a bloke and the other three used to shag each sheila they got then realise she was crap at the job.'

Radio and those wire recordings welded the country together whether it was a local station, the Public Service Broadcasting System, or a short-wave system in the outback. Radio was as Australian as a six pack of DB beer. Television came second best until as recently as the early seventies. After all, who the hell wants to watch TV when it's summer and there's cricket or the beach to go to?

Mind you, it could be lonely out there in the bush. Back in the mists of time (the 1950s) the ABC's then cricket correspondent headed off into the middle of nowhere to commentate on a test tour. As the tour rambled on, so our hero got lonelier. Each day he'd turn up, say 'good morning' to the man from Australian Post and Telecommunications, accept the microphone and begin talking to the unseen millions. The trouble was, he never saw them, or heard from anyone. For weeks on end it was just him out there in the middle of nothingness, staying in hotels and talking into the blasted mike. He took to drink of course and then finally he snapped. The Director General of the ABC found a telegram on his desk one morning from the correspondent, 'Have gone mad. Will not be back for sometime.' And he wasn't back for quite a while.

'Of course,' said the old broadcaster who told me the story, 'they couldn't put up with that, so he went overseas and worked for the BBC I think. Couldn't stand the pace I suppose.'

The Australian Broadcasting Commission was the national service and did a fair number of good things. Like a caring relative, the ABC always did its best, but it was confronted with the age-old problem of being perceived as a distant national broadcaster rather than a friendly local one.

It was the local commercial stations that made up the guts of radio for the mass of Australians, and work on one of these was man's work even if you were a woman. The first commercial station I worked for employed two of the toughest women talk-show hosts I have ever met. They were big women, though in the parlance of the time they were 'light on their feet', which meant that they were gay. But being big physically meant that no one ever challenged them. The pair loathed each other so intensely that written into their contracts was the requirement that neither was to be on the premises when the other was there.

I was at the station the day that someone screwed up and Sheila was leaving a little late as Raewyn was arriving, a little early.

'Hello, bitch!' Raewyn smiled.

'Fucking cow,' quipped Sheila.

Then one grabbed the other by the collar and heaved her bodily into the mass of technical equipment that lay at the side of the corridor before marching butchly through the front doors. No one said a word, we were all too scared. They were, as I explained, big women. The next day, apart from one black eye, things were exactly as they always had been and life returned to normal. No one mentioned the incident.

All the women who worked on air in Australian radio seemed to be huge, and with their size went an almost obsessive sexual appetite. You were safe with the lesbians, for the most part they left you alone, it was the heterosexuals who could cause trouble.

At a party on the North Shore one night, a larger-than-life lady of mature years, who was one of Australia's most successful talk-show hosts, bore down on me. 'You can take me home if you like,' she said.

I thought for a moment and then, missing the point utterly, realised that she lived further out of the city, while I had to make the trip back to Paddington. 'I'm going in the opposite direction. Hasn't your driver brought you?'

A pause you could have filled with a ton of crazy paving and a look that would weaken Cruella de Ville.

'I said, you can take me home if you like.'

I still hadn't cottoned on. 'Er, sorry?'

'For Christ's sake, you are coming home with me.'

I was frogmarched out into the road amidst much laughter from those present who were more experienced than I and into an expensive Jaguar, taken home and dealt with. All I can remember is being bounced around several rooms and off the walls by an extremely vigorous and experienced woman. I'd just got round to enjoying it when I noticed how many bruises I had.

When I next saw the lady a few weeks later, I took my courage in both hands, walked up to her and said something along the lines of, 'I'll take you home, if you like', and she smiled very sweetly and said, 'No, darling, no one takes me home more than once.' I got the message.

These were larger than life people with larger than life egos. They were for the most part healthily psychotic. For all of them, as they became better known and more successful, the great difficulty was separating their lives on and off air. One breakfast-show man gradually went round the twist on and off air. At first, Paddy took to wearing a Confederate American officer's uniform in the street. Everyone tolerated this until he started wearing a ceremonial sword to go with the uniform. The police only became involved when he began to threaten passing traffic with it at rush hour. The sight of a loony in a frock coat, on a boiling hot summer's day, leaping into the road, drawing his sword and charging a Holden station-wagon, was too much for the authorities and he was charged with carrying an offensive weapon in public. This only served to widen his fame and his already eccentric private life spilled on to the air. Paddy was accustomed to a little support while he was doing the breakfast show. This took the form of a bottle of Fanta. Paddy would carefully drain off half the Fanta and replace it with gin before going to work at about five in the morning. By the time he finished he was paralysed, but only those in the know could tell. In fact, he was often better drunk than sober.

One fatal day, with the microphone open, Paddy dropped the Fanta bottle on to the studio floor. 'Oh, fuck,' I heard him say, then, 'Oh, I've never said fuck on air before. Fuck, fuck, fuck, fuck.'

The station was owned by the Catholic Church and the Father descended like the Assyrian, only faster and harder. Paddy was off the air four minutes later and was never heard of again. Correction. A while later I heard that he got a job in Hobart. But that, as any drinker would tell you, was like never being heard of again.

BAPH Staters they were called by Sydneysiders. People who worked in the cities of Brisbane, Adelaide, Perth or Hobart. Mention someone who had become a Baph Stater and there'd be a moment's silence for the poor bloke.

Being fired, though, was part of life in Australian radio. Just because you'd got the elbow, didn't mean that you were bad at your job. You could have fallen foul of the station's manager, or the station manager's wife. Many a broadcaster has been dusted off and sent on his way after a wife has whispered in her husband's ear, 'Why are you still employing so and so?' Even worse is getting on too well with the manager's wife. This can result in instant expulsion, with jealousy as the only justification.

You could, of course, be fired for being bored as much as being boring. A friend of mine working on an 'easy listening' station became so despondent at the endless, mindless stream of mediocre music that he was forced to play that he would sit creating lists for mates working on other stations while he was spinning the latest horror from Bert Kaempfert.

There was, for example, his 'top five occupational hazards aboard the *Starship Enterprise*':

5. Phaser accidentally discharging in trousers
4. Warplash
3. Head caught in food replicator
2. Improperly applied Vulcan Neck Pinch, causes willies
1. Burns from French-kissing alien female whose internal body temperature is over 450°

He also created the 'Singers Play On Words' list:

Bonnie Raitt and The Drifters
'Give It Up On the Roof'

Eddie Fisher and James Brown
'Oh, Mein Papa's Got a Brand New Bag'

Jimmie Rogers, The Yardbirds and Creedence/Loggins and Messina
'It's Over, Under, Sideways, Down On the Corner/Pooh Corner'

Al Green and Gilbert O'Sullivan
'I'm So Tired Of Being Alone Again Naturally'

Leo Sayer, Johnny Cash, A Taste Of Honey
'Just a Boy Named Sukiyaki'

The Beatles, Petula Clark, Gene Pitney
'Don't Bring Me Down Town Without Pity'

Lesley Gore and Joe Cocker
'It's Judy's Turn to Cry Me a River'

The Dovells, Neil Young, Ashford and Simpson and Paul
McCartney
'You Can't Sit Down By the River Deep Mountain High, High,
High'

It was inevitable that he would be fired because he was supplying half
the pop stations in the country with funny lines while working for a
pack of deadbeats, and so he was, though the first he knew of it was
when the station management changed the locks on the door so that
he couldn't get in. Only when he phoned the engineer was he told
that he 'didn't work there any more'.

One disc jockey I knew only learned of his dismissal when his
bank manager called him and said, 'Now that you aren't on station
XYZ's payroll any more, can we talk about how you're going to pay
off your mortgage?'

Andy Richards was the most paranoid broadcaster I ever met. His
management kept firing him. This would happen every three or four
weeks and though it drove him insane with insecurity, Richards was
no fool. He simply showed up after the weekend, by which time the
station MD had forgotten that he'd fired Andy and the relationship
went on calmly until the next employment hiatus.

One station I worked on issued a two-page memo to all, or nearly
all, the staff. The first page was the standard 'things are going terribly
well' sort of memo. The second was the news that 'from next week
Jack Sanders will no longer be with the company'. Jack of course
only got the first page.

There was one religious station that insisted all its staff attended
a morning devotional prayer meeting before starting work. A closing
prayer was often used and always came as a surprise to at least one
person present, 'And Lord help so and so as he searches for a new
job.' Once, when a hard-rock station changed its format to Christian
music, the entire staff was fired! Just shows that being a good Christian often isn't enough.

One day I attended the staff party of a big radio station in Melbourne where the Managing Director made a speech about how bad
the commercial returns had been in the previous year. 'And that
sadly means,' he continued, 'that we'll be letting half of you go in
the New Year. You'll find a list of names on the notice-board as you
leave. But now, LET'S PARTY!!' Nobody did.

Only one man that I have ever known triumphed over management's ultimate weapon, the sack. His name was Ian Grayson and he was seriously the nicest, most insensitive and incompetent broadcaster I have even known. He could miss a point if it was mounted on an Exocet and fired at him from twenty paces. Ian couldn't get anything right and worse he had a slight speech impediment which made him sound like a screaming queen on air. A previous regime had employed him and the incomers decided that, though they liked him personally, it was time for Ian to go. He was duly called into the chairman's office and politely told that there were 'a lot of commercial pressures and we feel it would be better if you moved on.'

Ian listened for a while and then, completely missing the point, leaped to his feet. 'Don't worry, mate,' he said, putting his arm protectively round the chairman's shoulders, 'I know what's happening.'

The chairman looked puzzled and frightened at the familiarity.

'The board's putting a lot of pressure on you, right,' lisped Ian, dribbling slightly on to the chairman's new crushed velvet jacket, 'and they're making life hell for you? Well, that's the time for mates to stick together. I wouldn't leave you in your hour of need for a million dollars. Trust me, mate, I'm going to stay and we'll see this thing through together.' As far as I know, Ian is still there twenty years on. The chairman died, a disappointed man, in the early eighties.

Sex as the prime motive for life was never far from the surface. One radio station in Victoria boasted two fine broadcasters who were sharing the same lady. The problem was that the evening host was married to her, while the breakfast DJ had an arrangement that kept the lady busy while her husband was on air. Things would have been just fine and probably gone on for years if the lady in question hadn't got drunk at a station party and made her affection for both men all too obvious. It was so easy. The married couple lived just round the corner from the radio station and the husband waited for a few nights before making his move. At about eleven o'clock one night, just after the MacQuarrie news, he put The Beatles' 'Hey Jude' on to the turntable. The cuckold then had six minutes and forty-two seconds including fade to nip round to his house, discover the two lovers in each other's arms, break the offender's three front teeth and return, slightly breathless, to introduce 'Oh Happy Day' by the Edwin Hawkins Singers. The word in the business was that there was a smile in his voice when he made the announcement.

Then there was one notorious station in New South Wales.

Viewed from the inside or the outside it looked perfectly normal. The giveaway was the DJs' roster on the wall. All the names were female. Susie, six till nine; Tina, nine till twelve, and so on. Perfectly reasonable until you realised that all the DJs were men. You had to be very understanding to work there.

I was working a good deal at the Gore Hill television studios, half an hour's drive across the Sydney Harbour Bridge, and it was there that I met the most screwed-up man I've ever known. David was a first-rate current affairs director but hated the job. He travelled all over the world and got good stories but, like virtually everyone in broadcasting, he wanted to be something else. 'The bastards won't realise that I'm a great drama director.' This was palpable nonsense. What he was was a great current affairs director who never doorstepped anyone in his life. He just kicked the thing in and shouted, 'Where are ya?' The idea of David actually keeping his temper with an actor long enough to get a shot done was about as likely as Charlton Heston playing the devil in his next movie.

David also had woman trouble. He was an expansive man, at his best in the pub, but he had the Australian chauvinist mistrust of women, coupled with an inability to exist without them. Accordingly, he would take them back to his flat just off King's Cross, where they would wrestle together for what I always assumed was mutual satisfaction, though I suspect that David didn't give too much thought to his partner's point of view. There were a good many of these one-night stands and a pretty well-stocked repertory company of regulars, but he never got close enough to them emotionally to warrant giving them a key.

'If you love me, you'll wait,' he would say, and they always seemed to do just that. I'd drive past late in the evening, and when David was *in situ*, there always seemed to be some hopeful doe-eyed creature sitting on the wall outside his block waiting for him to come home. Of course they had to leave in the morning when he did, except on one occasion, when, late for a meeting, David charged out of bed, rushed into the shower and his suit and out of the flat, slamming the door behind him.

It was only that evening, when he had stopped rushing about, that he remembered. 'Jesus, Charlotte's still in the flat.' And so she was, like Rapunzel, unable to get out because she had no key. But unlike Rapunzel, this girl had no intention of shouting for help. And David by this time was in Melbourne. Charlotte spent a couple of days in the flat, made a great many overseas phone calls, caused a certain amount of damage to David's clothes and ate him out of house and home. But when he returned and Charlotte was finally released, 'She walked out on me with style,' said David admiringly, 'that girl has class.' It took him a week or so to clean up the flat. The whole incident confirmed David's views that however desirable, women were a rum lot, to be desired but not to be trusted.

David subsequently married an extremely well-to-do bully. He's become a quiet, nervous sort of chap who asks permission before he goes out, and spends most of the evening looking at his watch and worrying if he 'ought to phone the wife, just to check in, y'know?' He runs a local news outfit on one of the smaller regional TV stations and is a proud Rotarian.

Around about this time, colour television was a-coming in. This was the next big step technically and was 'of great importance' to an ABC struggling in the ratings. Endless memos appeared on notice-boards stressing how great the importance was, until one appeared appealing for help from the staff. 'With the onset of colour tests,' it read, 'would staff assist the transmission department and use the car park as follows: cars painted red on the left, cars painted green on the right, all others in the middle.' The next day the Gore Hill car park was a struggling, heaving mass of Holdens trying to be helpful. It took two days before the penny dropped and people realised that they'd been had. The flow of memos about colour ceased.

My primary job at this time was to read television news on what was then the only TV network in Australia. I wasn't very good at the job, so I fell back on Bob White's advice and spoke very loudly and clearly when I didn't know what the hell was going on. This some-times puzzled Jim Dibble, then in his fifties and the distinguished senior broadcaster with whom I used to share the job. Jim was prob-ably the nearest thing that Australia had to a Dimbleby, but perhaps a little softer. His eyes would twinkle when he was on the box and he always seemed to be able to soften the worst possible news. He was an instinctively kind man, though underneath the blandest of exteriors there beat the heart of a true rocker.

I was once asked to Jim's home in one of the better suburbs on the North Shore. It was a typical sunny bungalow, set in a third of an acre of immaculately kept garden. Jim was also beautifully kept, like his garden, and the interior of the house also reflected Jim's obsession for neatness and perfect Australian taste. But locked away in his front room was Jim's terrible secret – an organ. Not one of those things that people pound away at in sad hotels on wet days at the British seaside. This was enormous, it took up half the room and the speakers took up the other half. When Jim sat down to play it, he did a Lon Chaney and changed from a quiet, respectable suburban Australian into a raving, cackling maniac. The wall of noise he could pump out would have drowned out Mildenhall on a busy day and yet no neighbour ever complained. This was Jim's pride and joy and he sat, bashing at the keys, making enough racket to waken the dead, grinning from ear to ear. Maybe that was why he was so charming and reserved in his professional life.

Someone in a position of power somewhere, and with the ABC it was all a little hard to identify who ran what and when, had decided that 'I would do'. This was a catch-all and meant that, whether or not I liked it, I was going to succeed. I was called into an office and told that I would be doing the Australian end of the moon-shot coverage. Even I wasn't stupid enough to look blank and say, 'But I don't know anything about space shots', I just remembered James's advice and went to the public library. But that wasn't necessary and I discovered the great secret of good broadcasting. Always do a job where there's a first-rate briefing book, then look for a first-rate producer. Get those two right and you can't fail, get either of them wrong and you're doomed. NASA's press book, of course, was the best. Every step in the mission was laid out, every move planned and every event catered for. You could virtually record your coverage and swan off to Bali for a holiday. Barring accidents, it was foolproof.

Our TV coverage was pretty primitive: a tiny studio, three cameras and a bit of hardboard with some sand on it simulating the moon's surface. The floor manager had prised a model of a moon-buggy out of a local university and we had little American flags to represent where the spacemen would be when they landed. These were later replaced, after someone had the bright idea of going to the local model shop and buying some Airfix models.

Of course we had the obligatory expert, but he wasn't much use. We discovered pretty early on that the moment he put on make-up and the lights went up, he became a gibbering wreck. His problem was that he was unable to make up his mind about anything. Ask the poor sap a question and his opening comment would always be, 'Well, that depends . . .' From which point we all knew we were on a roller-coaster to disaster. First, he would put a couple of alternative answers, then he would disagree with himself, then he would start to panic. Finally, he would become completely confused and ask what the question was as the perspiration poured down his face. This left me helpless, because all I could do was sit there and watch the poor man sweat to death.

We all agreed that it would be much less stressful if he would explain what was happening to me before we went on air and then keep an eye on things sitting in a chair just outside camera range. That worked well until we realised that he was so relieved about not going on camera, that he'd taken to bringing in a hip-flask. By the time we were a couple of hours into the coverage, he would be into his second hip-flask. On one occasion, the floor manager, trying to make polite conversation, asked him what would happen if the golf-cart scheduled to trundle across the moon's surface wouldn't start.

One reddened eye glared at him. 'Who gives a shit,' quoth our scientific expert.

We learned to rely on NASA's briefing book. All went well and the press pack served its purpose perfectly, until there was an explosion aboard the space vehicle and we were on our own, while the poor guys in space struggled to get back in one piece. That's where the good producer came in. I was a bundle of nerves and he gave me the confidence to do the job, simply by telling me calmly what we were going to do next. I assumed that he knew what was happening and relied on his expertise. The programmes were considered to have been a success and so we carried on covering the space shots.

I became more and more confident, which meant that I learned to stare accusingly at the camera if I was in the wrong place at the wrong time or said the wrong thing. It *had* to be someone else's fault. This is a fine tradition and one that I see being followed nightly on the world's screens. But I like to think of myself as one of the standard-bearers when it came to developing the technique. This is an attitude which can carry you through a multitude of cock-ups and here I'll hand you a free tip on how to deal with your own mistakes.

Let us assume that you are a newsreader. Take a piece of news copy, then make a blunder, any blunder will do – turn a million into a thousand, or a president into a king. The sort of thing that news-readers the world over constantly do. Realise your mistake (many newsreaders don't do this) and snort impatiently. Pause, then say, preferably with a tolerant and above all confident grin on your face, 'That *should* of course read . . .' and correct the error. If you do this properly, the audience will assume that you have just saved the day by correcting the copy handed to you by an ignorant sub-editor. They will be staggered at your quick wit and you will probably win an award as newsreader of the year. There is a down side to this, in that you will have to mollify the guiltless sub afterwards, but if you play your cards right, he will be too old to care, be on the phone in the gallery to his girlfriend or boyfriend when you committed the crime, or in the pub across the road and not watching anyway.

There are some errors that take a good deal of explaining. On night shift in the ABC newsroom there was one strange radio bulletin that had to be read at ten forty-five each night. It was a matter of opening the mike and saying, 'I'll start in ten seconds', and then launching into it. This was the *Marie Celeste* of news. No one seemed to know where it was listened to and no one cared that much. In a vast country with three time zones, the bulletin had been scheduled at the same time for years. Someone was obviously recording it somewhere, it kept the reader out of the pub and there was no point in fussing about it.

One night, I began to read the bulletin as usual and made a huge blunder. Instead of struggling on, I stopped, swore viciously and after a ten-second pause, started again. I had forgotten about the incident when I got a call at home a few days later from a very pleasant man who announced that he was the duty engineer in Adelaide and that the bulletin I had read was indeed broadcast and that as always it went out live. My knees sagged.

'No worries, mate,' said the voice at the other end, 'it goes out on the country network. Only ranchers hear that and they'll be perfectly at ease with the language.'

By this time I had learned one of the most important lessons in life – I knew that I didn't know what the hell I was doing, but for some reason a lot of other people hadn't rumbled me. This was a lesson that was drummed home by a feature that appeared in a magazine called *The Bulletin*. Together with a flattering portrait of me, went copy along the lines of 'this is a young man who is going places'. That I could handle. What made me sit bolt upright was the proof of the pudding that appeared further down the column. According to the author, I had been reading the news on Channel 2 one night, when a late item had been handed to me to read. I had apparently glanced at it disdainfully and made an instant editorial decision: ' "I can't possibly read that," said Bates, throwing the ill-prepared copy aside and carrying on with icy authority.' The truth was a little less icy or authoritative.

A handwritten late item had been thrust into my trembling paw and I had indeed looked at it. From there on the true story takes a less heroic turn. The moment I looked down, one of my contact lenses had started acting up, my eye ducts had sprung a leak and I'd virtually burst into tears. Rather than throwing the copy aside, I'd whimpered at the floor manager in a high-pitched whine, 'I can't read that,' before dropping the blasted thing and fumbling my way through the next story, half-blinded by the tears.

I asked an older and much wiser broadcaster who fronted the nightly news magazine whether I should let the story stand or own up to the truth, and he looked at me sternly. 'If it's truth or legend, stick with the legend, mate,' he said. 'It's a bloody sight more entertaining than the reality.' And so it was and is.

Most of the work was fun, some of it was fascinating. I worked for a while on a series for immigrants. Australia was suffering from her immigration policy – like the country itself, it was politically well-meaning but misguided. Batches of immigrants were arriving on a regular basis from all over Europe. When some of the poorer countries received notification of their allocation, they would post notices all over inviting applications. Then the applicants would be subjected to a literary test. If they passed that, they were promptly refused permission to go to their new life in Australia. Couple that with the fact that although the migrants who did make it received a warm-hearted welcome when they arrived in Australia, it wasn't designed to prepare them for their new lives. Non English-speaking migrants arrived and would unsurprisingly disappear into areas where only their mother tongue was spoken. The result was that their kids were turning up in Australian schools at the age of five unable to speak English. It was the perfect recipe for future social problems and the perfect breeding ground for organised crime.

Our little multi-lingual programme was designed to encourage these new Australians to become part of the greater community. It all went well for a while and we were humming along, with instant translations by a team of inspired volunteers, of what I was saying into Turkish, Greek, Serbo-Croat and heaven knows what other language, until I got a phone call from a total stranger. It took a while for me to grasp what the man was saying but gradually, as I understood more and more, I became paler and paler. The gist was that this bloke was thrilled that we were putting out such 'strong' material. The alarm bells rang. We weren't putting out any strong material, it was all deeply dull information for people who might not know how to use a public toilet or where to go to pay their rates. So what's this with the strong?

Then slowly I grasped the fact that one of the interpreters of one of the more obscure languages had gone native. He had decided to ignore my dreary treatise on how to deal with everyday life at City Hall and was preaching his own form of revolution. While I was saying, 'And don't forget to pay your electricity bill within fourteen days', this chap was crying, 'Down with the imperialist dogs of wherever and up with the revolution. In a few weeks we'll all have guns and they'll all be dead.'

We managed to keep it quiet, no one really cared about our programme anyway. The man who'd been plotting the overthrow of the State was hauled in and told that he was finished, through, out, *finito* and if he dared breathe a word of what had happened we'd tell the Secret Service and he would be taken up over the Murrumbidgee River in a helicopter and kicked out. We trembled for a few weeks, but there was no sound of gunfire from the Parramatta area, so after a time we relaxed.

I had been in Australia for nearly three years and a more seductive lifestyle I couldn't imagine. The weather for the most part was perfect, though those few suffocating humid weeks in high summer were too much for most people to deal with. Work with the ABC could only get better. So why leave? Two reasons really: the first and most important was that after seven years away, I wanted to see my family before they fell off their respective perches; the second was a little harder to define, but I was starting to feel smug, comfortable and at ease with my situation. Australia was so darned easy to like and so easy to live in. It was patently obvious that here was a country with a great future. I felt that I'd had it too good, my conscience got to me.

I had met dozens of broadcasters from all over the world who had been through the mill before they even got near a microphone. Here was I, having never auditioned for anyone, never really applied for a job, certainly never been interviewed properly, having a simply wonderful time. I'd just fallen into one job after another. I was beginning to stabilise and, unless I watched it, I knew there'd be a house and a mortgage coming up behind me. There had to come a point at which life got tough.

I would go back to Britain and see the family, then I'd take off and go to India or somewhere. One thing was for certain, I wasn't going to try the BBC, I had developed a massive inverted snobbery about 'the finest broadcasting organisation in the world' and I had better things to do than stagnate there.

Michael Eisdell came to Britain a year or so later for the cricket and though I saw him for dinner one night, I didn't give him the attention he deserved. I was going through a bad patch and simply didn't have time for anyone else's troubles but my own. A few years later, Michael was waiting at a bus stop late one night in Sydney, when he was knocked over and killed by a hit-and-run driver. The sad fact was that he couldn't get out of the way of the careering truck because the wounds he'd suffered to his leg in the desert campaign prevented him from moving fast enough.

Chapter 7

WALKED DOWN to the Qantas office in the warm winter sunshine with the air fare to Britain in cash in my pocket, more money than I had ever carried in my life before, absolutely certain that everyone on George Street had X-ray vision and was about to bludgeon me over the head and nick my loot.

Then it was a matter of saying goodbye to the ABC.

'You're a mad fucker. What the bloody hell d'you want to go back to Pommyland for? It's cold and wet and no one washes.'

'You do realise that you won't be eligible for a Credit Union loan?'

It's always so easy to do things when you've made up your mind and everyone thinks you're out of it. The problem only arises when they agree that you're doing the right thing. It was simply a matter of packing a few things, I'd already been seduced by possessions, and catching the next plane out, after getting mildly drunk of course.

Ever since working in Australasia I've loved the sunshine. Like a lot of country people I loathe the heat and humidity that goes with it, but I love the sunshine. So when I got back to Heathrow a couple of weeks later and it was bone-numbingly cold, I was in shock. As far as I could see, the streets of London were paved with drunks. From a moderately comfortable flat in Bondi with the sun raging outside, to an environment which at best was basic. I moved into a basement flat in the Bayswater Road which flooded every time a bus went past and this was a busy route for the Big Red Ones.

I stayed in London for a week before I plucked up the courage to go home. I haven't the faintest idea why, but I was as nervous as a kitten at the idea of seeing my family again and I tried to put off what I thought was the evil hour for as long as I could. I ran out of excuses pretty quickly and caught the train from Euston. My grandmother and my two cousins, who were just kids then, were at the station to meet me as I tumbled off with my suitcase. My grandfather had died while I was working in New Zealand, but Queen looked exactly the same and so did my mother, who was as embarrassed as I at all the fuss and bustle about unnecessarily organising everyone. It was an awkward reunion. I was no conquering hero, after all. I was back in Britain after seven years with a mah-jong set, a hangover and no job.

I had learned my lesson in Sydney and I wasn't that keen to get back to work, so I set off to the employment exchange in Paddington the moment I got back to London and for the first time in my life someone asked me what I did. I'd never really thought about this before and I was completely baffled. 'Er, I work in broadcasting.'

'Yes, dear,' said the lady, 'but what do you do?'

'I, er, I, um, I talk,' I mumbled.

'Ah, that'll be upstairs in the executive placement department.' She smiled, and I was whisked from what looked like a betting shop to a long room with seats and a carpet where I was offered a cup of coffee, had my ego stroked and was given a long and detailed form to fill in.

I had uncovered the crock of gold. Because of some agreement they had with Australia, I would be paid unemployment benefit and a bit more for six months and I wouldn't have to do a thing. This could be the life of Riley. I could play pool and hang around the Kentucky Fried Chicken shop all day if I wanted to. I didn't want to and as it was coming up to Christmas time, there were plenty of temporary jobs going.

So, for the last time, I donned the now sadly unfashionable corduroy jacket with the narrow lapels and the leather buttons that had served me so well down the years and went along to Selfridges for an interview as a temporary salesman in the wine department. I got the job and nipped down to Take Six smartish to buy a cheap pinstripe suit with horrible flares, all on credit of course. I seem to remember that at the instigation of the salesman I also laid out forty-five quid on a black crushed velvet jacket with wide lapels and padded shoulders. Before you laugh, ask any of my generation and I'd be surprised if there isn't a similar jacket lurking somewhere in their past. The Afghan coat was still to come, but at least I was the nearest thing to respectable I'd been for years.

I loathed and detested wearing that suit or any suit. It's not just that the most stylish and well-cut of clothes hang round me like a dressing-gown, it's the whole thing of being a peacock, of standing in front of a mirror preening and cosseting things into place. Besides, getting up in the morning and making sure that I've got the right things in the right order in my shoulder-bag is enough.

I'm with the producer Kenton Allen, who has a healthy personal ego about the way he looks and made his choice years ago. Faced with a lifetime of filling his wardrobe and then selecting from it, Kenton came down on the side of minimalism. He has half a dozen of everything and everything is black. Jackets, T-shirts, jeans, boots. This is life at its most sophisticated and makes things easier in every way. Also, you can't go wrong forgetting what you meant to buy when you're shopping for clothes.

I have enormous admiration for women. They seem to go through hell everyday, but I was born a slob and I still can't join the queue in the gents' just for a final chance to put that strand of hair back in place once and for all.

Now, in my defence, I have to remind you that I had never done a day's work in my life before being accepted at Selfridges, so the reality of the daily grind hit me hard. There was a level of expectation there that I found very hard to come to terms with. It had something to do with an 'honest day's work for an honest day's pay' and it bore no relation to what I had just spent the last seven years doing. For a start, they expected you to turn up to work on time and there was a time-clock that you had to punch at the staff entrance. I would struggle up at seven o'clock in the morning, and bail out the flat before wrapping myself up as warmly as I could and battling up the stone steps from the basement to the street. I would then walk to the corner just by the porn shop, which would be opening around about that time to the middle-aged men bent on avoiding each other's eyes as they scuttled in and out, and catch the bus from Bayswater to Oxford Street.

After I had worked out that the time-clock wasn't a coin-in-the-slot machine, I was able to stand, just below the head of department, Mr Prince, with a gormless expression on my face as the hordes of Christmas shoppers came in. Mr Prince was everything that a boss in a department store should be, large, dignified and given to going for long lunches with buyers or reps, from which he would return a little red-faced and unsteady on his feet, walking with great delicacy between the port and the whisky. He seemed a decent soul, but one never actually talked to him, because whenever the great man had news to impart, or a rallying cry came down from above, 'Watch for shop-lifters in the cheap wines', it would be one of Mr Prince's assistants who would pass on his thoughts. Mr Prince was the kindly Chairman Mao of Selfridges, a presence always to be respected, but he didn't actually seem to do very much.

The staff and the management at Selfridges were fine, it was the customers who were truly awful. To be fair to them, it was the height of the pre-Christmas rush and Oxford Street must have been a nightmare to negotiate.

The worst, incalculably the worst, were the Little Old Ladies. These well-dressed apologies for the SS would never ask you for help when a low blow in the stomach from their elbow or a bang over the back of the head from their umbrella would do. Some would stamp on your feet and then smile accusingly at you and say, 'I need your help, young man.' Others would merely punch you very hard in the small of the back and say, 'Champagne'. The first of these L.O.L.s to try the heavy approach came as close to death as she had ever done. I had just returned from democratic Australia, where L.O.L.s behaved or were mown down, so I nearly reacted as any Sydney taxi-driver would when assaulted. Only the reality of no pay cheque that week stayed my hand and prevented that particular Little Old Lady from ending her days dangling by a noose from the Babycham display.

As with most things, it was a good lesson in life. Now I always keep a wary eye out for L.O.L.s. After my experiences in Selfridges I became and remain 'Little Old Lady Aware'. Whenever I went home to the farm to see my family, I would peer very closely at my grandmother to see if she was about to succumb to an attack of Little Old Ladydom. Over the years my antennae have become attuned to Little Old Ladies, I can usually spot them at thirty yards now and make a break for the hills before we come in contact. But sometimes I don't move fast enough and they creep through when my defences are down. I've been nearly trampled to death by a flock of them in the endless hunt for a New York taxi. If there are empty carriages a-go-go on any train, they'll select mine and glare at me while I drag my luggage and myself out of my seat and into the aisle. The only times I have missed trains are when L.O.L.s have asked me to go and get something for them from the kiosk and I've turned back with their orange juice or whatever to see the last coach disappearing out of the platform.

I was once cornered by two in Boots in Wolverhampton and

forced to drive them both twenty miles to their homes. Who is going to say no to two piteous old ladies moaning about their broken-down car when they're standing in front of thirty shoppers on a Friday morning? 'What a bastard that bloke over there is, Mum, he told those two lovely little old ladies they were ruthless, conniving so and sos and they should catch a bus.'

Don't believe that I hate L.O.L.s, I don't. I'm terrified of them and I'm not alone. When I lived in Hampstead I got to know one of the number-thirteen bus conductors quite well and he would go ashen-faced at the prospect of doing his job in the middle of the morning, when the L.O.L.s would all wave their bus passes and descend on Grodzinski's for coffee. A normally peace-loving man, he knew what these women were capable of if the bus was delayed or slow, so he'd spend most of the journey hiding upstairs.

At Selfridges, we'd stand in pairs, rather like coppers walking in danger spots late at night, as we watched the L.O.L.s tottering around the aisles.

'These are the ones who couldn't get a credit card at Harrods,' one of the permanent sales staff told me.

I quickly learned that Selfridges had a secret underworld that, much like the other ones I'd experienced, was based on sex. Everyone at my very junior level seemed to be shagging everyone else. You couldn't go into the stock room without hearing gasps and moans brought suddenly to a halt, followed by a pair of bright red and guilty faces peering from behind a pile of cardboard boxes.

Memory has us mere mortals eating in one canteen and the bosses in the other. It was quite fun and they were nice people, but I found the everyday business of being reliable suffocating. In the previous seven years I'd had so much freedom and been protected for the most part from any degree of responsibility, so the idea of doing this for very long filled me with horror. I'm afraid that I had developed into a waster, and besides I still couldn't add up, so bottles of expensive port were winging their way out of the store at bargain prices. At least the Little Old Ladies were happy about that!

The crunch came when one of Mr Prince's assistants took me on one side and said, 'Y'know, I think you should consider applying for a permanent job here, it's a good career.' *A good career!* I had been trying to avoid that all my life. Of course the poor man meant well but he had just set off the biggest set of psychological alarm bells possible. I had to get out, but where?

My vaguely planned intention had been to spend some time in London and then hop it, to India or South-East Asia, but I didn't feel like doing that just yet and besides, I was still trying rather inadequately to be the kind of person that Diana wanted me to be. My inverted snobbery meant that I was still violently against asking the BBC for a job. Of course, it wasn't snobbery at all. I was in awe of the organisation and frightened of rejection, but it took me a while to grasp that. Diana urged me to at least try and then gave me the name of the then Head of Presentation, David Lloyd Jones, whose father had been the inventor of 'BBC English'. I called him and heard a pleasant enough voice on the end of the phone invite me to come and see him.

My first impression of walking into Broadcasting House was one that has never left me. I can't understand how there can be a sense of occasion to an entrance made through brass swing doors beneath a perfectly carved willy. While I worked there I was always obsessed with the idea that the statue in place over the entrance must somehow have been provided with a vulgar little fountain in his scrotum and that when after all these years it finally worked, I'd be the one underneath.

When I arrived, I went through the ritual that has impressed thousands of people over the years. It worked on me too. I was taken by a uniformed commissionaire the longest route around the endless corridors to Lloyd Jones's third-floor office, where I was met by his secretary, given a cup of dreadful coffee and asked to wait. When his office door finally opened and he invited me in, David was pleasant and chatty in an afternoon-tea sort of a way. He talked to me about what I had and hadn't done, offered me a gin and tonic, and sent me on my way thanking me for coming and saying that he would bear me in mind if anything came up.

I walked back down Oxford Street feeling quite happy. I'd spent the afternoon out of the cold and away from Selfridges, met a nice old duffer, chatted to him for half an hour and got a drink out of it into the bargain. All round it wasn't too bad, and even though I hadn't got a job at the BBC, I still had a job at Selfridges until the end of the sales. Two days later, David phoned Selfridges and offered me a short-term contract as an announcer.

A couple of years afterwards I asked him why he hadn't made a bigger deal of our chat that afternoon and why he hadn't auditioned me. His chin sank on to his chest and he gazed at me patiently over his spectacles. 'I rang the ABC and talked to the people you'd said you worked for. If I'd auditioned you, all I would have found out was whether or not you were good at auditions.'

I left Selfridges immediately, after which the profits in the wine department must have soared, and only came in contact with Mr Prince once again, on a Piccadilly Line platform on the Underground. I'd been at the BBC for about four years. 'Shame you left,' said Mr Prince, listing slightly to the left and slurring his words just a touch. 'If you'd stayed, you might have done quite well for yourself.' Looking back, I suspect that he knew what he was talking about.

A few years later I met someone who'd worked at Selfridges when I'd been there as a temporary salesman and he claimed that the old fellow had taken to congratulating new recruited staff. 'Bates was here for a while, you know, and did quite well afterwards,' he would reminisce, and then he would wander off, allowing the impression to sink in that he'd been singly responsible for my career move.

Once I had got over the initial surprise of finding myself a BBC announcer, life became pretty easy. There was plenty of variety and one wasn't overworked, which rapidly became the problem as I became more and more fidgety. But at first, of course, there was the shock of finding oneself working for an organisation with a vast bureaucracy and a Bible of unwritten internal traditions. I discovered that, as an announcer, I was entitled to two theatre seats a month, God knows why, and pounced on this opportunity. There was also a sort of dormitory arrangement over at The Langham Hotel – then the property of the BBC – where if you were on a late shift, you were entitled to a bedroom all to yourself. Admittedly it was not luxurious, but it was clean and free.

I also discovered about this time what true corporate perfidy was when a night sweep by the commissionaires found me in bed with a rather attractive young lady. Even though I plunged a five-pound note into the bloke's hand at the time, he still reported me the next day. I claimed that I didn't understand and for some reason the whole thing was covered up.

Then there was the small matter of the TV licence fee. I forgot to pay mine and learned another lesson about what bastards people can be. It was the easiest thing in the world to forget and I was going through a bad patch, having split up with Diana. I'd combed the pages of *Time Out* for somewhere to lay my head and come up with a pretty unsuitable flat. In the process of getting my black and white

Grundig TV through the front door and into the tiny bedroom, I had completely forgotten to pay the licence fee, so when the knock on the door came at eight o'clock one night, I cheerfully let the two detector men in. They seemed rather nice and I sat them down on a packing case and plied them with coffee. It would have been silly to pretend that the cheque was in the post and besides they were extremely sympathetic, so, like George Washington, I owned up and dug down into the pile of clothes on the floor to find a cheque book. They went on their merry detecting way, whistling and carrying my cheque, and I forgot about the whole affair until the summons arrived in the post a few mornings later. Even then, I wasn't too concerned. Irritated that I'd given the two swine coffee and they'd then shopped me, but not that worried. Still, better tell the boss, I thought.

When I told him that I had been summonsed for non payment of my licence fee, the colour drained from his cheeks and I thought he was going to have a major coronary. He shot to his feet, shut the door and told me to sit down. It was as though I had just advocated the overthrow of the monarchy at a meeting of a Tory think-tank. Later it was explained to me that you could do almost anything in the BBC and survive, with the exception of not paying your licence fee. This was a capital offence.

Much drama ensued. I was told to keep a low profile as the wheels were put in motion to pretend that this had never happened. I wasn't absolutely certain how to keep a low profile, but I did my best to slink in and out of work and sidle rather than walk along the corridors. From time to time, I would be tipped the wink. 'Don't worry, I'm across this problem, we'll probably get away with this one.' I wasn't being ungracious, but after a while I started to giggle. From being a bloody silly thing to do, my forgetting to pay my TV licence fee had become a major crime with 'possibly serious consequences'. I know I should have taken it more seriously and been much more grateful to the people who made sure that the story didn't reach the fourth floor, but the whole thing seemed to have developed a life of its own and become melodramatic enough to be the basis for a le Carré novel. All that had happened was that I'd forgotten to put a cheque in the post, for heaven's sake. After I had paid my fine and some time had lapsed, the licence-fee incident passed into history and I got on with learning about the goings-on in the nooks and crannies of Broadcasting House.

On night shifts in the newsroom there was a remarkable journalist with great gifts as a safe-cracker. This man seemed capable of getting into any executive office and then into the executive's drinks cabinet. You would never be without a drink during his overnights. He also ran an early version of a bucket shop for airline tickets, coming unstuck only when he sent a collection of journalists on a holiday weekend to Spain. He got them there all right, but when they tried to fly back from Malaga, the authorities intervened over some technical problem with the tickets. His customers were not happy, and when they finally returned to Blighty he had disappeared for a few weeks and the drinks cabinets were safe for a while.

I was mightily impressed with such men. They were endlessly more intelligent and better read than I. What I didn't recognise at the time was the fact that most were capable of so much more than was required of them and that they were bored rigid with their jobs. One senior newsroom sub would spend most of his shift translating Agatha Christie into classical Greek as an exercise in mental agility. As the years wore on he became steadily less reliable and more unwilling to actually do his job. Towards the end of his tenure he couldn't be bothered to update the bulletins and he would sit in the studio quietly barracking the reader. 'In Vietnam, fifteen Americans have been killed.' This was what the bulletin had said an hour earlier. That same bulletin would be delivered for the next hourly news and the reader would launch into it again as the sub sat in a corner of the studio and watched him like a slightly pissed hawk. 'In Vietnam, fifteen Americans have been killed.' The hawk in the corner would quietly murmur, 'seventeen', and the reader would cough slightly and say, 'That should be seventeen Americans killed.' So it would continue with both exhibiting perfect timing, the ultimate update. The man moved on after writing an opening for a Radio Four bulletin that ran, 'Well, General Amin's been huffing and puffing again.' Now, placed on the right network such a phrase wouldn't raise an eyebrow, but then it was regarded as the final nail in the coffin.

Of course they were right, whoever 'they' were. The BBC was the greatest broadcasting organisation in the world then and still is for that matter. But there was a kind of sickly, unhealthy smugness in the way some people in the middle management of the organisation looked at it. There was an air of the higher moral ground being the BBC's as of right and there being no need to try any more.

On the lowest level, one of my colleagues, leaning against a bar, stared earnestly into my face and said, 'D'you know, I sit sometimes on the tube and look at those ordinary people there and I think, Christ, if you only knew that I worked for Radio Four, you'd be so fucking jealous! Know what I mean, Simon?'

No I didn't and I still don't.

It was quite fun working there, but it wasn't exactly mind-bending and I found the principle that everything we did, no matter how trivial, was 'extremely important' rather hard to swallow. I mean, we weren't exactly speaking peace unto nations, broadly, we juniors were puffed-up walking time-checks. On one occasion I sat for six hours and said 'Radio Four' three times before legging it as fast as I could to the pub. This was a lifestyle that did drive a man to drink.

Even then though, I became acutely aware of those irritants in radio style that still drive me to chucking my Nesquik at the wireless when I hear them perpetuated. There is an awful cosiness about a continuity announcer who creepily informs me about 'our next programme'. It is neither inaccurate, nor is it particularly bad use of language, but this anonymous plural is horribly creepy. Then there is the classic programme opening during which some oaf announces that 'we ask the home secretary', or 'we find out from the general secretary', or simply 'we ask the question'. By the time he is halfway through the sentence I am halfway up the wall screaming, 'it isn't "we" you damn fool, it's you. Stop spreading the blame for your own fatuity and take it like a man.' It is you, or rather, it is 'I' who ask the question. I will listen to the programme and decide for myself if I wish to be swept along on your tide of 'we's'.

And while I am railing, whose crazed idea was it that as many voices as possible should be crammed into a long, though well constructed and clearly written news bulletin? If the story comes from a correspondent on location, or from a recognised expert who has something unique to impose upon it, then all well and good. But if it is simply a deadhead from the newsroom who is dragged into the studio to record the piece he has just subbed from the wires, then what the hell is his purpose on air, other than to baffle the audience? The point is that unlike television, radio is a form of communication and unlike television, a plethora of voices is confusing. For the audience, the transition from one voice to another is just another hurdle against comprehension. Mentally the listener has to take a moment to adjust, and in adjusting he can easily lose concentration and the sense of what is being explained. Then you have lost him.

I am not advocating the absence of contributors to radio news bulletins. If I did that, I would be depriving radio news of Fergal Keane, Philip Short, Jonathan Charles and the like. They and others are honourable exceptions. But what in God's name is old so-and-so – breathing heavily after a long night shift and dropping the end of his sentences like a stone – doing, but creating a barrier against understanding?

Then there is the matter of reading one's own script. From the sentence where unhesitatingly the wrong emphasis *is* placed on every word, to the sing-song delivery, to the declining sentence where the last few words come from the presenter's socks, presentation sometimes poses a great barrier to understanding. There are some presenters who, if you dare to listen to them, demonstrate with anything they introduce a shocking misuse by its owner of a perfectly adequate voice and an often able script. Yet no one has taken them to one side and shown them how to lift words off a page. Or if anyone has, they have been totally and foolishly ignored. Presentation is no worse and sadly no better than it ever has been, but it could be so much better.

Why do I care? I can't really tell you, except to say that it is not the poor quality of anything that offends me, it is the thought that maybe the root cause is laziness. That someone cannot be bothered to try a little harder seems wilfully stupid and ungracious. It is like giving up playing in the band when the *Titanic* is sinking purely because the water is getting near your ankles.

Back then in the grim seventies, positioned at the bottom of the ladder, we weren't really responsible for those wonderful, sweeping radio programmes that were produced by the giant minds hiding behind anonymous room numbers elsewhere in the vast building. Neither did we have the talent or the experience of the senior announcers. We just pumped out the news and the time-checks, and then pottered across the road to The Langham and held up the bar of the BBC club. So I began to drink too much and turn up late.

On one occasion, I spent the night on another announcer's couch with a promise from him that he'd get me into work in time for me to read the Sunday morning shipping forecast at six thirty. Sure enough we both overslept. Not to worry, there was still time if we moved quickly. Out came the motorbike and off we zoomed, him in front and me hanging on for grim death on the pillion seat, round Shepherd's Bush and over the Westway before screeching to a halt outside Broadcasting House at six twenty. We toddled in through the entrance over-confidently and took the lift to the third floor, where we both expected the forecast to be read. The studio was cold, dark and locked. We trotted round the corner to another possibility, only to find a vicar being observed coldly by an ageing producer as he stuttered through his script. We cantered downstairs to yet another locked studio and then galloped panting to the control room, which was empty but for an engineer who looked up, grinned and said, 'Yer too late, mate. I got Robin Boyle to do it.'

One distinguished announcer was kind enough to say, 'If they don't say anything, don't volunteer an apology. It probably means that no one has noticed.' I didn't and nobody had.

Of course it was somewhat disconcerting to meet the voices of my childhood. These were men and women I had listened to on that little Bakelite radio in my room upstairs at the farm, and in real life, as always, they were far from being special. Barry Alldis, an Australian with a big brown voice who'd spent years hosting *The Top Forty* on Radio Luxemburg and who should have looked like Clint Eastwood, turned out to be a tubby little bloke who habitually wore white shirts of the see-through kind with a vest underneath that stood out like a Belisha beacon.

I met another of my heroes under less than promising circumstances late one night. I had finished a newsreading shift and walked into the announcers' room on the second floor to see the poor man obviously in the throes of a heart attack. His chair had its back to the door and he appeared to be leaning over it, hands gripping the back tightly, with an expression of agony on his face. I rushed forward to help and then realised that the expression that I had assumed to be agony was actually a reaction to quite a different sensation. A young lady was kneeling on the chair and the two were joined in an intimate though complicated embrace. I blundered my way out of the office as quickly as I could, but listening to him was never the same again.

I had made a terminal mess of my relationship with Diana and was now living in Hampstead. I was also developing on-air nerves for the first time in my life. Up to that point the whole business of going on air had been faintly ridiculous, but fun. Now I found myself tensing up and worrying about what was going to happen, or what kind of mistakes I might make that day. My concentration vanished and I found myself making silly, inexcusable errors on air. I introduced *Gardeners' Question Time* once with great panache and the tape operator played in the correct programme *Any Answers*.

I referred to 'the uninvited' when the copy read 'the UN invited'. Whether it was the sense of occasion that working at the BBC encouraged, or the dawning realisation that this was a living and was for real, or just a lack of concentration, I don't know, but while I didn't drink before work, I took to putting away a good deal afterwards.

I had had a few beers one lunch-time after working overnight and I hopped on a number thirteen bus to go back to my little flat in Hollycroft Avenue, NW3. Unusually there was gridlock around Selfridges, just before the bus turned into Baker Street. Still, I meandered boozily through my memories of the store as we hovered at the intersection. Another delay and another and suddenly my bladder started reminding me that there were four pints of Guinness and God knows what other junk stuck inside waiting to get out. The bus crawled along and I became more and more uncomfortable. Gradually the situation became worse and I began to cross and uncross my legs in a sort of tribal rhythm to control the surge from my bladder. Just before Swiss Cottage the bus came to a stop and I nearly screamed in agony. I HAD TO GO AND I HAD TO GO NOW. I looked out of the bus window, frantic for a tree or anything that I could hide behind. Nothing. Worse than nothing, by now it was three thirty and the school kids were all coming out. Wonderful. I could see the headlines: 'BBC Announcer Convicted For Exposing Himself Before St John's Wood Schoolchildren.' 'I had to go', wept convicted man as he stood before the court. 'Please, we've seen it all before,' said schoolboy Peter Farthington-Twit II, when asked for his reaction by our reporter.

By this time, tears were streaming down my face and I would have sold myself into slavery for a Sanilav. I leapt off the bus, and hobbling along like the Hunchback of Notre Dame, clutching my loins as discreetly as I could, I shambled over the road to the Odeon Cinema, oblivious to the teeming traffic screaming to a halt as I crossed. 'Lavatory, for Christ's sake, where's the lavatory?' I croaked to the girl behind the pay desk, like a drowning man crying for a lifebelt.

'Upstairs, but you'll have to pay like everyone else.'

It was a quiet day at the cinema and I reckon they could have remade *Everything You Always Wanted to Know About Sex* . . . and put the laughs back in for the amount of cash I threw at her.

Hampstead was discreet in the seventies, it had to be. The number of senior politicians who had little flats and private personal arrangements that everyone knew about but no one mentioned in that part of London surprised even me. Getting up early in the morning meant running a gauntlet of seemingly half of London's security forces as they guarded various important people, or rather sat in their cars outside playing a waiting game. After a while I got to nodding acquaintance with some of them. Which is more than I can say for their charges, who would rush in and out in double-quick time looking studiously anonymous.

Round about this time I got myself attached to a lady singer who was doing well in the pop charts. She was delightful, funny and original, and well aware of how silly almost everything she had to do in pursuit of her career was. The late seventies meant that pop fashion demanded she wear a wig every time she appeared on stage or TV. She would wearily haul one of these horrors out whenever she was booked, and once claimed that she would marry anyone who would design one which was aerodynamically sound. She had been taping for a BBC programme in a field somewhere near Southampton. 'On that stage, if there's anything like a high wind, I could end up in the next county.' She's still just as intelligent. We didn't live together, she had a flat just around the corner from mine and we ended up in whichever was closest at the time. I was taking myself and everything I did far too seriously and she did her best to open my eyes, bless her, but failed.

Her manager was terrified that an involvement with anything so unhip as a BBC announcer would become general knowledge, so we were cautious to separate her professional and private life. It wasn't too difficult because when she was 'at work' she duly wore a ridiculous wig that increased her height by about six inches. When we were together she was almost unrecognisable.

The relationship lasted for a while and then, when inevitably the time came for both of us to move on, the break was genuinely amicable. I missed her deeply for a while. She was that rare thing, a genuinely good person who always saw the best of everything, but there was a compensation in her going. She had probably the most perfect body I have ever seen and I spent most of our time together plotting and planning how I would get undressed in the dark, so that she wouldn't be confronted with my awful reality. The strain nearly killed me.

She lives in the United States now and has taken the decision to avoid marriage. We still see each other maybe once a year and she always has a new and ever younger man in tow. 'I like 'em,' she will say, 'when I'm tired of them I can just say, thank you, baby, that was wonderful and goodbye.'

It was not long after this that another of those myths confronted me and I nearly forgot my Australian advisor by denying it. I'd been enjoying a fling with a lady newsreader I shall refer to as Sarah. Nothing serious, just a movie and a meal every now and then. I bowled into Broadcasting House one afternoon to be confronted by a friend of the aforesaid newsreader who said, 'You, bastard.'

I stopped dead in my tracks and said, 'what?' at which she repeated herself, 'You, bastard, how could you knock Sarah out like that?' I hadn't the faintest idea what she was talking about. The idea of me knocking out a substantially built woman like Sarah was patently absurd and I protested that 'Tweren't me, guv'nor.'

We went a few yards down Oxford Street to a coffee bar to resolve the issue and she explained herself. According to Sarah, she and I had been in the bath at her flat making vigorous love and I had become so passionate that I had somehow managed to bang her head against the taps knocking her out in the process. I knew nothing of this and when I asked Sarah about the incident the truth came out. Unbeknownst to me I'd been sharing the favours of the lady newsreader with a light-entertainment producer. Obviously, one or both of us wasn't up to the mark, but I was Wednesday and Saturday nights' assignation and he was Monday nights. It was the oversexed light-entertainment producer who was responsible for Sarah's loss of consciousness and not me. When she'd told her girlfriend, she'd forgotten to mention a name and as the light-entertainment producer was a bit of a dark horse everyone had assumed that the guilty party was me. The light-entertainment producer was a man with a great sense of his own place in life, so I never asked him about the incident, but the relationship with Sarah was somehow soured and we went our separate ways, though I never denied the story when I heard it coming around again.

Gossip and the BBC go hand in hand. The circular design of Broadcasting House and TV Centre guarantees that if it happens on the ground floor at nine o'clock in the morning, the machinery of gossip will work its magic and by lunchtime, the occupants of the farthest office in the building will know about it.

In the late eighties, a couple from different buildings and departments who had lived together for seven years and who had been

bove: Aged eight. To think it
arted like this . . .

Above, right: Lost in Hong Kong
aged 22, trying to look confident

Right: With Tom, my first publisher,
in Fitzroy Street, Sydney, Australia

Above, left: 1977. Punk is raging and I get a perm. Atkey's mistake!

Left: 1980. I hated soccer and I hated the macho team 'japes'. An obligatory part of being a wacky jock. With Dave Lee Travis

Left to right: bottom – Peter Burnett, Peter Powell, Tony Blackburn,
Stuart Henry, ?, Alan Freeman, David Jacobs; middle – Noel Edmonds,
Richard Skinner, Andy Peebles, ?, Steve Wright, Annie Nightingale,
myself; back – Dave Cash, Ed Stewart, Pete Murray, Duncan Johnson,
Tony Prince, Mike Read, DLT, Tommy Vance, Keith Skues (*BBC*)

Carolyn and me with a goose, 1980. The goose got away (*Keystone Press Agency/Chris Ware*)

Probably the most entirely forgivable creature in the world, Magic Story, 1982 (*Daily Star/Tom Stoddart*)

Me and producer, Egypt, 1984

rince of Wales colliery, Yorkshire,
everal hundred feet below the surface,
980 (*NCB/Bill Devey*)

Lunch! (*Sun/S. Lewis*)

Nicaragua, 'Around the World' (*Oxfam*)

Me and safety advisors, Sudan

Another failed Ruffle attempt to kill me

Addis Ababa, 1993, with Fergus Dudley and equipment

Croatia, 1993, with British lorry drivers who wanted to talk to their families back home (*Red Cross*)

With Fergus Dudley in Russia, 1990

The final show from the Carnegie Deli
in New York, 21 October 1993

In Aretha Franklin's front room,
enjoying a private concert by the
Queen of Soul, 1993

going through a tough time in their relationship decided to take themselves off to the Lake District to sort out their problems. They spent the weekend together and on Sunday evening went to a tiny restaurant near Carlisle for a meal. They were the only customers. Suddenly, he produced a ring and proposed to her. She paused for a moment and then said 'yes' before bursting into tears. Fade Out.

The next day the couple returned, overjoyed at the idea of sharing their lives together and went back to their offices. At lunchtime, *his* office door banged open and a friend of hers stood accusingly in front of him. Within hours of the event taking place in the Cumbrian outposts, the rumour mill in London had heard of her tears in that tiny restaurant in Carlisle and within seconds the assumption had been made that he was a cad and should be confronted. Forget the security services: someone from the BBC is always watching you!

For a while, I did a late-night chat show on Radio Two. The show had its place in the schedules of the time, though now I suspect it would sound agonisingly predictable. The joy was to discover more about how hideously guests on programmes like that behave when they're off air. For an innocent colonial-trained broadcaster to observe guests arguing about their fee before trotting out a couple of old stories and being stuffed back in a taxi, was an education and a delight. The fifties radio star Wilfred Pickles stood in the green room outside the studio one night and point-blank refused to go on for 35 quid. 'I want forty, or I'm not doing it,' he said flatly, and of course he got it.

These programmes were pretty limited. They were neither as good as similar shows done in the sixties nor as adventurous as those that were to come. It was as though no one could quite commit themselves to what the show should be. Interviews were to last no more than four and a half minutes and the joke in the production team became the sequence of questions: 'Good evening. What are you doing at the moment? What are your plans for the future?' End of interview.

Packing all they had to say in four minutes was a nightmare for the guests too. They would arrive aware of the limitations and the moment the first question was put to them, they'd be off like rats from traps, racing the clock, trying to cram their life stories and a plug for their latest show/film/book into the allotted time span. It was plainly ridiculous when Vincent Price rolled up to plug his new BBC series and film. Vincent was not a fast worker and by the end of the four minutes he had just about said 'hello and thank you'. I discovered how simple the art of breaking the rules was that night. All I had to do was keep the plug for the BBC series until the end of the interview and the producer, who would be shaking with fear at the idea of us not getting this vital piece of information across to the waiting millions, would allow the interview to run as long as was necessary.

There was a relentless blandness to the show, which occasionally lifted when guests like John Houseman and Sean Connery came on. But I did learn a good deal of the basic rules of the game of interviewing, though I still and endlessly forget them. Always, always, always know the name and if possible the sex of your interviewee. Always read the book or see the movie before you talk to the subject. This of course can go horribly wrong even if you follow the basic rules but don't understand the aforesaid movie or book. If this happens, always return to the movie or reread the more complex books.

Q: 'In chapter three you say that all European agricultural subsidies should be suspended?'

A: 'No, young man, you've missed the point. I say that's what my opponents say.'

Or, when it's all going frightfully well and you launch off into a flight of fancy which can leave your guest, however helpful, boggling at you.

Q: 'I've always thought your performances as villain fascinating. In 1966 you triumphed in a piece of film noir and yet now you've come up with an elegiac masterpiece, does this link in with your relationship in the seventies with the French protest movement and your marriage to Anouk Aimee?'

A: 'I'm sorry, could you repeat the question?'

Absolutely not.

Then there's the business of listening to the answers.

Q: 'Mr Churchill, your grandfather's career has never held you back?'

A: 'No, but I think that we should bomb the Argentine mainland.'

Q: 'But your father undoubtedly suffered in his shadow?'

Most politicians are far too self-centred to bother with the interviewer so you can hide behind your anonymity as they prattle on about 'Jeremy' and 'David' before you begin to talk to them. Beware the old pros, though. On the day I was scheduled to do a set-piece interview with him, Denis Healey had made a statement that was completely at odds with his party's defence policy. 'Ah, ha,' I thought, 'gotcha,' but he was far too slippery for me and had come prepared. Unlike most politicos he had been briefed on who was interviewing him, right down to some of the regular features on the show and he'd taken the briefing well.

A good proportion of the flock of British politicians desperate to get themselves on British radio and TV are so anally retentive that they don't realise the advantage to be won by understanding a little about their interviewer and their surroundings. Often the audience will be more familiar with the frontman and his peculiarities, and knowing something more about him/her than just a Christian name whispered in the corridor by an aide, can give the politician the edge. This may not be a fashionable stance, but it is true and the Healey incident proves it.

I asked him about his statement once and about the apparent disparity between his attitude and that of the Labour party and he made a fairly bland reply. I asked him again and he leaned forward smiling. 'Oh, now then, Simon,' he said, 'I think you're pretending to be stupid and we both know you and your audience are perfectly able to understand what I've just said.' I asked him again, and he smiled again but lethally this time, leaned back and mentioned a couple of the daily features on the show before saying, 'It's a bit like "Our Tune", you know, Simon,' and I knew I was lost. I tried half a dozen times, but he saw me coming and wiped the floor with me.

There can be occasions when the interview is so unwelcome that when it is nearly all over, you can come a cropper as much for the flood of relief at its conclusion as for anything else. I was parked unwillingly at some BBC fest to cover the opening and was ordered to interview the chairman of the BBC board of governors, a man who had suffered dreadfully in the War and who had lost a leg in the process. The interview rambled on – I mean, you are not going to tell the boss of bosses to shut up, are you? – and as it wound down, I heard myself saying, 'Well there's lots to see here, so I suppose you'll be legging it off around the exhibition?' The engineer on duty developed a hacking cough for about five minutes and had to be provided with countless glasses of water before he could resume his duties.

Then there are what one can only call the involuntary interviews. I was deputising for some disc jockey or other in the afternoon in the days when Radio One lingered as one of a row of studios next to

Radio Four, when to my astonishment the actor Robert Morley walked into the studio. He stood there for a moment, a large, amiable figure, looking slightly stunned.

'Who are you?' he said.

I told him.

'Well, I'm here to talk about my new book,' said the great man briskly.

I assumed that my producer had forgotten to tell me that Robert Morley was coming in, and privately cursing him, I did what I most hate, interviewed an author about a book I hadn't yet read. He was, as always, very funny and helped me out of my ignorance by telling me the title on air again and again and again. At the end of the interview I apologised for not being prepared, and as he left he turned and said, 'Oh, don't worry, dear boy. I had fifteen minutes to wait for my Radio Four interview and I saw you and thought I'd just pop in.' He smiled the most delightfully devious of smiles and added, 'It all helps the sales, you know. Cheerio.'

An oddity can turn up in an interviewee with a sense of humour. I had met Eddie Murphy a few times before I went to his home in Los Angeles, loaded down with technical gear to record another interview about some movie or other. I'd been told that he wasn't particularly in the mood for an interview, but he seemed pleasant enough to me.

'Hey, man,' said Eddie, holding his hand up, palm outward.

I made a pathetic attempt to hit his hand with my hand like I'd seen in the movies and he winced. White men can't jump.

'Now,' he said, 'where shall we do it?'

Please, God, not by the waterfall at the back of the house, I thought.

'Let's do it by the waterfall at the back of the house,' he said.

Enough noise was generated by that waterfall to deafen Beethoven.

'This looks good,' twinkled Eddie, who knew exactly what he was doing. He sat opposite me as I tried to unscramble the wiring that always seems to spend its time out of the daylight making love to itself. I had just got the mike in a position that limited the amount of noise coming from the dratted waterfall, when Eddie produced his secret weapon, his guitar, which he lifted to a point between him and the microphone. The recording had the waterfall battling with Eddie's guitar and Eddie himself, like a little mouse, popping up every now and then in between all the other 'noises off'.

Mick Jagger is equally wise in his dealings with the press and with interviews generally. He usually knows what he's about, though even a star of his calibre can come a cropper. I chaired a TV conference for him on one occasion and when I introduced him he overdid the entrance, came on like Wily T. Coyote, was unable to stop and crash-landed. I didn't help him up, I thought that it wouldn't do his image any good if a tatty old DJ was seen to lift one of the most notoriously fit rock stars from the carpet.

Mick is brilliant at interviews, he'll drop a few newsworthy gems before getting to the subject he's trying to plug. And the gem is usually about photographers. Once when he was being hounded by the paparazzi he told me, 'If a photographer doorsteps me and gives me a hard time, I just clout him over the head with an umbrella or a stick or anything I've got in my hand. They always run away, they're very cowardly. Sometimes I get really scared when I realise that they're two foot bigger than me!'

However, the cracks show sometimes and they're good to see. After an interview at Radio One, I noticed that his father had arrived and was sitting outside. The moment Mick saw him, he smiled, quite the warmest and most welcoming of smiles, helped him to his feet, put his arms around him and hugged him very tenderly. The two walked off to lunch, arm in arm. He's just a softy, really.

Once, when talking to George Michael as we took a break from recording, to fill the time I asked if he hung out with many pop stars.

'No,' he said, 'I really don't know many famous people.'

At which point his phone rang. I answered it and on the other end of the line was Elton John asking to speak to George. Great timing.

It's all a matter of having a sense of humour. When I asked Keith Richard once about the rumour that he used to carry a gun for his own protection in New York, he reached into his shoulder-bag and pulled a loaded Colt .45 on me.

When I asked Jagger about this, he said, 'Oh, you put him up to it, you made him do it. You just got him showing off, din'cha?'

Talking to Ronnie Biggs in Rio, he claimed, 'Most villains are stupid.' To prove it he told me how he once broke into a house with the intention of opening the owner's safe. After a few unsuccessful hours trying to crack the job, he gave up, gathered his tools together and went home. Behind him, Ronnie left the local newspaper he had used to carry his jemmy, at the top of which the newsagent had written his name and address!

I always thought that Biggs was exaggerating until, sitting in a bar in Dallas a few years later, a local newsman told me the story of Eugene Flenough Jr., who tried to rob a Texan restaurant wearing his motorcycle helmet back to front to hide his face. He forgot that written on the front of his helmet was 'Eugene Flenough Jr.'

Then there are the times when you really do have to work hard to keep awake. A few years ago I did an outside broadcast from Dublin and it seemed appropriate to ask Mary Robinson, the President of Ireland for an interview. Her office said neither yes nor no, but prevaricated and began to impose endless conditions. Because the programme was about Dublin as European City of Culture for that year, we were most definitely not doing a political programme or examining the troubles, so when her office asked to see a list of questions, we broke our own rules and agreed. Come the day, I sat opposite Mrs Robinson and my producer stood just behind her operating the tape recorder as I began to plough through the list of bland questions that had been agreed with her office. Her answers were long and frankly uninteresting, it was as though the poor lady was responding to the very tedium of the questions and giving back in kind. Unforgivably I began to lose interest. Gradually my eyes slipped down as she droned on about the wealth of cultural identity in the city, until I found myself gazing at the President of Ireland's legs, which are by the way spectacular, and entertaining impure thoughts. My producer, who was well aware of what was happening, gained my attention and I launched into another dreary question.

On the subject of interviews. Here comes another of Bates's broadcasting laws. 'Always know how the gear works and never ever put your elbow on your knee.' A few years ago one poor journalist with *Newsbeat* went on a facility trip to Jordan, had an exclusive interview with Queen Noor and came back with a blank tape. We all laughed, but we all thought, 'There but for the grace of God, go I.'

Clint Eastwood had a new movie out. In Britain, Eastwood is popular, but in France he is a god. The French have this thing about adopting American film-makers with absolutely no French connection and claiming them for themselves. The point was that, not unreasonably, Eastwood was going to stay in France to be worshipped and not bother with the kind of questions that the weasels would ask in the UK, 'Hey, Clint, how big's your willy?' So, to get him on the programme, I had to do a five-hour round-trip to Paris, which I hate. Not the city, I could stay there happily for as long as I was picking up the expenses, but the five-hour round-trip was something I could do without.

Clint does not exactly overproject when he talks, so I allowed Fergus to persuade me that taking a DAT (Digital Audio Technology) machine would be a good idea.

'The quality will be much better than cassette,' I heard him cry as I disappeared into an Oxford Street tube station.

Four tiny bottles of airline wine later, I reappeared with only a few minutes left before my scheduled interview at the Georges Cinq in Paris, by this time realising that I hadn't the faintest idea how to work the bloody DAT machine. I rushed into the interview room, threw out a bumbling Belgian TV man (why do Belgians always mutter?) and had started to plug up the machinery, when in strolled Eastwood. He looked great and seemed to remember me, which was nice, but I hadn't got my head around the infernal machinery, so I kept grinning oafishly at him while frantically putting what I hoped was the right bit of cabling into the right socket. After a couple of fumbling minutes we were ready to go and I pressed the 'record' button. The machine's read-out screen lit up brightly with one word, 'error' and refused to work. Eastwood smiled, a thin-lipped but patient smile. I laughed too loudly and struck the machine a blow that would have silenced Marvin Haggler for ever, it continued to smugly declare 'error'.

Eastwood leant forward and said, or rather breathed, 'Problem?'

Faced with a man who knew what he was doing and who was no fool, I owned up, expecting him to throw an almighty wobbly and stalk out of the room, after which I would be beaten to a pulp by his henchmen and thrown on to the Paris streets with a cry of '*Voici, le wanker*'.

Eastwood reached into the breast pocket of his jacket and produced a pair of pince-nez which he dangled from his nose. 'D'you have the instructions?'

I fumbled about inside the case and found them.

'Let's see.'

Which is how I found myself on my hands and knees, as one of the world's finest actor/directors read the instruction manual and took me through the ritual of 'Fig. A, press two, then press four,' and between the two of us we got the thing going and successfully recorded the interview.

'Japanese shit,' breathed the great man.

The French are, of course, totally right, Eastwood is God and everyone should see an Eastwood movie at least once a week, or if that is impossible, rent one of his videos. When I am made president, this will be mandatory, so start practising now.

As a Luddite of long-standing, can I now make a plea against DAT machines? They were designed by the devil and a BBC outside broadcast engineer in league together to render the life of the lowly presenter miserable. The last time I was in California in a small town called Palo Alto, I was persuaded by Adrian Juste to take one of the wretched things with me and, sure enough, when I got there, it didn't work. When I took it back for an old friend at the BBC to diagnose, he smiled and said, 'Ah, well, then, that'll be the motherboard.'

'Yes, but why did it go wrong?'

'Well, they have a tendency to do that sometimes, trouble is you never can tell when it's going to happen. Those motherboards have always been a problem.'

The motherboard, for heaven's sake! My old Sony Pro cassette machine doesn't have anything as complicated as a motherboard. It is as a steam engine to the DAT machine's TGV and it works like a dream. OK, sometimes it'll grind a little slow and Arnold Schwarzenegger can come out sounding like Angela Rippon, but we can always fix that in the dubbing. No, DAT is great for opera, but lousy for people, and the kind of people who use it you wouldn't want to meet. Let me prove my case.

Last year I was in Cannes for a music festival. Now, music festivals are wonderful, because there can be no misunderstanding about them, you know where you are and what's expected of you. If you stay up after eight o'clock you must become drunk or consume vast quantities of a sherbet-like substance that I have always managed to avoid. And the uniform is always denims, denims, denims and Reeboks. Maybe you'll become a crazed individualist and wear a sweat-shirt, but that's about as outrageous as you can afford to be without stopping the *Croisette* dead.

I was wandering through the *Palais des Festivals* feeling, for one of the rare occasions in my life, a bit of a snappy dresser in my clean jeans, when a vision appeared. The vision was dressed in cream leather shoes and carefully pressed slacks, with a Hawaiian shirt and Raybans to complete the ensemble. This man looked like a turkey on Christmas Eve.

'Hi, are you from the BBC?'

I shrank into a corner, desperate to avoid being seen with this monster. 'Maybe.'

'Well, I'm from the Rick Dees show, you know about Rick?'

This latter spoken slowly as though to a total idiot. I found myself answering in a ponderous tone to match his. 'Yes, I do know Rick Dees. Very successful DJ in Los Angeles.'

At this, the thing leaned forward and breathed crème de menthe all over me. 'Well, we've left our portable tape recorder in LA and we wondered if we could borrow yours?'

'OK,' I held up my Sony Pro cassette recorder, 'here you go.'

The frightmare staggered back as though he was a vampire and I was Van Helsing. 'No, no, no, Rick can't possibly use that, he only works with DAT.'

'Fine, fuck him!'

Later I learned that the American team had arrived at the Carlton and eyed their rooms. The frightmare had shrieked at reception, 'Please get up here and clear out all these French soaps and Colas, Rick will only use proper American-made products.'

OK, do you really want to be like that, use DAT and wear a Hawaiian shirt? Stick with manly cassette, I say.

And while we're on the subject of music festivals or conferences, let me say right now that I love 'em. This is where the drunk is hailed by the drug addict and the artist is entirely forgotten in a welter of making deals that never get signed. Like the two teams of lawyers from opposing record companies who last year spent twelve hours arguing over a difficult contract with the help of a good deal of whisky. By the end of their brainstorming session, they had come to an agreement and headed for bed, leaving the business of writing up the contract till the following morning. When the following morning dawned, none of them could remember exactly what agreement they had arrived at the previous night. So they patiently started out all over again.

But we were discussing interview techniques and Bates's law of broadcasting. It is as unforgivable to arrive for an interview with equipment that doesn't work as it is to do anything to startle your interviewee. I'd been angling for an interview with Robert De Niro for years and one night the call came from the Savoy Hotel. 'Mr De Niro will talk to you tonight.'

I packed the equipment, and here it has to be said that 'the equipment' is not an elevating sight. It consists of a couple of microphones, batteries, cables and a Sony Pro all tastefully popped into a ripped British Home Stores plastic carrier bag. So minimalist is this ensemble that I end up being offered fifty-pence pieces by passersby who think that I'm selling *The Big Issue*.

I arrived at the Savoy Hotel and was introduced to De Niro, who was charming. Then I retrieved everything from the bag and began the interview. I have this thing about eye line and body language, especially with people who don't like doing interviews but have been kind enough to agree to do one. To achieve the required effect, I hold the microphone and sit with one leg crossed over the other, making sure that the interviewee is aware that I'm listening to him by keeping my eyes on his face and not looking at the tape recorder or any other nonsense. On this occasion my mistake was to rest my mike arm on my knee and somehow trap the blood vessel.

The interview ended, De Niro rose elegantly to his feet and offered his hand to me. I tried to do the same thing. As I got up and put my weight on my right foot, I realised that I couldn't feel a thing, it was as though I'd had a massive dose of Pentothal in my calf. I grinned foolishly and fell over, a writhing heap at De Niro's feet. I lay there for a minute or two trying to laugh the whole thing off, as he asked me if I was OK. What De Niro thought of this fool lying at his feet rubbing his thigh, kicking out with his right foot and crying, 'No, it's perfectly OK, it happens all the time', I can only imagine. He behaved impeccably, looking away tactfully as I staggered to my feet, stuffed my things in the BHS carrier bag and limped to the door.

There has always been a sort of inverted snobbery in Britain about the business of 'plugging'.

Defining a 'plug' is pretty easy. It is when a musician, author, film maker, actor or whatever makes him or herself available for an interview because something is being released, published or staged that he or she has an interest in. The moment that you accept the idea of doing an interview on this basis, you as the presenter also accept the fact that there will be an element of promotion involved in which the interviewee requires you to mention or involve the product and the possibly shy and retiring artist will then give a little more as a result, rather than staying tight-lipped. They will go the extra mile, if you are a little forgiving of their needs.

This has always seemed to me prefectly logical.

Radio One is usually pretty tolerant of plugging interviews because it is pragmatic enough to realise that if it doesn't allow them, then artists simply aren't going to show up. But sometimes it goes through a sort of intellectual constipation and begins to require 'challenging' interviews with artists. That is usually a short-lived and silly phase and often has a good deal to do with some hidden agenda on the fourth floor of Broadcasting House.

I'll cheerfully admit that on occasion I have cut material out of interviews if I've been asked to by the artist, and I've also excised material when I thought I was being unfair to the artist.

George Harrison once made an ill-advised remark about the Prime Minister of the day, implying that the holder of the office should be hanged from the nearest lamppost. At the time, George was going through a high profile phase and it would have been a perfect headline grabber: 'Beatle says string ****** up.' Even though to his credit he said to me afterwards, 'I said it, so you can broadcast it if you want,' it seemed a pointlessly tacky and exploitative thing to do, so I cut it out.

Equally, I was recording an interview with a well-known chart topper when he suddenly broke down and talked intimately about a boyfriend who had just been killed. After the interview he asked me if I would cut that segment out, 'because it is intensely personal'. It seemed to me that no one would benefit from hearing his distress except maybe the brownie points hunters on the fourth floor, so I cut it out of the tape.

There was another American artist who came into the studio for a prerecorded interview and almost immediately announced that it was his intention to cut his own throat later that day. We poured coffee into him and he at once changed his mind, so we cut that bit of the interview, though I admit I kept the edited tape just in case he changed his mind back again.

There are so many examples. People who arrive in tears, in a sulk, drugged up to the eyeballs, aggressive and carrying offensive weapons. So, calm them down some and then start the recording with a grin on your face. Do the best you can and make up your mind later about how bad it was.

These are not politicians and if they haven't come out with some whopping great social or political gaffe, why go for them? Be realistic.

Droves of guests are driven to Broadcasting House, flattered, coffeed and delivered to the studio with reassuring words whispered in their ear before they do their stuff. Some are good and some are bad, all are fodder of a kind to the demands of the microphone and cheap programming. But some are different, some are so open and honest that it is impossible not to be moved: A woman whose child had been a victim of cot death and who was campaigning for research. Another woman who had survived the most horrific treatment as a prisoner during the Cultural Revolution. A man from Sudan who tried to explain why his country needed help from the West – he spoke superb English quietly and thought about his answer, 'I am not asking you to give my country a hand, I am asking for a fingertip, that is all.' In print it looks very ordinary, it is the power of the human voice that lifts the commonplace and makes it extraordinary.

The Radio Two show was an interesting experience. I can't say that it brought light into the lives of many, or was that memorable, but it did teach me that radio was much more flexible technically than many were prepared to admit. The Red Devils invited me to do a parachute jump with them and after being told by a senior engineer that it would never work, I took a small cassette machine with me, and sticking the microphone in the headset I recorded a perfectly adequate commentary. The Red Devils struck me as amongst the most macho and suicidal people I had ever spent any time with. On the initial 'rehearsal' run, with me sitting in the back of their light aircraft trembling at the thought of what I was about to do, a bunch of them linked arms and simply fell out of the plane, laughing like maniacs. I looked out and saw these supermen rolling about the sky, giving each other thumbs-up signals with their parachutes still wrapped in their containers.

I felt sick, and when it was my turn, still attached to the aircraft by my static line which would guarantee my parachute opening, I sat in the open doorway, looking straight ahead of me, fiddling with my equipment as an excuse for not jumping. I was panicking so much that I didn't even hear the order to jump, though the tape machine recorded the command, I just felt a massive thump in my back as the NCO literally kicked me out of the aircraft. Listening to the tape eighteen years on, all I can hear is a sort of strangled gurgle as I fall through space, followed by the distinct impression of a man pulling himself together as fast as he can, when the parachute opened and I found myself swinging through the air over Aldershot. The commentary was rudimentary to say the least and my voice rose by an octave or two, but the sound quality was fine.

One of the reasons for doing the jump was my endless and stupid fear of heights. I have always found it irritating and offensive beyond belief that I simply cannot look over the side of a second-floor balcony without everything beginning to swim before my eyes. I thought that if I did a parachute jump it would solve my terror of being more than five feet off the ground. It didn't. I did another four jumps, shaking with fear as I forced myself out of the open door of the aeroplane, but it was no use, and when on that final jump I had to use my emergency parachute, I took the advice that was obviously being handed me by a higher force and chucked the whole thing in.

I am still terrified of heights, though I've learned to control the worst extremes, the nausea, the sweats and the shakes, on most occasions. But they come back to haunt me occasionally. I was in Los Angeles earlier this year having lunch on the twenty-seventh floor of a sheer-sided building and sitting with my back to the window, which stretched from the ceiling to the floor, when suddenly the old fear hit me like a tidal wave and I felt as though I was falling backwards. I had to spend five minutes in the lavatory dousing myself with cold water.

More ridiculously, years ago I was helping an elderly outside-broadcast engineer put a cable over a hedge. I didn't know that he suffered from vertigo and he didn't know that I did too. We were sharing a step-ladder and standing about six feet off the ground, when both of us suddenly suffered an attack simultaneously and clung terrified to each other like lovers. God knows what the neighbours thought . . .

'Eric, there's two of them people from the BBC with their arms around each other.'

'Come away from the window, Agnes, they're always at it, them poofs.'

The night-time show pootled on for a while and then, not before time, quietly died, unmourned. It had been moderately pleasant to do and I'd been able to watch and understand more about how broadcasters I admired, like John Dunn and Bob Holness, worked. I also met David Hatch, who contributed over the succeeding years more than any other individual to the present health of public service radio. If anyone is responsible for its survival and its health in the nineties, it's this height-deprived bundle of energy. David looks like an upturned beer barrel with a smile grafted on the top, and apart from his boundless enthusiasm, he is also mightily intelligent and socially mobile. He is that rare thing, an ex-performer (along with

John Cleese he graduated from the Footlights to *I'm Sorry I'll Read That Again*) who isn't jealous of performers but is a master when it comes to dealing with them. He is almost obsessive in his love of radio, and if he has a weakness then it is that he is sometimes unable to understand people who aren't as committed to the medium as he is. He is an internal entrepreneur, something that is viewed as old fashioned and unfashionable, but which can be the perfect force to help new talent through the system, for the right reasons. He enjoys having a hand in other people's success. He tends to take a papal view of his territory and the listener benefits.

When I met him, he was a light-entertainment producer in a department that was encouraging bright young things. Whether he was going to become enormously successful or not was impossible to predict accurately back in the late-seventies. But if he hadn't reached the position of managing director of network radio, I suspect that he would have burst!

I was trundling along, working quite happily as a presenter on the daily early morning show between five and seven, which back in those prehistoric days was broadcast on Radios One and Two, and learning another lesson. 'Do not make the mistake of thinking that huge figures equal success: small audience equals loyal audience and that is just as important.' There was a joy at working so unreasonably early and I learned that a small audience cares more about what is delivered to it than a large one. Whoever you are, sputtering away at an unholy hour of the day or night, you become a piece of property to the listeners. They get to know your foibles and become extremely possessive about you. There is therefore no need to endlessly parade your name, as in 'And it's me, so and so, with your whatever.' If they like you, they will find out who you are, and if they don't like you they won't bother. Life was easy. A BBC car collected me every morning and I was working for a delightful and easygoing man, who seemed permanently on the verge of collapsing with laughter, called Geoff Mullin, who functioned as producer. My day ended before most people's had started and virtually none of the BBC bigwigs ever listened. They were tucked away in their little truckle beds dreaming of their expenses or their secretaries when I was on the air, and besides they had much bigger fish to fry than SB, whoever he was.

The executive on the programme was Derek Mills, a pear-shaped man with a wide, easy smile and a kindly, supportive attitude. Derek would have been perfectly cast as the kindly Vizier in a pantomime production of Aladdin. He seemed light years away from some of the people I'd been working for who were endlessly tied up in their own minutiae. I once emerged from a two-hour meeting with this sort of person, to realise that the only subject that had been tackled was the producer's dislike of my use of the words 'my producer' in the end credits to a programme we were doing together. It took a good while to unravel what his problem with this was, but then it transpired he felt that it patronised him and his exalted position and sounded like I owned him lock, stock and barrel. He is now a performer in a small way, introducing education programmes for schools and the like and using the words 'my producer' with unfailing regularity.

Those were the days when radio announcers were, quite properly, owned by the BBC. I was on contract and not allowed to work anywhere else. Coincidentally, the BBC's internal staff policy meant that I couldn't do any more work than I was doing already. I would work my two hours and then potter into the sunshine. It sounds like heaven, but in truth it was deadly dull. Just as my system was getting going, my working day ended. I was being suffocated by goodwill and generous terms of employment. So rather than spend the rest of my life in the pub I resigned at the end of my contract.

The BBC then was a wonderfully old-fashioned, caring and maternal organisation. Getting out of it was well-nigh impossible. It was patently obvious to them that anyone who contemplated resignation was severely unbalanced and if, as was the case with me, there was no work on the horizon, they must be fit for the funny farm. There could be no reason for resigning, it was a good job and employees were well looked after. So I began a round of caring interviews in which nice people from personnel talked to me slowly and softly, all the while watching me carefully for signs of madness, explaining to me the many reasons for staying in the BBC.

'It's a career for life.' 'We look after our own.' 'If you leave you won't be able to use the canteen.'

I was almost persuaded when one executive generously offered me a job as a Radio Two producer. Now this would be a job for life and it might even be fun. But I said 'no thanks' while thinking that maybe I was making one of my biggest mistakes, and handed in my ID card in a sorrowful ceremony that made me feel as if I was being drummed out of the Seventh Cavalry having had my sword broken over the colonel's knee.

Simon Bates

A few days after I left, the BBC offered me a contract to deputise, when required, for Radio One and Two presenters when they took their holidays. I had met and been rather intimidated by Derek Chinnery, the slim and thin-lipped Controller of Radio One, who had asked if I would like to work on the fledgling *Newsbeat* programme when it finally became a fixture in the schedules. I'd read the news headlines on the pilot shows which Noel Edmonds had presented and been staggered at the amount of hysteria taking place in the control room. The producer was an excitable woman who had an unnerving tendency to stand on the desk and point at whoever she was cueing next in such a way that one half expected flames to come out of her fingers. There seemed to be far too many people shouting and yelling, but without much work to do, so I'd hummed and hawed a bit, and while not closing the door (on the grounds that no one likes to starve), I hadn't expressed wild enthusiasm about the idea. Derek had got the message, but along with one of his deputies, Johnny Beerling had agreed to the idea of sharing the cost with Radio Two of keeping me around in case of a temporary gap in his schedules. It didn't pay regularly, or very much, but it was some kind of umbrella for the hard times.

Oddly, I was rather frustrated when the offer was made. I'd been all for upping and going back to South-East Asia again, but the BBC's contract and my laziness put a stop to that. Hitherto I'd been scuffling around the basement of populist broadcasting. Now suddenly I was on the periphery of the big names and in all fairness I didn't have the faintest idea how big they were. It's hard now to realise just how much impact these radio people had on the everyday life of the country, Blackburn, Wogan, Murray and Young. They were stars, and with the exception of Michael Parkinson and one or two other professional television hosts, their influence was total in the mid to late seventies and they knew it. The BBC was still slightly embarrassed by them and by what they did. When I'd been working for Radio Two for a while, I was invited along with Wogan and Murray down to Aeolian Hall, where the Radio Two administration offices were, to meet Lady Plowden, whose forthcoming report the BBC were mightily concerned about.

'Get a suit, for God's sake,' Wogan told me. So I meandered along to Gieves & Hawkes and got myself a suit, which whenever it was exhumed was recognised and jeered at by the staff.

The three of us stood in an uneasy file as Lady Plowden walked down the line, gently patronising us and talking about how important broadcasting to the masses was and how we should all do a programme for Radio Four 'to explain what popular radio is all about'. She reminded me of one of the L.O.L.s in Selfridges. It was a faintly ridiculous ceremony and felt a little like one of those parades so beloved of British film-makers where the troops are inspected by the general with a staff sergeant alongside keeping an eye out for malcontents. The then Controller of Radio Two played the part of the staff sergeant but we were no malcontents and behaved impeccably until the end of the parade, when we had naïvely expected to be invited to join them for lunch. But as the three of us surged forward, in the hope of some free food to make up for our time wearing suits, the door was firmly shut in our faces. No one was going to risk having three presenters there when the port was being passed around the table. It was Pete Murray who shot up in my estimation when this happened by pausing for a moment while he collected his thoughts and then checking the drawers in the Controller's desk for spare cigars.

My new job, as far as I could understand, meant twiddling my thumbs and waiting until some superstar croaked, became ill or took leave. Now there was a fine line here. Taking leave was something that superstars on Radio One with a few exceptions weren't too happy about.

One didn't really meet the superstars of the network. They came and went in their flash cars and one sort of stood aside for them as they passed. There was another huge divide between them and me. Most had worked for the pirate stations and for the first time I was to hear about the 'Golden Age of Radio'. This would be the first of many occasions that the Golden Age would be referred to and each time, the Golden Age would be different. I knew nothing at all about pirate radio and, since it had long since sunk beyond the horizon, I must admit I had very little interest in it. Also the cynicism about too much nostalgia for the 'good old days' that had been grafted on in my years in Australia meant that I really couldn't take much interest. The stories about seasick DJs working with buckets between their legs and jolly masculine japes sounded less than golden to me.

Working as I was for both stations, I was in a kind of limbo, so, understandably perhaps, no one bothered too much about me. I knew Noel Edmonds faintly, because I had spent some time doing the early show before his enormously popular breakfast show. I didn't know him at all well, but his superb command of radio was unquestionable. I've often speculated whether or not he actually enjoyed it and I sometimes suspect that he didn't, which I find difficult to grasp. The reward of radio is the total control and the almost instant response. Success or failure in whatever it is you're trying to do is so easy to gauge, it is an instant surge based on your own perception of what has just happened, a raised eyebrow from the engineer or a listener's phone call. Since Noel probably achieved the best single entertainment series ever on Radio One with his Sunday morning show in the eighties when he worked with producer Dave Price, it would be quite extraordinary to discover that he didn't gain pure pleasure from doing it. But I have a feeling that his almost total self-control might prevent him from getting the lift that he so emphatically earned. I've always regretted not knowing him well enough to ask.

When I arrived at Radio One, it's fair to assume that my future looked pretty limited, so understandably most people didn't bother to do much more than learn my name. Johnny Walker, Tommy Vance, Ed Stewart and Alan Freeman were, predictably, the four who made an effort and showed me how to tie my broadcasting shoe-laces. No one else directly hindered me.

There was a high level of paranoia amongst even the most secure of superstars and that suited the suits just fine. 'A nervous turn is a malleable turn' is a truism and that's the way they were treated. It's easy at this distance to understand just why they were all so nervous and insecure. There really was nowhere else to go, nowhere else to work and earn the considerable sums that anyone working on the national pop network could expect to pick up outside their BBC earnings. Most had taken to living the high life with great ease. For DJs and producers, this was the high life and then some. There was no reason for a Radio One producer to dip his hand in his pocket, ever. There would always be someone there to do the providing for him.

Sitting in an Indian restaurant in 1990 with a BBC executive and my then producer, I gradually got more tired of the producer wailing about his inadequate salary. The executive, a canny man who always appeared to be a great listener, but who was actually a recruiting officer for his own ambition, was listening sympathetically but growing bored, so I suggested that we do some sums on the 'freebies' that the producer could enjoy in his exalted position. Working on a five day week, we calculated that the man could enjoy free lunch and dinner in a good restaurant and a show, play or gig each night, with transport provided. All this would come from the record industry and we added the value to the endless free supply of records which at that time used, in a few cases, to find its way almost immediately to a second hand record stall in one of the street markets. The executive and I came up with perks to the conservative value of £35,000 tax free. The producer stopped moaning about his inadequate salary. An opportunistic and under-employed producer could then enjoy the high life seven days a week and leave his BBC salary in the bank.

These were the days when Radio One's administration block at Egton House took on the look of a location for a Mafia funeral at about midday as the record company cars lined up to take the producers for lunch. Lunch! This was often not lunch, but for some a marathon that could take the guest through to midnight, after which he would be poured back into the car and delivered to his wife. There were producers who were notorious for being firebrands and who, if they did make it back to the office after a good lunch, were to be avoided at all costs.

For the promotion men, lunch could be a necessary nightmare, an obstacle to be surmounted, rather than a pleasure. Most of the producers who overstayed their welcome were not in the least interested in the music. Their obsession was with status and that meant ordering the most expensive wine on the list or, as one producer did for all his twenty-five years at Radio One, going for the prawns and eating them entire, tail, head, eyes, the lot. No one dared tell him that he should restrict himself to topping and tailing them.

Then of course, some producers who took more on board than they should became embittered at their lack of opportunities and took to being carried back to Egton House by the promotion man, weeping ungratefully. In my innocence I took one producer to the Monte Bello, the local restaurant for most of the BBC and ITN, which lurked behind Broadcasting House at that time. I was quickly made aware that though the Monte is a perfectly adequate restaurant for most people, it was not really up to my guest's standards. He complained that the plate was not warm enough and asked for the wine list. I didn't even know there *was* a wine list at the Monte. Like most people I drink the house white and behaved myself. But worst of all, when I asked him if he wanted some pudding, I was not quick enough to stop him clicking his fingers.

Now no one, but no one clicks his fingers in the Monte. That sort of behaviour in that sort of restaurant is the stuff that starts wars. So when my guest clicked, a strange and deadly silence fell on the assembled diners. Mama, from her position by the door looked in.

'Who clicked?'

I wanted to crawl under my pasta and die.

'I did. Can I see the trolley?'

A pause.

'The trolley. The trolley? You feel ill, you walk out!'

There was for the most part a division as real as the Berlin Wall. The producers produced, that is they made up the list of records, collated the requests and popped the whole into a box ready for the DJ to add, as one executive used to say to me, 'that special glitter' in the studio. Contact between the producers and DJs was limited. The one had to justify his position as a BBC staff man by claiming that the other was 'musically illiterate' or some such nonsense: the other had a living to make, opening and closing garages and just being seen, so he needed to exploit his few hours and possibly limited future on radio to make sure that the bulk of the mortgage was paid before things went downhill. These were professional disc jockeys, professional 'personalities', larger than life figures who were just the same off air as they were on. Their job was to glitter and shine, to entertain, to be special, and if they didn't succeed in doing that 'on' and 'off', there was always a good-looking, bouffant-haired lad with great teeth just aching to take over. In a divided world, the lives of these two, disc jockey and producer, were interdependent. The one could not really do without the other, and relationships, though often strained, used to last longer than marriages often did. In fairness, these were the seventies and they were essentially people of their time, rattling around in shiny cars, paying visits to the Playboy Club on Park Lane and most important of all, being recognised. Their reward was a national following so total that it seems unreal now.

I once walked down Oxford Street with a couple of these superstars and watched astounded as a crowd grew and eventually brought us to a stop near Liberty's. The crowd seemed amazed that these two could actually walk and talk at the same time. Eventually I was pushed none too gently to the back of the knot of people fighting for an autograph.

In my first months at Radio One, Derek Chinnery called a disc jockey staff meeting at which one of the big names announced that he had a real beef. I sat up and took notice. He was, he said, fed up with the canteen service. The cups were of poor quality and when he ordered his bacon and eggs while he was on air, the rinds were not cut up. I collapsed under the table. This was a stunning example of a man sending himself up sky high, wasn't it? No actually, it wasn't. All the other DJs nodded seriously in agreement and I started coughing heavily to cover my embarrassment.

This was an Elizabethan world of plot and counter-plot, where turns were taken out to dinner by the boss and the news roared round the department so that the other turns became mad with fear that they were being ignored for some deep, dark reason. The problem really comes when you push a turn too hard and he cracks and does what he has been close to doing for some time, goes crazy. I knew that at least and had observed it happening in the less rarefied atmosphere of Australia. It happened fairly regularly in Broadcasting House.

One none-too-bright presenter was told consistently by his bosses and over a long period of time that he was the bee's knees. Correction, that he was the Mr Wonderful of broadcasting. I suspect that at the time, his management had convinced themselves that this was true. This was a man with little or no cunning to him. What you saw was what you got and he believed nearly every word that his management said, which I suppose anyone would, given that he had been lauded to his face for a good five years by the time the crunch came. He was flattered and cajoled, cuddled and stroked. He would often lunch with his Controller in the canteen. This was the most important form of patronage, if you saw the Controller and his turn together at a table in the Broadcasting House canteen that meant you didn't even have to wait for the white smoke, this was a 'turn for the future'. The man was nearly untouchable.

Inevitably, resentment at the poor fellow's success grew and grew. The relationship between the man and his employers began to sour. Equally inevitably, someone funnier, brighter and wittier than he was came along, and after the management had accepted the idea that our hero was replaceable, he was told, out of the blue, that he was a bloody nuisance and that his show was being moved. The fall when it came was so sudden and so total, and the pill such a bitter one to swallow, that the effect was unsurprising. The humiliation and the suddenness of it all got to him, he went mad and became a bundle of bitterness. He flailed around trying to work out whose fault it all was and gave up, blaming everyone and anyone for what he saw as a career dive. The point was that he had become too successful, he had made too much money, and he wasn't grateful enough. Like the boy in *The Magnificent Ambersons*, it was time for his come-uppance. It was an unreal atmosphere and of course it always will be. A hothouse of ideas and egos all trying to race each other to the surface.

While all this was going on, I was very much the junior, and although I was hanging on, hoping for the occasional job deputising for a holidaying superstar, I was also pottering about outside the BBC trying to make a living and doing it none too effectively. For a while I worked at Southern Television for an awfully nice man called Tony MacLaren. My job, along with a few others, was to pop up between programmes and fill the gap with some rubbish about the pleasures to come. The final job of the day was to read the local news to an automatic camera that sat huddled in the corner of the pit we occupied that was called a studio. Many of the people who did this kind of thing were out-of-work actors and I had always admired the distinguished grey-haired man who, at the end of the evening news, would remove his glasses, look warmly at the camera and wish me 'a very warm goodnight'. It looked wonderful and I was completely conned until the night when I noticed his specs sitting on the desk and picking them up to return them to him, realised that there were no lenses in the frames. 'Thank you, dear boy,' said the actor, not a whit abashed, 'it keeps the mums and dads happy.'

'It's all a dream, mate,' said Brent Saddler, who at that stage was a sub in the newsroom desperate to get out and do things. 'You don't want to hang around here for too long.'

I didn't, I was fired summarily for moonlighting on Thames TV. Southern TV was a territorial organisation and liked to keep its own people exclusive unto itself and when the Managing Director happened to be watching something in London one night and saw my face grinning out of the screen introducing some programmes on the then-holder of the London franchise, it was the end of the end in pretty short order. I felt terribly guilty at letting Tony down, but a man has to make a living.

I was a lousy on-camera continuity announcer. It was so boring sitting there waiting for the next link and it seemed to involve far too many visits to the lavatory to pour more hair lacquer on the head. There were those who were past masters at doing the job and talking to their agents, girlfriends, boyfriends and others on the phone in between the moments when they popped up on camera looking sharp as a tack and saying just the right thing at the right time. There was also the matter of how long one had to talk and the business of tailoring a link to fit what the presentation director had allotted for the announcement. One spectacularly inefficient director, having cocked up the whole evening's programmes, said to the continuity announcer on the talk-back, 'Bill, you've got three seconds for this link.' And before Bill had time to protest that this was ridiculous and that there was nothing sensible he could say in three seconds, so why not just hold the station identity slide for a while longer, the lights were on and he was being faded up. He triumphed. I watched at home as he said 'hello' gravely, and then smiled and said 'goodbye' before the *News At Ten* logo appeared. It was a masterpiece of brevity.

I did a few shifts at ATV in Birmingham before some wise old soul said, 'Why are we using this man? His soul doesn't seem to be in it.'

The world of a freelance gob on a stick – which is basically what you are as an available voice-over – can be a strange one. Your agent gets you the work and you find yourself haunting the West End's dubbing studios, drinking too much coffee and recording anything and everything on an hourly basis. The best voice-overs in the business, people like Tommy Vance, En Reitel, Patrick Allen, Michael Jayston and others, never stop working. You'll see them dragging their way along the streets of Soho from studio to studio, preparing to work themselves into a frazzle of excitement over almost anything really. The world of the voice-over is the world of the unemployed, until they get a job. Starting up is a torture only to be enjoyed by the paranoid.

When Peter Dixon left the BBC, having read the news on Radio Two for a couple of years, he recorded the inevitable demo and sent it off to the advertising agencies. Nothing happened for a week or two and then a pleasant-sounding woman called him from the production department of a local commercial radio station. She enthused about his voice. 'Christ,' thought Dixon, 'if I play my cards right I can eat this week!' and he accepted her offer of a voice session a few days later.

And here we come up against the lack of reality demonstrated by 'turns' – because the booking was for some time in the future, Peter never asked where it was. To him, as to most of us, the future is a concept far too vague to grasp. When the day came, he got out the map to discover that the radio station was Radio Hallam and was in Sheffield, over two hundred and fifty miles away from *chez* Dixon. It was the height of winter and he set off in his car up the M1. As he got further north, so the weather turned more and more evil. The roads were blocked with snowdrifts and our hero was reduced to leaning forward and peering through the rapidly icing windscreen. Two miles from Sheffield his car skidded and wrapped itself around a passing lamppost. He got out of the car (and by now of course it was hailing), disentangled it from the lamppost and continued slowly on his way to Radio Hallam. He made it, though two and a half hours late, and as he stood in the foyer, dripping wet, the sleeve of his coat ripped, and in a foul temper, he was greeted by a middle-aged lady in slippers and a cardigan who eyed him, tut-tutted and said, 'Well, love, you're a bit late. Have you come far?' He was paid £100.

The studios where these epics are recorded are monuments to the needs of the 'turn'. There is always an area full of couches for voice-overs to linger on and gossip with each other. 'V.Oing' is a little sub-culture, where everyone knows everyone else and what they're doing. 'I see he got the British Rail then . . .' There are the senior V.O.s, who stalk majestically through the foyers of the studios and tend to lend their voices to up-market material, Lingua phone records and the like. Then there's the middle-brow brigade, got a Pavarotti's Greatest Hits and these are the boys and girls for you. And then there's the likes of me, pottering along, picking up whatever the big boys have left.

I have been a cartoon giraffe and an elephant. I have left my mark for posterity as the voice on the 'Shake 'n' Vac' advert. Then there was a strange advertisement for Technics, for replay in Japan only, in which I had to speak a line of Japanese that I couldn't make head nor tail of. Heaven only knows what I was saying, but they paid at the end of the session and my agent said that it didn't really matter. You could find yourself in a little booth saying 'programmes on BBC1 tonight' or trolling up the motorway to cry 'the carpet man in Handsworth is the man to trust'.

There are, of course, the knock-backs. Often an ad agency will audition V.O.s for very big campaigns where millions are going to be spent on placing an advertisement on ITV. There is nothing more humiliating than to have done an audition for, say a toothpaste ad one week and then to see the same ad pop up a few weeks later with someone else's voice on it. Or the moment when you've been struggling to keep your speed up or down to make the commercial run to time and failed. 'Don't worry, love,' says the engineer, 'we'll varispeed and no one'll notice.' There is, however, a great deal of fun to be had doing these little underground bits of work, in that you meet and get to know enormous talents, who turn out to be pussycats.

For years I have been exploiting Patrick Allan, calling him up on a whim and asking him if he'd be kind enough to narrate this radio programme or that and he's never turned me down. The last occasion was a serialisation of Michael Crichton's *Jurrasic Park*, in which Patrick read five episodes, playing all the parts himself. We put in the music and the sound effects later and, because of the complexity of the read, I had allowed two hours' studio time to record the narration. Patrick looked at the script and sailed into it, voice characterisations included, finishing the job in forty minutes. The man is a vocal genius and a generous one at that.

My world and my attitude to it were beginning to change. I was heading into the competitive business of being a freelance and that meant taking everything including, for my sins, myself much more seriously. But by that time, Johnny Walker had gone in search of the ultimate wave in California and Paul Burnett had replaced him, which left a gap in the schedule for Sunday mornings. I suspect that Derek Chinnery and his immediate deputy, Doreen Davis, cast around for a more suitable replacement, but time wasn't on their side and they were more or less stuck with me.

I had absolutely no idea of what I was doing. All I knew was that I didn't fit in at all with what I understood to be the image of the Radio One jock, i.e. young (which I wasn't, being nearly thirty when Radio One picked up my contract), good looking (enough said), sexy (yeah, OK) and well-schooled musically (not at all, I just like the noise). There was decidedly nothing fab about me, still, it was a job and I would have to play the game.

It was at this point that I made the first of a big series of mistakes. David Atkey, a friend and still a friend even after what he did to me, suggested with what I can only imagine were the best of motives that I get a perm. I couldn't understand why, so I asked him. 'Image, mate,' he said, and I accepted this at face value. I'd heard of image and knew that I didn't have one, so maybe this was what you did. I charged off to the hairdressers and said, 'Make the hair curly will you, Hugh.' To his credit, Hugh didn't laugh, he just took the money and made my hair curly. It was a disaster. At a time when punk was thrashing around, there was I with a hairdo that would have looked more suitable at Badminton Horse Trials under a Liberty's scarf. I lived with the thing and the howls of laughter it attracted and let it grow out praying that it wasn't permanent. Since then, the hair you see, along with the grey streaks which I consider to be natural highlights, is all mine. Accept no substitutes.

I was lucky in that I was assigned Ted Beston as producer. Ted had worked with Jimmy Saville for years and was now embarking on a new career as schoolmaster to the incomers. To describe Ted as small but well-built is accurate but perhaps doesn't give you an accurate picture of the scale of the man. I often had the feeling that if you picked Ted up and then dropped him, he would bounce a few times and then settle down on his legs just as before with a grin on his face like those Subbuteo footballers you played with as a kid. Ted was an extremely kind man given to spending those special moments that all producers need at lunch-time just around the corner from Broadcasting House in the Marie Lloyd Club. The club was a cellar really and pretty uninviting too in those days towards the end of the seventies.

The Marie Lloyd Club, which somehow never seemed to ask anyone for any kind of proof of membership, was just across the road from the George, the legendary pub where the poets of the BBC met and exchanged witty banter in the fifties. It was rumoured that when the BBC scheduled *Under Milk Wood*, Dylan Thomas had only done a rough draft and had vanished into the hills. The story goes that he was dragged back, imprisoned in the Marie Lloyd and set to work to complete the play. Whatever the stories, the Marie Lloyd has an atmosphere of its own. You could get anything there as long as it was in onyx and if you wanted a different size, that might take a day or so. Receipts were unfashionable in the Marie Lloyd and cash used to change hands at an alarming rate. I could never quite grasp what people were buying, but a lot of smiling went on.

Ted was in his element there, leaning up against the pinball machine and holding court. But he was also a superb and sympathetic producer. He provided the bedrock of confidence on which you could build, whatever you wanted to build really. If you were in doubt about anything, the chances were that Ted would know where the BBC stood on it and if he didn't he'd know someone who did.

He had an ability to give you the impression that he trusted you, though God knows why, and that was the springboard.

I worked for him for a couple of years, before I was told that I would be doing the mid-morning programme that Tony Blackburn had vacated. This came as a complete surprise. Once the decision had been taken by Derek Chinnery to move Blackburn to an afternoon slot, there was no holding the rumour mongers. I was certainly not in the running as far as most people were concerned. The industry money was on David Jensen, who called himself 'Kid' Jensen in those days. A blond, good-looking Canadian, he was working on the drive-time show and his credentials were impeccable. He was a professional disc jockey with a cool understanding of what the job entailed, how one should look and how one should sound. I certainly assumed that he'd get the job, though Ted Beston differed and warned me that I might be offered it. A warning I didn't take seriously. Which is why I was so astonished when Chinnery took me to lunch and told me I'd be doing the show.

Sadly, Blackburn has always believed that I had in some way manoeuvred myself to taking the programme away from him. I tried once to explain that this was a ridiculous notion, but Tony was never the best of listeners when it came to accepting that there might be another point of view and wouldn't be persuaded. I have always regretted that I wasn't able to communicate with him on any level and I suspect that I should have tried harder, but time and patience ran out I'm afraid.

Normally everyday radio is an endless belt, churning out stuff. It is the music, news and voices that crowd the airwaves. It is this ordinary, average, everyday stuff that makes it possible to recognise the good and the really great material that appears every now and then. The dross is essential, without which no one could recognise the broadcasting jewels, and it can be great fun providing the dross and aspiring to the jewels. There is a down side though, and that is that whoever provides the dross is eminently replaceable. Properly and tactfully engineered the change needn't be that great a trauma and on this occasion the change was executed simply and intelligently. There was no great waving of flags or posturing by the management, there was a scheduling change and no one really noticed that much.

The real row had been a couple of years earlier when Edmonds had assumed the role as breakfast presenter on Radio One. As

Blackburn had been the first early morning man on the new giant alternative to pirate radio and had created his own myth in the process, the first shake-up had been the one that mattered. This change in 1977 was a comparatively quiet one externally, though of course inside Radio One there was an added sense of drama and the staff were watchful to see if there was going to be an explosion on the fourth floor where the producers' offices lined the long corridor. There wasn't of course. The people concerned were far too worried about the business of getting away with their daily programme to worry too much about each other.

I hadn't mastered the body language of Radio One and knew almost no one. The daily job of dealing with overwhelming shyness was a big one, and I would sometimes walk around the block before taking a deep breath and running the gauntlet of the 'Wailing Wall' through the foyer of Egton House and making my way to the office. The Wailing Wall was/is the front room of Radio One. It's the foyer of Egton House and on the walls are typed copies of the playlist and the programme running orders. Inevitably the record company promotion men and women gathered there in force, to check if producers were playing their records and to gossip. To me these people were astounding, they were so damned trendy and confident that I would sneak through in my button-down shirt and corduroy trousers feeling totally conspicuous in my ordinariness.

When I was working on Sunday morning, most of them didn't know who I was, now I was in the front line and for a while as I walked through the middle of them, there was a sort of baffled sigh at my arrival. 'Why in God's name is this man doing the morning show?' Understandable really. Suddenly, having stood on the sidelines, I found myself slap-bang in the middle of the fun factory with everyone giving advice and no one helping that much. It was also a bit of a shock to change producers in mid-stream and find myself working for Ron Belchier.

Ron had a reputation as a toughie in the department, especially after a good lunch. He knew a great deal about the business of recording music and was extremely intolerant of anything he regarded as sloppy. He could also be overbearing and to a new boy quite frightening to an obsessive degree. Having worked for Beston, I found myself very much in a sink or swim world. Ron had worked in his own 'Golden Age' of radio back in the fifties and early sixties and made his dislike of 'the way things were going' quite clear on a regular basis. He was always very clean and immaculately dressed and I could usually judge if the sun was shining by the way the trench coat swept into the office. If there was a flounce about it and nothing was said before the door closed, chances were that it was going to be a black day.

I cannot say that this was a marriage made in heaven and I suspect that neither Ron nor I cared greatly for each other, though I respected his undoubted intelligence enormously, but at least he toughened me up. I was a bit of a wimp when I started working for him, but by the time he moved on to another programme, I had learned to fight or die, to stand my corner and not turn tail and run. The only way to survive with Ron was to be as aggressive as he was. This was all very well and good, but his legacy was to leave a raving maniac who was quite convinced that if he didn't spin round fairly quickly, a well-timed kris would be plunged in between his shoulder-blades. The advice that Morris King had given me years before was now expanded into, 'Get the buggers before they get you'. Without question Ron had a great understanding of what would work on radio, and especially on populist radio, and it was his initiative that brought 'Our Tune' on to the air.

Chapter 8

I N PAUL DONOVAN'S encyclopaedic *Radio Companion*, 'Our Tune' is described thus:

Our Tune is . . . sneered at by the intelligentsia and hugely popular with the audience . . . a daily sob-story in which Bates reads out listeners' accounts of make ups, tender longings and tragic deaths. The background music which accompanies these outpourings is an arrangement of 'The Love Theme' from *Romeo and Juliet*. It . . . attracts about four hundred letters a week from listeners keen to share their joy or anguish with millions of listeners.

Which about sums it up.

The slot had originated in an earlier series I'd done in Australia called 'Sentimental Journey', though there the feature hadn't had time to grow and develop its own style as it has in the UK. Although the feature was introduced by Ron Belchier, the title was suggested by a listener, and the music was chosen after hours of market research done at home with some neighbours by Dave Price, a few years after Ron had moved on to another programme. In essence, of course, it is simply a letter from a listener requesting a particular record to be played and giving the reason. That's how it started, nothing special, just a mid-morning feature which, to be totally honest, owed more to the Australian radio soaps than to any other genre. Which was how I viewed it in the early days when the letters tended to be of the 'Met him or her in a disco, fell in love, split up, reunited, got married' variety. Almost as soon as we began, the letters sent in by listeners were surprisingly honest, straightforward and full of genuine emotion.

One woman had gone on holiday with a friend, fallen for a man she met in her hotel, only to walk into a restaurant and find her boyfriend from home sitting at a table with another girl. They had a furious row, a tearful reunion and ended up getting married. Another couple met on holiday in Marbella and discovered they both lived three streets apart in Macclesfield and had both been to the same school. Of course they got married and hopefully lived happily ever after.

As the years passed, the feature seemed to become less and less to do with me and more of a sounding-board for listeners. I suppose because it's been going for so long and because there is a sense of easy familiarity to it, people feel more and more inclined to write in and share their problems. It's sometimes easier to say what you feel in a letter than face to face. Not long ago, the boyfriend of an Aids victim wrote in to thank the straight community for their kindness, their help and generosity while the man had been dying. Another man wrote asking me to say how much he cared for his brother, who at that point was a patient in Papworth Hospital, because he simply couldn't bring himself to say the words.

The character of the feature has changed almost totally in the last decade. In the late seventies and early eighties the postbag would be dominated by letters about marriage break-ups and financial problems. Then as the decade wore on and as people's attitudes widened, I started getting letters from the gay community as well as from people who were struggling with their sexuality. A mother and father wrote after discovering that their son, who they thought was happily married, was living with another man in London. He had contracted Aids and hadn't got long to live. Far from turning their backs on him, the old couple had come to terms with their feelings and were trying to offer him what comfort and support they could. When I read that letter out, the phone lines were jammed and not just by members of the gay community but others simply wanting to show their support.

At a time when Radio One wasn't entirely at ease discussing or commenting on anything in the real world in daytime programming, 'Our Tune' became the perfect vehicle to circumnavigate the unspoken rules. A few weeks before, Annie Nightingale had been castigated for using the word 'orgasm' on an embryonic chat show where the subject had been rather daringly titled 'sex'. When challenged like this, Annie had defended herself vigorously by enquiring whether the executive would have preferred the word 'come'.

There were a number of easy defences of 'Our Tune' as it grew more and more realistic in its approach to everyday life. First, very few important people in the BBC listened. They were either coming in to work, in a meeting, or working out where to go to lunch and with whom, and that meant that unless someone wrote in to complain, the chances were that we could get away with a fair amount that would normally be considered unacceptable by authority rather than the listener. Second, apart from the Radio One management and David Hatch when he achieved status, it was universally loathed by management and therefore ignored. No one, I suspect, wanted to be associated with such a 'down-market' item and the best policy often was to ignore it. So, more from ignorance than desire, 'Our Tune' was given time to grow. It didn't take a stance on any of the issues raised and as no judgement was made, there was no need to produce a 'counsellor' to do the job of making up the listeners' minds for them about the rights and wrongs of each case.

I could never identify a theme from the thousands of letters addressed to 'Our Tune'. But if there is a common characteristic about nearly all the letters I've had over the years it is the message of optimism that each seems to contain. People who've been through hell and worse, struggling to cope and determined to carry on somehow. There is also a degree of intensity that at times can be quite frightening.

Having read hundreds, if not thousands, of these letters, the one identifiable trait is that they matter desperately to the people who write them. These letters aren't just dashed off in a moment, they're agonised over, often rewritten and always deserve a decent hearing. The people who've written them haven't just dropped a line in the post, they have poured out their feelings and the impression often is that this is the first time they have ever felt able to do that. What this says about loneliness and the state of Britain today I do not know, but there is a study there for anyone who cares to take it up.

The two 'Our Tunes' I can identify as being from people who had given up hope were quite horrifying. One came from a young man who subsequently rang me at the BBC. We talked for an hour or so that day and many times in subsequent weeks. He'd had a bad start with violence and misery endemic to his childhood and every time things appeared to be getting better life would take a mighty swing at him. If ever there was a person who has suffered from more than his fair share of bad luck, Mike is that person. But now he is beginning to cope and there seems to be a levelling process going on. We keep in touch and I like that.

The other negative letter came from a man in his thirties whose marriage had split up. He was full of remorse about his failed relationship and about the mistakes he felt he'd made in life. It was very much a farewell message, but there was absolutely no hint of what he was about to do. No one in the office knew about the letter until the police called and asked us if we'd heard from this particular man. I asked why they were so interested and a calm voice on the end of the phone said, 'He committed suicide a couple of days ago and had always said he'd write to "Our Tune". We're just trying to find out what happened to him before he died.' We found the letter eventually in the pending file. He'd posted it and then hung himself.

From being an excuse for a request, 'Our Tune' became very much the listeners' property. It was impossible for me to dictate the subject matter or even the style in which it should be approached, that was in the hands of the listener. When it came to selecting the letters, the final arbiter was always the producer, whoever he or she was, which took the responsibility out of my hands. 'Our Tune' was always 'sneered at by the intelligentsia' says Donovan, and so it was and still is. The sneering outside the Corporation was as nothing to the beating the slot took inside, where it was almost universally loathed. It's easy to understand why. To those who counted themselves its enemies, it is in appalling bad taste and horribly embarrassing simply because it is about raw emotion and the chattering classes have never been at their happiest when confronted with that. It was also an easy target.

For a while, I grew desperately defensive about 'Our Tune' and began to hate the negative attention it provoked almost everywhere. I took the endless internal criticism far too seriously and used to dread eleven o'clock every weekday morning. Then my producer at the time wisely suggested that if it was becoming such a bugbear to me that we simply take it off the air. I duly made the announcement on air the following day that we would be resting 'Our Tune' and the roof fell in. The phone ran red-hot and we were flooded with complaints. Though that is true, to maintain strict balance, ten per cent of the mail was from listeners overjoyed at the prospect of 'Our Tune' being removed. At the time, we bowed to the demands of the majority and kept the feature intact. From then on, as a matter of judicious courtesy, I would always suggest to Chris Lycett or Paul Robinson each time there was a break for The Roadshow or a series of specials that 'now would be the perfect opportunity to say goodbye to "Our Tune" '. On each and every occasion, the command came down, 'Keep it or die'.

The Radio Review Board almost universally hated it. The idea of the Review Board is an excellent one, in practice it is as bad, if not worse than the Spanish Inquisition. In its original form it was a gathering of senior programme executives, the great and the good, who would in turn discuss programmes on the various networks, usually with the producers present. Back in the mists of time this must have been a high-flown discussion between mighty intellects all prepared to give and take a little to achieve the greater good for the BBC. By the time I had arrived it was a bear pit. Some producers who had less than others to do, it must be said, spent their entire week lobbying on behalf of their programme. Others retired to their offices sunk in gloom and chain-smoked.

For the two cultured networks it could be tough. There might be members of the Review Board with real opinions. If the programme had been transmitted by Radio One, chances were that only half the Review Board had heard it and you would be ahead on points. The problem could be if there was one very opinionated person who started off the debate. If he or she was a strong enough personality, then the rest of the Board would be carried along on a wave of criticism and you were as good as dead.

One programme that I did came in for a particular pasting from the Review Board which both me and my producer expected. It was a one-off celebratory programme heralding the announcement of Dublin as European City of Culture. The wiseacres took the show apart for not examining in detail Dublin's housing problems or the Aids issue and so on. There really was not much point in explaining that this hadn't been the brief, and wasn't really the kind of feature one could throw together on a whim having arrived in Dublin twelve hours before transmission. So the arrows just flew around for a while, until some silly old duffer added, 'And what, pray, were the Dubliners doing on the show?'

To which my producer, by this time bored to death, could not help replying, 'I suppose you wanted the Belfasties for political balance?'

The Review Board is never predictable, though. If things start badly and it looks as though you are in for a rough ride, the Board can suddenly be swung round by one very loud voice saying, 'I quite liked it actually.' Immediately all the drones will fall into line and chirrup eagerly, 'Yes, yes, yes, it was awfully good,' and you will be head of the class. A bad Review Board does not mean the sack *per se*, but it does mean that you will be in a kind of purdah for a while. The feeling after a lashing from Review Board is much the same as having a bell tied round your neck and being made to cry 'unclean' every few minutes.

Over at TV Centre it was even worse, but at least one producer I know had a secret weapon. If a colleague criticised his work too effectively, he would creep down to the car park and scratch the paintwork on his Volvo. Another was capable of lurking in the canteen queue and then holding a critic up against the wall with a cry of 'OK sunshine, what's the big idea, having a go at my show?'

There were times when even the Review Board could show some signs of humanity and humour though. On one occasion when my programme was up for its usual beating, my mother's local BBC Radio station had submitted one of its shows, an outside broadcast that included an interview with my mother. In the minutes of that meeting, the final summation read that, 'the board felt Simon Bates's mother came out ahead by a short head.' I kept that from my mother for some time. Her ego doesn't need to be encouraged.

Understandably, the Review Board hated 'Our Tune' and on the rare occasions the subject came up, it was often David Hatch who had to come to the rescue by declaring it a 'no go' area. Though he himself had the strongest reservations about it, he knew it was a ratings earner, or at least I imagine that's what he thought. I can't for the life of me imagine him defending it for any other reason. Equally I see no point in defending 'Our Tune' to those who detest it. It either works for you or it doesn't and there is no persuading those who cringe at the very thought of it. In retrospect, I'm amazed that it became the subject of such hot debate. I could never grasp why so many got hot under the collar about it. Maybe it was that old problem: the chattering classes being unable to accept that a chord has been struck with the listeners. After all, in the end it was just a bit of radio.

Listener correspondence is fascinating. The British divide themselves up fairly neatly into the nice and not so nice. People rarely write simply to say nice things about a programme or a presenter, there's usually a purpose. It can be an enquiry for information or for a request, but usually people make the effort to add a compliment or a backhanded compliment as an afterthought, as in:

Dear Simon,
I think your show is great. Please play a request for my mum
and tell me what show you do so that I can record it.

or

Dear Simon,
You're not nearly as good as Steve Wright, but I can't listen to
him 'cos our boss won't let me. Please play a request for my
mum.

or

Dear Simon,
My mate thinks you're really awful, but I don't think that any-
one can be that bad. Please play a request for me mum.

The critical letters are, thank God, in the minority. The balance is about ninety per cent to ten per cent, but in fairness, the ten per cent is much more interesting. They line up with their brickbats, sometimes sincere in their criticism and sometimes plain abusive, but nearly always expecting an unqualified grovel. There is little you can do with a complaint other than own up and say that the author is right, if he is. If he ain't then there's nothing for it but a rebuttal and in my experience complaining listeners don't like to be argued with. Assuming that an admission is what the person wants and you think he's right, then you've done your duty. If on the other hand you believe him or her to be wrong, then stick to your guns, but be prepared for the occasional endless and obsessive correspondent.

I found one very effective way of dealing with the persistent and extreme complainant who failed to mask his/her rage in moderately polite letters. It was called 'the clincher'. The idea was simple, write back on BBC paper, 'Dear So and So, someone has got hold of your letterhead and is writing obviously unhinged letters to the above address, perhaps you would like to investigate this blatant misuse of your name.' This worked wonderfully for years until I used the technique on the wrong man. He was a doctor in an old-age pensioners' home whose matron had apparently written in for a dedication one Christmas. The letter had gone astray in the tidal wave of mail and as a result I hadn't read out the request. A sharp letter of rebuke from the doctor had been followed by two more abusive ones and eventually I sent out 'the clincher'.

I forgot about the whole affair until the Controller of Radio One called me into his office a month or so later. He was almost incapable of speech and shaking with laughter held out two letters for me to read. One was 'the clincher', the other was from the doctor. 'How dare you employ such people,' was roughly the tone the aggrieved medic took, but he added in a postscript: 'Don't think your man Bates can make amends for not reading the dedications out by doing them now. It's too late, by now most of the patients are dead or deaf!'

But the letters that always caused the most trouble were the ones addressed to the Chairman of the Board of BBC Governors or to the Director General. It is fair to assume that these worthies are too busy to listen to all the output all of the time, so chances are they won't have heard the offending item. But they will want a response and they'll want it now! That's where the production team – in my case me, a producer and a PA – would go into a huddle and try to remember what was actually said.

On one occasion we worried so frantically about a particular libel I was alleged to have uttered, that though at first none of us could remember it, we agonised so much over the wretched incident that we eventually fantasised that we could actually identify when I'd said it. As we began to compose a grovelling apology over this incident that we thought we could almost remember the phone rang. It was the Director General's secretary. The author of the letter had called to apologise for writing, she'd remembered that she'd been listening to her local commercial station at the time.

The problem with listeners' complaints is identifying the difference between a criticism and a torrent of abuse. Criticism can be constructive and often is, the other kind can have a motive. The usual stance taken by the torrent merchants is a political one. Over the years I've been accused of having allegiance to every legal, and a few illegal political parties in the country at one time or another. My sexuality has been questioned by people who couldn't possibly know the sad and inadequate truth, and my religion has been defined, always inaccurately twenty or thirty different ways. Come to think of it, about the only thing I haven't been accused of is being a stud.

Most critical letters contain a sentence somewhere in which the author links this accusation of political bias with a suggestion that I shouldn't have said or done this or played that, because it could 'affect the opinions of the listener'.

I usually found these guardians of public morality were more concerned about the effect of our transgression on others than on themselves. The author would always assume that the rest of the audience is made up of a bunch of simpletons, eager for their daily dose of guidance on what and how they should think from SB. I've never held with that, simply because it isn't necessary to agree for a moment with a performer to like, enjoy or respect what they do professionally.

I love what Kenny Everett does professionally, but I think he's a jerk for appearing at a Tory conference and shouting, 'Let's bomb Russia.' I loathed the high moral ground that Brian Redhead always assumed, but was lost in admiration for his work on radio. I can't bear journalists who accept awards in the honours list and drown in their own 'loviness'. But while their OBE may colour my view of their trustworthiness, it won't affect my respect for their work.

Interestingly, Joshua Rosenberg, the BBC's legal affairs correspondent, is, like so many others, of exactly the same opinion when it comes to the fourth estate accepting gongs.

When I first started working for Radio One I was almost immediately disabused by Teddy Warrick, an executive of the time, of the idea that a disc jockey can make the public buy what he likes. 'Make a note of the records that you call to the attention of the listener,' said Teddy, 'and after a couple of years you'll realise they take as much notice of you as they want and no more.'

However, you can never stop a listener from taking it upon himself (and interestingly it usually is a him) to call you a flaming red, or a bloody Tory, or worse, all without the slightest justification. The odd thing is that they will never be dissuaded from the conviction that they're right in their assumption of your politics. I have some correspondents who track me down wherever I work and are capable of commenting on one single remark and interpreting it as evidence of allegiance to four different parties. I was accused of being a scientologist once after mentioning that I'd been bored stiff by a novel of L. Ron Hubbard's!

Then there are the prize-winners, bless 'em. Prizes are another way that a radio station, like a newspaper, has of desperately trying to keep your loyalty. Nigel Blundell, a newspaper man and a friend of mine, once commented that the three most important words to the tabloid press were 'sex', 'free' and 'win'. If you could create a story with the headline 'Win Free Sex' then you'd have it made. We never got round to giving away anything as physical as sex at Radio One, but we did have a fine line in holidays as prizes. Once again, ninety per cent of prize-winners are wonderful people, happy and eager to accept whatever they've won without question. But occasionally I'd come up against a horror.

A few years ago, I gave away a holiday in the States to one lucky couple who promptly began to haunt my waking hours. Nothing was right. They wanted pre-assigned seats. They wanted us to pay for taxi fares to and from the airport. They wanted this and they wanted that. Eventually a letter arrived asking for five hundred pounds so that the wife could buy herself some clothes and look nice for the holiday. I blew a gasket and said, 'No, a thousand times no' or words to that effect. The couple from hell won in the end. They wrote to my boss and at the time Chris Lycett and he, rather than argue the toss, gave in and the pair got what they wanted. I could see his point, he'd had a long day, but personally I wanted to throttle them.

I was asked by a Radio One producer to spend an evening while I was in New York working for an American company, entertaining two holidaying prize-winners from Wolverhampton at a local restaurant. For me it was no great hassle and I got a meal out of the arrangement. When I picked the two lads up at their hotel, they were grumbling a good deal but I couldn't get a clear idea of what their problem was until the third bottle of beer.

'We were surprised the flight took so long,' said one.

'Eh?'

'Well, it took seven hours.'

'Yes,' I said, 'That's because it normally takes seven hours.'

'Well, we were expecting Concorde seats.'

I kept my hands down by my sides so that the pair wouldn't see the whites of my knuckles.

A friend of mine who works on a big commercial station in the States was confronted by a prize-winner and his wife who held a sit-in and refused to budge from the reception area until the station paid return air fares and hotel bills for their relatives as well as themselves for a holiday they had won. Rather than be embarrassed, the station paid up. It's proof that if you want to win, you just cause more trouble than the bloke next door and in the end we'll give in to the relentless.

There nearly always seem to be problems when it comes to prize-winners, if they don't want too much before they go, they want the impossible when they get there. There was the winner of a holiday in the south of England who asked me if I could fix him up with a girl; or the girl on a holiday in the West Indies with a Radio One producer who suddenly discovered a deep passion for promiscuity and bedded the entire hotel staff, one by one. The producer was a little miffed that she didn't bother to offer herself to him.

I lost a prize-winner in Los Angeles once. One minute he was there rambling on about how he hadn't met Clint Eastwood yet and the next minute he was gone . . . vanished. I rushed around panicking that he might have been abducted or murdered, then spent a sleepless night and was just debating bringing in the police when he turned up at the hotel all smiles, with a very languid and attractive young Puerto Rican man on his arm. It seemed unsporting to tell his wife and as far as I know they're still together.

The real joy of working in pop radio is the pop element. I was always being asked if I got bored with the music and the answer was always no. How could one possibly get bored with music that changes at such a speed? Sometimes records hung on too long for comfort, but that was the audience making a choice. For me, the sheer pleasure of chart music is that if you don't like this one, there'll be another one along in just a moment. From time to time the music business takes a tumble in terms of creativity and excitement, and starts producing what can only be described as terminally boring music. At these times, a disc jockey's lot is not a happy one and he will search for other forms of entertainment. You can always call your agent, but that can be a fruitless course of action. 'Who? Oh yes, let me check your file and call you back. No, no, we're really pushing to get you work. God bless, I'll call you later Andrew.'

During one of those phases, I was sitting at my console at Radio One, drumming my fingers, when I looked up at the TV monitor displaying BBC1. There, in glorious colour, was a very young Philip Schofield interviewing Peter Dickson. Well, it wasn't actually Peter, but his alter ego, 'Mr Mad'. Peter spends a good deal of his time developing and performing characters for Steve Wright, and 'Mr Mad' was a classic and almost immediate success. So there he was in full 'Mad' make-up and foaming generously at the mouth, courtesy of Foamo shaving cream. He was ranting and raving on in character about life and its little absurdities. But 'Mr Mad' had no intention of being out of reach of his agent – well, you never know what might turn up. I noticed that his portable phone was sticking out of his pocket and I wondered if he had been sensible enough to switch it off. I dialled the number and I heard it ringing! Dickson, cool as a cucumber and without batting an eyelid, answered it. I was cracking up with laughter as Dickson heard me say, 'Think of your reputation as a performer, lovey. Get off as quickly as you can – you're making a terrible fool of yourself.'

I have lived in fear of retribution ever since and currently I'm at my most vulnerable working on Newstalk Radio five days a week where 'on air' is only a phone call away.

Chapter 9

I GOT MARRIED in December 1979 to Carolyn, a strong-minded and independent lady. My professional life was in its usual uncertain state and there was no use pretending that I had the remotest idea what was going to happen next, so it seemed logical to take a risk. We had both agreed that the ideal would be to buy or rent a farm. So we bought a small place in Surrey, within commuting distance of London, and since neither of us wanted or could afford to live the life of the idle rich, we began the business of creating a farm that would make a return on our investment.

Both of us had country backgrounds and we didn't harbour romantic images of 'life on the land', but we both still made enormous and endless mistakes. Probably the worst mistake was to try and work in concert on something that is as personal as breeding horses. We clashed endlessly about virtually everything that it was possible to clash about. The day-to-day running of the place, the breeding patterns of the various horses and which horses we should buy and sell. I was monstrously unfair, turning up at the end of the day, airily disagreeing with at least half of the decisions Carolyn had made and discussing what was usually a *fait accompli* far into the night. In the end, we both agreed that it was absurd and wrong for me to interfere too much and I let Carolyn get on with it. To her endless credit and my shame, she's done that rather successfully without my interference.

Currently there are four working stallions on the farm and heaven knows how many mares arriving and leaving with grins on their faces. Carolyn's pride and joy is an Irish draught thoroughbred called Jumbo, a big bloke at seventeen hands, who arrived as a six-month-old wimp but has changed magically in the last nine years. He's now one of the most sought after competition stallions in the country, but he's still a big softy at heart whose favourite pastime is gently accepting a mint with his soft, rubbery lips offered from the lips of the donor. He's never missed or nibbled yet and I see no reason why he should in the future. His is the life of Riley, to date he's been romantically involved with three hundred other females. Not a bad score, but he isn't a sexist.

Far from being a haven of peace, the place is like Piccadilly Circus, with endless arrivals and departures and the less-than-bell-like tones of horsey women who are themselves bred, I am convinced, to talk loudly.

The difference between the sexes is never clearer than on those occasions when a colt has to be castrated. It is a simple and painless operation and men hate doing it. News travels fast though and there's always an audience of thoughtful, smiling women when the job has to be done.

We've had our share of tragedies and mistakes. There have been occasions when I've wondered if it was all worthwhile. After my childhood days in the Midlands, I had always sworn that I wouldn't allow myself to get too fond of any one animal, but since then and especially in the last fifteen years, I have blundered on that promise as on so many others. Morning Story is a little pony stallion we've had since he was born. As a foal he broke his shoulder, which would normally be a cause for putting the animal down. The vet had made an incorrect diagnosis and that error gave him a few more months of life, before we realised what was wrong with him. By that time, I'd fallen under his spell. He's still alive and kicking and as attractive a personality as ever.

In the early eighties, one foal was born with breathing difficulties and I nursed it for three weeks before it quite suddenly died of septicaemia. I felt absolutely desolate, I had got to know the animal well and had fed it every three hours or so, night and day. We had left it in the foaling box, as comfortable as it could be on deep litter, wrapped in all the sweaters we could find, and simply hoped that the animal would build its antibodies up as time went on. It was a forlorn hope, of course, but sometimes just leaving an animal in the warm, with peace and quiet, can work miracles. Each time I went into its stable, it would lift its head to me and reach for the bottle, so when it gave up suddenly and its head dropped into my lap, I was furious. I was angry with the wretched foal for letting go of its life and cross with myself for letting myself grow so fond of a little scrap of bones and hair.

Simon Bates

I suppose my anger at the death of that foal must seem very selfish to you. Perhaps frustration is a better word. My childhood had a great deal to do with my attitude to life outside the city and the town. I was brought up in the country and maybe I don't have the same view as some who see it as a sort of national park and others who believe that Mrs Tiggywinkle and Little Grey Rabbit are part of everyday life. Sadly, it just isn't like that. The countryside really is red in tooth and claw. Animals do fight and kill each other, foxes do break into chicken runs and commit mass murder, pets get run over, animals damage themselves all too easily.

I've been accused at work of not being soft enough about animals and my own relationship with the countryside. But being tough on oneself in how you view life is just about the only way that one can survive an affection for an animal. The point surely is that, for most of us, buying or being given an animal is a painful process. It is almost inevitable that the pet will die before you do and cause immense sorrow. You see, I do think that most animals are much more practical and straightforward than we are. Food, warmth and sex are their basic motivations. Maybe add a safe and peaceful life to the list. But, they aren't guilty of projecting their own personality on to us, in the way that we sometimes do to them.

'He's almost human' is something I've heard so often and can never reconcile with a dog or a cat, because in the end that's what they are, dogs and cats, not human beings. They are pets who can spot a good, warm lap a mile away, and I know it's unfashionable to say this, but we need their company infinitely more than they do ours. We as a species are not very practical or realistic in our relationship with animals, I fear that for the most part they are much more down to earth than us. I know the stories of sheep dogs who've lost their master and pined for weeks, and of cats who've followed families for miles . . . those are the rarities.

Years ago I had a dog of my own who was almost a soulmate and I was like a man possessed when he died. He was put down because he was ill, it was a quick and painless death for him and an agony for me. I have always crossed my fingers and expected the worst when it comes to animals of which I'm fond. I can be deeply pessimistic and sunk in gloom when one is ill or expecting a calf or foal or whatever.

Birth is a logical process, but whether it is human or animal there is so much that can go wrong and so little that one can do to put it right. It seems to me that I have spent a quarter of my life standing or sitting in foaling boxes and cowsheds watching as a horse or a cow grunts and heaves in the birth process, waiting for the moment when I really cannot avoid interfering. It is a subtle thing, because birth is such a natural activity, and the older I get the less I like the idea of heaving on a pair of back legs or putting my hand up the horse or cow to see if everything is OK. That seems to me to be playing with fire. But of course, often one has to and it is choosing the moment that is so vital. Jump in before you should or before you need to and you can cause more harm than good. It is wonderful when a foal or calf is born, but even then it isn't a matter for wild celebration. Is the animal whole? Can it feed? Is the mother bonding with it? It's not a commercial issue at that point, it is worry for the animal's welfare that makes me so sombre on these occasions.

Before my daughter was born, I was frantic with worry that something might be wrong and relieved beyond belief when it wasn't. She was born on an autumn day in 1982. She arrived, or rather she announced that her arrival was pending at about four in the morning. We both got up and checked that the horses were safe and secure, before I drove Carolyn to the local hospital. There the nurses and doctors were quite used to odd schedules. When I asked the matron what was going to happen next, she told me not to worry and to go to work. 'Come back after lunch, dear, and things should be moving by then.'

So, I went to work, did the programme as usual, piled back in the car and drove down the M3 in time for lunch and Nicola to enter the world. Apart from the fear and joy of being responsible for a child, watching her with the horses, or rather the horses with Nicola when she was very young was quite fascinating. As a baby and as a toddler, she had absolutely no fear of these huge, blundering things. Often I would be horrified as I saw her walk up to a stallion and gurgle at its legs. Sometimes, as all kids do, she would appear out of nowhere when I was leading or holding a horse, and I'd turn round to see her hanging on to the front leg of a large and otherwise anti-social animal. They never seemed to mind. These great big animals adored and were endlessly careful with her. Their heads would reach down to hers and nuzzle her hair. If for some reason she got in their way, they would cautiously pick up each foot in turn to be certain not to hurt her.

My worst moment was once when I was idly looking at a row of loose boxes and saw a three-year-old Nicola hanging on to the tail of a horse that had just wriggled out of its headcollar. She was trying to pull it back into its proper place, and instead of going crazy with irritation, the horse, which had realised who this damned nuisance pulling at it was, was allowing itself to be dragged backwards.

On one occasion when she was six years old, a prospective client for Jumbo arrived unexpectedly and Nicola took Jumbo out of his stable and showed him to the prospect. It would be more accurate to say that Jumbo allowed himself to be pushed hither and thither by a diminutive six-year-old. I only discovered that this had happened and nearly had a heart attack in the process when the client rang and thanked me.

As she got older, so the horses became less and less patient with her and a part of Nicola's childhood that I suspect she won't remember, sadly vanished for ever.

As a child I was always taught and accepted that there was a great deal more to life than that which was obvious. It was less a matter of believing in ghouls and ghosties and things that go bump in the night, than accepting that there are still things that are not explainable and that one should keep one's mind open to what may seem odd ideas. There were always older people around in the countryside of my childhood who had special skills, people who could help a wound heal, mend a broken bone quickly, or solve a difficulty. They are still around if you look for them, or if you know people who know. They are a million miles from the chic and fashionable cult figures of the big cities and they're often not very 'user friendly'. They can be brusque or downright rude, and they have cultivated that quaint old rustic countryside look about them that people seem to find attractive. Their nails often need looking at. Call them witches, call them healers, it doesn't really matter.

There are those who know more and who are more sensitive than the rest of us to what is in the air and beneath the earth. Wherever I have travelled, Australia, India, or perhaps more especially in Eastern Europe, I have met them, and while a good proportion are misguided or charlatans, there are always those who have about them that which sets them apart. These are just normal people who have extra skills. I have a damaged spine, and for years an old farmer with no medical training has manipulated it and sent the pain packing. My feeling about this is that he does me no harm and I believe he does me some good, therefore no damage is done to anyone but everyone wins. Before you raise your eyebrows, I haven't yet got to the stage of inviting the local coven round, there is nothing dark about these skills.

When we moved to the farm we lost a couple of cows for no reason that the vet could define. They just gave up the ghost and died. The next year, another cow died and two horses somehow damaged themselves in the same field. The chances of this mayhem happening across a decade was remote, but for such a series of inexplicable accidents to take place in such a short space of time seemed ridiculous. I did some checking and found that within the last fifty years there had been two dark incidents in the same corner of the field. A man had hung himself and a boy had been accidentally shot.

The action that we took may seem ludicrous to some, but to me it is utterly logical. When I asked a healer to come and look at the land, I merely handed over to him something that I didn't understand and something that he might be able to deal with. There were no *Exorcist* histrionics. He merely walked across and around the field, and as he said to me afterwards, 'I picked up very unpleasant sensations. A good many nasty things have gone on in this field over the last few hundred years and it is coming up through the ground.' He came and walked around the field every week for about a month and eventually told me that the bad feelings he'd experienced before had disappeared. Of course nothing is proved from this, or from the fact that to date there have been no more catastrophes in that field.

If you ask me do I believe in all this, I'll tell you quite simply that I have an open mind, that I have learned not to dismiss anything and that I touch wood each time I walk through that field.

Chapter 10

PART OF LIFE'S RICH PATTERN at Radio One was the magic world of 'gigs'. When I joined the station, Rosco was still there, and having heard about 'gigs' and puzzling over the idea of David Hamilton driving off behind a pony, I asked him what this meant.

'Gigs,' he said, 'are bank raids. You drive up the motorway and preside over a disco and are paid an amazingly large sum of money to do this.'

I had what to me was a massive overdraft of five hundred pounds and absolutely no way of paying it off. 'Where, how?'

'Get an agent.'

I didn't have a problem about getting an agent, the damned things were queuing up, it was getting the right agent that was the problem. Back in the dim mists of time, in the late seventies, having a Radio One disc jockey on your books meant that as an agent you could relax. So I picked an agent and initially I was lucky. The agent was a decent man with about as much experience in his trade as I had in mine.

'What do I do?' I asked.

'I dunno,' he said, 'ask around.'

Which is how I found myself charging all over the country appearing in front of baffled but tolerant crowds who would rather have seen Noel Edmonds or Kid Jensen or anyone, but who for the most part did the decent thing and let me live.

There were lessons to be learned of course. How to keep an eye on the audience, talk and duck simultaneously as the beer can winged its way over your head. I always asked where the nearest hospital was, just in case a can didn't wing but banged and I had to go to casualty. How to stand near the edge of the stage and still avoid the one person who was always going to grab hold of your feet and pull you into the crowd. One poor disc jockey stood on one spot for too long, just time for a villain to tie his shoe-laces together and watch as he took a step back, ending up in a tangled heap. How to avoid panicking and avoid being a dead hero if there was a riot. How to be aware that most stages have a hole in the floor somewhere which the management will have forgotten to tell you about. How to recognise bare electrical wiring when it is connected to equipment you are using. How to get over the fact that if there was a live band involved they would hate your guts because you represented death to what they were trying to achieve. How to always leave your car next to a Jag or a Roller, that way whoever hates you will scrawl 'Simon Bates is a pig' on the other car, not on your Ford Cortina. (What DJ would drive a Ford Cortina, for God's sake?)

I started doing gigs in the East End of London, working in a pub for a splendid and frightening man who ran an establishment where the CID drank on one side and the villains on the other. I first saw Jim Davidson work live there and was staggered at how he could hold a crowd. He made it look so easy. Comedy and how it is done has always fascinated me. How is it that a man or a woman can go on stage night after night and for the most part be confident that they can hold a crowd in the palm of their hand simply by the force of their personality?

A few years ago I did some presentation or other with Mike Reid. After I'd introduced the first act he asked me what the crowd were like. I said I thought they were a bit slow to catch on.

'All right then, I'll tell 'em the joke, explain it to 'em and get the laugh the second time I crack it.' And that's what he did and more mystifyingly, it worked.

Sam, the owner of the pub, was a bigger character than anyone in *EastEnders*. He owned a couple of pubs and several fruit barrows in Soho. Not a big man, but one you felt you'd never argue with. When he called and said, 'Can you please?', you always said 'yes'. A musician friend was asked by Sam to provide a five-piece band for a family party.

'Yeah, but, Sam, where are they gonna play?' said the musician, well aware that the pub was a labyrinth of tiny rooms.

'Upstairs,' said Sam, 'in the ballroom.'

'Is there a piano for me?' said the musician.

'Trust me.'

And so the musician did and turned up with four mates the following Saturday night, all asking for 'the ballroom'.

'Upstairs, love, on the left.'

They trooped up the stairs and opened a door which led into a small reception room big enough for sixty or seventy people at most and with no sign of the Joanna.

The pianist called into the hallway, 'Sam, where's me fuckin' piano, mate?'

Sam looked cross. 'For Chrissake, it's here.' He walked across the room and flung up the window with a flourish. And there it was. A grand piano sitting outside on the flat roof.

The band played for three hours that night and the event was voted by one and all a huge success. Every now and then someone would peer through the window at the musician sitting on his piano stool in the open air, hand him a lager and say, 'Sounding great, mate.'

'The worst thing was the fucking buses going past and the top deck taking the piss,' he told me afterwards.

From gigs in pubs to gigs in the middle of nowhere. Endless drives across and around the country and always endless surprises. Here a greeting from the management that would make surly seem like an open-ended invitation to move in with them, there people who seemed genuinely pleased to see you and who moved mountains to make sure that you were looked after.

Some DJs had rider clauses in their contracts. These were usually of the alcoholic kind. So and so would expect a bottle of whisky/gin/vodka on arrival, and if it was in the contract and wasn't there, so and so wouldn't perform. The problem was that if it was there, so and so would perform adequately for the first half-hour and half-bottle and then as the time and the bottle slipped away, so would he. One DJ was legendary for always making it to the end of his allotted time before passing out and being ceremoniously carried off stage to the roars of the crowd.

The first really big gig I did was in Great Yarmouth and from it I learned to find out a little about my working environment before going on. On this occasion I stood, knees trembling, as I was introduced and then walked out into a totally foreign world. The crowd was cheering and I was facing them, unable to see much when someone opened up with the lighting system. In this particular hall they seemed to be using an old Second World War searchlight and as I walked forward it hit me right in the eye. I was momentarily totally blinded, and being inexperienced I didn't do the one thing I should have done, stayed exactly where I was and waited for my sight to return. I took a step forward and plummeted eight feet off the stage. Here I broke another rule, 'if at first you don't succeed, give up'. Feeling as though I had broken every bone in my body, I crawled back on to the stage, with the crowd thinking it part of the act and yelling, 'Do it again.'

Gigs were, oddly, a good way to test the water, to meet those who actually made up the audience. This could be a salutary experience. We all got to taking ourselves far too seriously and it wasn't a bad thing to be taken down a peg or two by an audience that didn't give two hoots for whatever the next obsession was. They could also, when the night went well, be great fun.

There was a cast of Dickensian characters to deal with before you actually made your scheduled appearance though, and the manager was always the most important. These are moles, underground people who normally never surface in daylight. Their day runs from about seven in the evening until closing time and beyond. They see the worst and just occasionally the best of human behaviour in their clubs. These are great people to talk to. The older ones have seen it all. 'I booked the Beatles in 1961, they were crap then and they've never improved.' 'I'll tell you what, you bloody disc jockeys don't know yer born. Give me Chubby Brown any day.' 'If you're short tonight, lad, there's a really nice girl coming in. I've had her meself and she's a cracker.' 'Don't touch the one with the blue dress on, she's given half my staff the clap.'

When I started doing gigs these were proud men of the sixties boasting cummerbunds and wine-coloured evening suits with suspicious stains on them. Now they're much more contemporary, but they have the same attitude. They don't stand on the door so much, the internal phone system keeps them in touch and they have video cameras monitoring their territory, but the message is still the same as it ever was. 'John, hey, John, keep an eye on that fat bastard, he's out for trouble.' 'Rachel love, try and make sure you shift that Malibu stuff, please, darlin', and watch that bugger Ron, I think he's at the till again!' 'I'm sorry, sir, you'll have to leave and I'd like you to do that willingly or I'll have to ask Eric to help you.' 'If the coppers come in again, Colin, give 'em a drink but try and keep them away from me, will ya. And if they're hassling about the stag night, call me!'

In the last thirty years, entertainment and people's expectation of it has changed immeasurably, so the clubs, dinosaurs before the war, should have vanished, but they haven't. The reason is simple. Raves have an identity of their own, but most clubs are peddling one thing and one thing only – dreams. The clubs overrate the importance of the music or the bar and what they are about – simple, harmless sexual fantasy. There is no difference between the reason for going to the majority of clubs now and the dance-halls of the thirties and forties, other than the music and the décor. The motivation for going to a club is purely sexual and that has always been the case. The object is to strut and pose, maybe seduce and certainly get laid. But having observed from a privileged perch in hundreds of discos, getting laid after an off-chance meeting in the average club in the nineties is just about as unlikely as I am told it was in the thirties. Men still preen and gossip at the bar, moodily eyeing the women for availability. Girls still dance warily around their handbags and go to the loo far more often than is necessary.

One night, bored to death, I did some basic research and noted that men go to the lavatory as a function. They go by the quickest route there and back to their drink. Women never go by a direct route, they walk around the club, taking their time to note the talent and the opposition, and the number of visits to the loo climbs proportionately depending on how boring the other women are that they're with.

Some coupling is possible but the chances are that most will go home with the friends they arrived with. The exception to this rule are the clubs in the holiday resorts. There, the joints and the hormones are jumping and it's all a decent bouncer can do to stop the customers copulating in their seats. But these are the odd weeks out in everyone's lives and they must grab their chances while they can.

Holiday-makers of course have their own habits. The staff at one resort disco I regularly worked in had much more important things to do with their early mornings than go behind the chalets and screw. The town was one of the major landing points for illicit hash, but regularly the delivery boats would be scared off by the Customs and Excise patrols and would push their cargo overboard. Whenever this happened the entire disco staff would walk along the beach, carefully picking up the dope, which would then be dried out in the manager's office. They were a happy crew.

I was in deep trouble financially and going through a phase when it was necessary to work as hard and as fast as I could to get myself out of the financial mire. At this time in the mid-eighties I had no idea how secure I was at Radio One, and having some rather large bills to pay, I spent most of my evenings driving up the M1 or across country on the M4 to do gigs. These could often be pleasant evenings, but the downside was the drive back to London, arriving at about three in the morning. There was no point in booking a hotel, so I'd often sleep in the car in the BBC car park and wake as the attendant knocked on the window and told me that it was six thirty and time to go to work. I must have been in a coma for a couple of years doing this. Certainly I can't remember a great deal about what went on.

These events weren't always packed to the rafters. There were times when the people just didn't come. I once swaggered out on to the stage not having been warned that there were only twenty people in the place. I somehow sweatily got through my allotted time and limped back to work the following day. I warned Peter Powell, who was doing the following week's celebrity appearance, that it might not be a busy night, so at least when he turned up, the small audience might not come as a nasty surprise. Not only was Peter well prepared, he triumphed. There were twenty-three people milling around despondently when he appeared, and he smiled at them, leaped off the stage and spent the evening getting them drunk.

One disc jockey was a gimmick merchant and always loved to make his entrance with a bit of panache. One night in the Midlands, he spotted a rope, grabbed it and swung across the stage Tarzan-style. Gradually and then rapidly, the whole of the proscenium disintegrated around his ears and he ended up sitting on stage in the middle of a heap of scrap metal.

Another disc jockey was lead by his libido in a way that I have never seen in anyone. He was incapable of controlling himself when sex seemed possible. Appearing at a club in the north, he got chatting to an attractive blonde, who asked him back to her flat. They took the bus and when they got there, as he was frantically ripping his clothes off, he noticed a number of photographs of a well-built man around the bedroom. 'Boyfriend?' he asked.

'Husband,' said the blonde.

The libido subsided a little. 'Erm, is he er around?'

'No, love, he's in jail,' said the blonde, and before he could breathe a sigh of relief, she explained who her husband was. One of the most notorious armed thugs in Britain, from a family with a reputation for violence. Suddenly, feeling incredibly vulnerable, he asked where the brothers lived.

'Next door.'

His libido had by this time stolen away in the night, but he performed, very, very quietly and lay until morning in a sweat of terror before catching the first bus back into town.

The sexual aspect of these events is an odd one. I've always suspected that less goes on than appears to go on, but then I would say that, wouldn't I, and it's a good excuse for inadequacy. Certainly there were the ladies most of us avoided like the plague, the ones who had notches on their bedposts. There were those who were out to get the entire set, but they tended to be pretty obvious.

Then there was the business of being paid. It was a hideous and humiliating process. The point is that disc jockeys are paid a profoundly excessive amount for these appearances, and to be given the money at the end of the evening is to realise just how impossibly large that amount is. I tended to mumble thank you and stuff the cheque or the cash deep into my pocket while blushing frantically and running for the car.

One personality became immune to his own conscience on the subject and used to bring his loot back to Radio One and parade it down through the open-plan offices. 'Incredible for just an hour's work, en' it?' he'd exclaim. It wasn't long before he left and that was probably a good thing, the secretaries were on the point of organising a hanging party.

Another DJ who was endlessly careless left a thousand pounds in cash in the Radio One lavatories after a gig and found it was still there when he came back for it, panicking, an hour later. This same man appeared at a club in Blackpool, and at the end of the evening he walked to the car park to get his car, placed a grand in one-pound notes on the roof as he got in, forgot the money and drove off into the Lancashire night spraying used oncers across the motorway.

Gigs blend into gigs and memories fade, thank heaven, but I still tremble at the memory of doing a bikers' night somewhere in the north of England. When I walked on stage, there was a low moan from the assembled horde, and I did what I always did whenever I felt embattled, I scampered to the turntables and pretended to be terribly busy sorting out the next record while taking a good look round for escape routes.

'Watch yerself, mate, this lot are bastards,' said the kindly regular DJ, who sported what seemed to be a fresh wound on one cheek.

I was busy watching myself and covering my fear by riffling through the records, when out of the crowd came three of the largest, hairiest and least-washed bikers I'd ever seen. They walked slowly across to me.

'Hi, fellas,' I squeaked.

They took no notice. 'Play some Elvis.'

My voice shot up another octave. 'I'll try and find some, ha, ha, ha.'

'That's fair,' said the smaller of the three, who was about six foot two and weighed roughly sixteen stone.

There was a pause and then it was silently agreed that that *was* fair and the trio tramped back to their lager. I lived and left the stage, collected my money and walked out of the back door of the club in the direction of my hotel. The back door snapped shut. The terrible trio were waiting outside. I stuffed my hands into my pockets, just to check that my fee was there. I'd happily give it all away if they didn't mark my face.

'Don't worry, mate, we're here to look after you.'

I was relieved of course, but then I realised what 'looking after' me meant. Somehow, maybe because I'd played that Elvis track, I had become a pet of some kind for this particular bunch. As we walked round the corner and on to the main street about a dozen other huge, unwashed bikers joined us and trooped along 'protecting me'. Little old men out for a harmless walk with their doggies were pushed into the gutter as we swept towards the hotel, 'Get out of the way, Simon Bates is coming through', and when we got there I was kept to one side while a mighty hammering on the door roused the porter. The poor man nearly had a heart attack when he looked through the glass, but he let me in. The bikers threatened him with death if my morning tea was so much as a degree cooler than I liked it, and even though I frantically protested that it was much too much trouble to expect them to, they promised to be back in the morning and they were. They frogmarched me down to the station, elbowing aside any harmless civilians stupid enough to be walking on the pavement, and when we got to the station elbowed their way through the queue at the ticket barrier and on to the platform. When the train pulled in, even though I had a second-class ticket, I was pushed into the first-class compartment, and the last words I and my fellow travellers heard as we pulled out of the station were, 'If anyone gives you any shit, mate, just tell us.' Nobody did.

Simon Bates

This business of being a celebrity could rebound horribly on you. For some reason I found myself at the largest of Central London's discos doing a quick personal appearance for a medical charity. The place was packed, the organisation dreadful as usual and I had turned up with a friend who in real life was a BBC engineer. For reasons best known to himself, Ray decided to take the bit between his teeth and pushing me in front of him started making his way to the stage shouting, 'Get out of the way, Simon Bates coming through.' Just about everyone in the place was getting annoyed and I was trying to shut him up when our way was blocked by an extremely large pair of blokes who looked to me as though they didn't give a damn about who anyone was.

'Get out of the way, Simon Bates coming through,' chirruped Ray.

'Says who?' said the largest of the pair.

Ray paused for a moment and then pointed his finger at me and said, 'Him' and vanished. Try explaining your way out of that one to a man who wasn't interested in anything other than the concept that you were a pain in the backside.

A few years later I was appearing in Liverpool at some charity function or other at a dance-hall in what I shall politely call the heavier end of town. I knew the club manager well and liked him enormously. He had worked in Liverpool for twenty years and loved the place.

'We 'ad a grand piano nicked from here once. The lad put it on the stage and I went to get the docket for the driver. By the time I'd got back it was gone and there was no one here who'd seen it go. I mean, that's real class right?'

The night before my arrival, a dissatisfied customer who had been barred for antisocial behaviour – 'You don't do that in my club, mate, now fuck off out of it and stay out' – had announced his intention of returning by driving his Porche in to the club through the double-front doors, which were closed at the time. When I got there I found that there was a message asking me to ring a number. When I got through, a pleasant voice introduced himself as a well-to-do trader who would be really grateful if I would open a new store for him the following morning. It was another charity event, I couldn't leave until the afternoon and I said of course I would.

The next day a Rolls Royce drew up outside my down-market hotel and when I got in to the back of it, I met the only Englishman I've ever known who could wear Gucci well. He was tall and slender and knew what he was about. He was also extremely charming and made it his business to keep me entertained until my train was due to leave.

'Of course, you know I'm like *nouveau riche*,' he said over lunch when I asked if anyone resented his obvious success and the trappings, like the Roller, that went with it, 'and people get upset about that. Someone fire-bombed me other car a couple of months ago.'

'That's terrible, did the cops find out who did it?'

'Naah,' he said, 'but a bloke drowned in the canal last week and he may have had something to do with it.'

He ran me to the station, and as we shook hands he looked at me very firmly and said, 'Look, mate, we get on, right?'

I nodded, there wasn't much option and besides he was right, we had got on.

'Here's me phone number and if ever you've got a problem with anyone, just give me a call, OK?'

My relationship with the Controller had hit an all-time low at just that point and I was about to make a joke about 'having a word with Johnny Beerling' until I remembered the comment about the body in the canal and through my mind flashed a picture of a figure in a bright-red blazer, lying face down in Little Venice and for once I kept my mouth shut. We've kept in touch and have dinner once a year, and although he's never repeated his offer there is a tacit understanding that it is still open. I never get drunk when I'm with him, just in case the drink loosens my tongue and I idly mention someone I'm 'having a problem with' at that moment.

There were good nights and bad nights. The best nights were in seaside towns or on mountain-tops in the middle of nowhere at young farmers' gigs. Don't ask me why they were so much fun. Maybe those audiences worked harder at enjoying themselves down there than we did up on the stage.

Chapter 11

FIRST MET BOB GELDOF in the seventies when he was fronting the Boomtown Rats. We were both guesting on a programme called *Roundtable* which I loathed. The concept was to make an instant criticism of a bundle of new records based on a single listen in the studio. But it was a lousy way to comment on a record that for all I knew might be a life's work for some poor hermit out in the middle of nowhere. If at first you didn't like the song, you might be finishing off an already fragile ego. What you usually heard in the studio was often the wailing of the poor first-timer obscured by the mutterings of some guest artist who was stoned out of his/her head or paranoid, or both.

Bob was neither of these, but on a first meeting I didn't care greatly for him and I suspect he didn't warm much to me. Bob is a very definite person. A conversation with Geldof when he's bored usually ends up with him being as contentious as he can. I can't remember the reason for the spat, it was probably completely unimportant, but we both left the studio making a mental note not to bother too much with each other in the future. Our paths crossed a few times in the next few years and I came to realise that he is an extremely kind and amusing man, who spends most of his time covering his charm with aggression.

In 1984, when I'd been doing the morning programme for six years, a couple of friends called me at home to tell me that Geldof was putting a scratch band together. I knew that he had been to Ethiopia and was devastated by the famine he'd witnessed there. The stories about the special Christmas single with wall-to-wall guest artists grew, as did the cynicism at Radio One. 'It'll never happen', and 'Why's he doing it?' were the standard responses, not for the first time. My producer at the time was mildly xenophobic and not too concerned about much more than who was taking him for the next lunch, so no great support there.

The battle to take Band Aid seriously was one that Geldof and his associates fought and won on their own. I was reminded of the endless cynicism when I told the producer that Geldof would be coming in with the Band Aid single the moment that he'd finished mixing it. A good deal of the cynicism within the department was simply of the 'who cares about the bloody blacks' variety, but a good deal was the classic BBC suspicion of anything that appeared to be simple or hadn't originated at Broadcasting House. 'What's Geldof really after, you must know?' was a tune I heard pretty often from people convinced that there must be a hidden agenda of some kind.

My daily producer was desperate to keep control and to be seen as a power player. 'Yes, I can see your point and of course I'll take a listen to the record when I get it.'

'When you get it! Don't be so fucking stupid,' I said. 'For starters, the artists on the thing make it important and secondly what Geldof is doing matters. We're getting the first play. It doesn't matter a damn if the record is utter crap, it's an event.' The producer went outside to get a cup of coffee and sulk.

Geldof rolled in just after ten thirty looking like death and accompanied by a couple of promotion people with tear-stained cheeks. The producer huffed and puffed, but neither Geldof nor I were in the mood for his brand of caution. I played both sides of the record while the producer hopped from foot to foot and the engineer next door coughed a lot and wiped his eyes. Geldof had been up all night and was exhausted. He also faced a day of convincing a million other people that Band Aid was the right thing to do. But looking fairly glazed and with a cup of coffee dangerously squeezed in one hand he began to state his case that morning.

'Virtually one hundred per cent of the money from this record, apart from the VAT, goes straight to Band Aid and I swear every penny will go to Ethiopia. There's fifty-six million people in this country. Even if you've never bought a record in your life before, get it. It's only one pound thirty pence.'

The producer was nearly disappearing up his own sphincter at this upfront tactic by one of the UK's best salesmen.

'That's how cheap it is to give someone the ultimate Christmas gift, their life,' he continued. 'It's pathetic, but the price of life this year is a piece of plastic with a hole in the middle.'

And he was off to Television Centre to bully and bamboozle Michael Grade into doing exactly as he wanted, which was a five-minute feature on the record. Unsurprisingly, Geldof won.

When Live Aid reared its head in the spring of the following year, the same negative attitude surfaced inside the BBC and outside. People were unwilling to grasp the fact that here was a genuine idea. Now the currency of rock for charity has been tarnished, but then memories of George Harrison's concert for Bangladesh had disappeared and this was a truly innovative concept.

At first, people looked for that old hidden agenda, but Bob would persuade them that there wasn't one by going into overdrive with a ranting speech before each meeting. As Bob got more tired so the meetings got larger and were attended by more BBC staff from different departments, so the opening speeches took on a life of their own. Some people did get a little tired of Bob endlessly explaining to them what they'd already agreed to do, but there was method in these tirades, he actually got things done. On the broadcast side there was a good deal of enthusiasm, with a few miserable dissenters who would cry, 'Bob doesn't realise what this is. He's making a fundraiser, we're making a programme.' But in the Fleet Street that then existed, there was virtually no support whatever. I went to see the editor of the tabloid for whom I then wrote, who looked up wearily after my spluttered justification for Live Aid and said, 'I'm glad you like the idea, mate, but I don't believe the public care.'

He was wrong and at the last minute the press turned to and supported the concert, but it wasn't them, it was Bob who changed the national attitude in the space of nine months. Looking back it's hard to define just what he did. I was at an awards ceremony sitting across the table from Geldof and Margaret Thatcher at a time when Bob was desperately trying to get the VAT money charged on the Live Aid tickets away from the Customs and Excise and into the charity's coffers. He confronted Thatcher with this as she was about to leave the table. She came up with a pretty bland response and got up to go. But Bob wouldn't drop the issue and started haranguing the Prime Minister. Bob at that time was immensely popular with the public and though the PM's two minders looked as though they would dearly have loved to grab hold of him and end his life painfully then and there, the presence of a grinning ITN camera crew stayed their hands.

Bob got his way in the end as I suspect he usually gets his way, by refusing to always play by Queensberry's Rules and by throwing huge and exhausting amounts of energy into his arguments. To paraphrase Harvey Goldsmith, when he has his next brilliant idea, I hope he doesn't talk to me about it.

The Wembley concert was an extraordinary success. It was, in retrospect, also a unifying event for a country ploughing through the decade of the yuppie and total self-centredness. I'm not suggesting that it healed the UK's wounds, but it did a damned sight more than all those marches that I went on back in the sixties seemed to have achieved. I sat in the press box at Wembley and had a sniffle alongside hacks who would now probably deny that they wept as darkness fell and the stadium sang along with 'Do They Know It's Christmas'.

By the time of the concert, Bob was exhausted, but still ploughing a straight furrow when it came to the object of the event. He had told me earlier that he didn't care if the concert wasn't the Greatest Rock Concert of All Time. All he wanted was the money for Ethiopia, and towards the middle of the afternoon he became infuriated because BBC TV was not in his view putting up the caption with the phone number for donations frequently enough. He also discovered that Radio One wasn't performing to expectation by broadcasting the same number as often as he thought that they should. So, Bob went a-hunting and found Dave Atkey. In seconds flat, Dave was up against the wall and the mad, staring eyes of Geldof were boring into him.

'Broadcast the fucking numbers.'

Dave tried to breathe. 'Bob,' he sputtered, 'this bit of the show is going to Ethiopia on the World Service, you don't want the victims to be appealed to, do you?'

The great man lowered his fist and the BBC executive lived.

The atmosphere in Philadelphia was quite different to Wembley. Anne Nightingale, who was fronting the American end for Radio One, told me that anyone and everyone could get a stage pass, whereas at Wembley, Harvey Goldsmith had been seen chivvying Elton John and George Michael out of the way like a headmaster dealing with two errant schoolboys. Also in Philadelphia, the star system took its toll. Madonna had guards to walk her to the loo each time she felt like a pee. Worst of all, while Anne was craning her neck to see what was going on, her view was obscured by a large young man wearing a pair of Walkman headphones. After she'd tapped him on the shoulder and asked him to move, she realised that he had no right to be there. He wore the headphones in an official-looking way and everyone had assumed that he was a security man, but he wasn't, he was just an ordinary Joe. The security implications were frightening and the egos ruled. The value of the concert in the

United States was incalculable and because it was part of a whole it just about managed to justify itself, but it needed a Geldof to really make it work.

Every time a celebrity makes a major commitment to a charitable cause, some low-life hack will pose the possibility that the celebrity is doing the job for self-publicity. Geldof was accused, as were Sting and Elton John and so many more, of jumping on the back of major issues to raise their own profile. 'Why are they doing it, eh?' is the question from the weasels, many of whom are perfectly pleasant people in private life and who would never dream of asking the same question of their neighbourhood Rotarian. The best way to answer is to turn it round. 'Why are you asking the question and who the hell do you think you are?'

Geldof single-handedly screwed his career as a performer by in-itiating Band Aid and then Live Aid. God knows if the Boomtown Rats had a second life in them and could have made another career as a hit band, there are plenty who doubt it, but in the music business there are more pessimists than optimists when it comes to predicting careers. What's unquestionable is that the moment Geldof saw Michael Buerk's TV report from Ethiopia, he was sunk as a rock star. The same press that had vilified him when he got married to Paula Yates, canonised him for Live Aid, and then after a suitable pause sneered at him when he tried to get back into the business as a recording artist. When he produced his 'Banana' album, Maurice Oberstein, then the boss at Polygram, did all he could to put Geldof back in the charts. It worked in a half-hearted sort of way, but though the British public broadly liked Bob, they didn't want him in the charts. I suspect they felt that he'd moved on from that and should be doing other things. And maybe they were right.

It would be ridiculous to make wild claims for Live Aid but I've always thought that there was a bonus to the work that was done by the Band Aid trust. Unquestionably there are hundreds of thousands of people alive today because of Geldof's initiative who would other-wise be dust in the desert. But there is also a generation of Britons who, unlike many of their elders, know where Africa is, a little bit about it and who don't think of it as an extension of Empire. That's an achievement to be proud of.

For a while after Live Aid, Bob plotted his return to the pop business, but on the side he was negotiating with the Soviets to pro-duce the ultimate television show. This was to be a twenty-four-hour

ecological broadcast from an orbiting Russian space shuttle. The programme would introduce specially made features from around the
world as the shuttle flew over each country. Bob of course would be
the frontman, who else? This more than ambitious idea would have
required Geldof to train at Star City for a year, something he was
quite prepared to do. The only real problem was a typical Geldof one
– he wanted to take his guitar on board the shuttle. Even the Russians were starting to become used to this idea when the decline of
communism accelerated into a collapse and the idea had to be cancelled. He'll probably do it at some stage.

The last time I saw Bob Geldof in the line of business was when
he had put in a bid to take over the job of producing Channel Four's
breakfast programme. I assumed that, having a well-developed ego,
he'd want to front it himself, but no!

'Naa, we've got Chris Evans doing it if we get the franchise.'

I was stunned. At that time, Chris had a weekend show on
Greater London Radio, the station boasting some of the lowest listening figures in the capital. He was certainly a popular cult figure,
but for a national TV show?

'The bloke is near to a genius,' announced Geldof with characteristic understatement.

I didn't argue. I watched and as usual Geldof was right.

It was because of Live Aid that I made my second visit to Ethiopia
and I have Stuart Grundy, an executive producer of the time, to
thank for it. Our job was to produce a single programme about
where the money had gone and how it had been spent. It was Stuart
who did all the background work for the journey and Stuart, not me,
who became ill after he returned, thus proving there really ain't no
justice. Having a fairly strong constitution, I chucked almost any
food I was given down my throat and was none the worse for it.
Stuart, on the other hand, was endlessly careful, avoiding anything
that looked or smelt suspicious until we visited a small village and
were offered something nasty in a glass which was being ladled out
of a ten-gallon drum in the corner of a ladies' hut. For once I said
'no thanks' and got away with it. Stuart, however, was in the front
line and being a decent soul, held his breath and downed whatever
it was in one, smiling his thanks afterwards before slipping outside
to be sick.

When we got back to London, I was a picture of health. Poor
Stuart, though, was not at all well and was taken into the Hospital

for Tropical Diseases. The staff there are beyond reproach in their commitment and their skills, but there is a drawback to becoming involved with them. It's a little like those days in my childhood when I would be taken to three and four day agricultural shows. There were always selfless and generous Red Cross staff in attendance. The problem was that they would become bored, and when any of the exhibitors went to the first-aid tent for a little bit of iodine for a cut or a bruise, they would be pounced upon, given a sedative, shoved protesting on to the little camp bed at the back of the tent and made to keep quiet while the Red Cross staff gathered round them and tried to find a reason to get the ambulance that was always parked at the back all fired up ready for a mercy dash to the local hospital.

I saw this phenomenon replicated during the desert war in the Gulf a few years later. In Dahran a huge hospital complex had been built to accommodate the expected influx of British casualties, but estimates of Saddam's armed might had proved to be way off the mark and for most of the time the expert nurses and doctors sat and twiddled their thumbs in the heat. On one occasion though, a squaddie cut his thumb on a catering knife and found himself pounced upon and tended to by a platoon of underemployed nurses and two plastic surgeons qualified to completely reassemble anyone careless enough to have allowed themselves to be dismembered.

The people at the Hospital for Tropical Diseases love a challenge and in Stuart they found one. He was quite ill for some time and still has occasional twinges as a result of that perverted milkshake ten years ago in Ethiopia, but there's never been a final diagnosis and Stuart is in the same position as a good Catholic who every now and then lapses out of the faith. Periodically he remembers where he really belongs and you'll hear that he's 'back in the Tropical for more tests'.

Before all this happened, our job was to visit Korem, the camp that Michael Buerk had discovered so memorably the year before, just to see what had happened. One of the smaller NGOs had agreed to give Stuart and I a lift up to the refugee camp at Korem in their plane, and we were due to meet the pilot at Addis Ababa airport at six in the morning. Addis airport is like a hundred other African air bases – scrappy and unwelcoming and at that hour of the morning, with the sun low on the horizon picking out the rubbish around the terminal and the burnt-out remains of an old Ilyushin aircraft at the end of the strip it looked even more unwelcoming.

We picked our way through the pallets of food aid being loaded into the RAF Hercules and found our man and his Cessna. Jean Pierre looked like a caricature of a Frenchman. Forget the leather jacket and the shades, it was the way he loaded the fuel into the aircraft's tank while puffing away at a Gauloise. But he seemed pleasant enough and waved us into our seats as he started the engine and began to trundle down the runway. The engine screamed, the propeller dug into the thin air and we swung wildly into the sky, dipping and diving as we hit the air pockets around Addis, before Jean Pierre, who had been swearing furiously in English, gained some kind of control and we set off for Korem. It was when the aircraft had settled down and I tried to make some kind of conversation with our pilot that Jean Pierre opened up.

'Fucking French bastards,' he raved. 'My country, it is no good, they do not want people with ideas and ambitions, you know.' He spoke Franglais with the unmistakable tones of a BBC Drama Rep actor.

Everytime he came down on a word with heavy emphasis, JP would take his right hand off the controls and make a kind of sweeping movement. The trouble was that his left hand would act in some kind of sympathy and the little Cessna would swoop towards the ground in response to the jerk he gave to the controls. Trying to calm him down a bit, I asked him what the problem was and he explained that in real life he was a lorry driver, which I should have guessed by the unsympathetic way he treated his aircraft. JP had had a burning ambition to be a pilot all his life, but the authorities in his home country would not grant him a flying licence.

'So you see,' he said as the aircraft did a kind of kamikaze act in response to his increasingly erratic hand movements, 'I have to come to Ethiopia and work for nothing, just to fly, it is so unfair. What do they know anyway? They say that I am mentally unstable. I'll tell you who is mentally unstable.' At this the poor Cessna tried to stand on its head and tear its wings off. He wrestled with it for a while before continuing. 'They are, all of them, they are the mad ones.' He turned his head towards me. 'You can see that I am a good flyer.'

Sick with fear I nodded and grinned a death's head smile.

'So, you will write to the French authorities and say that I should have a licence?'

I wanted to live, so I agreed. I would have agreed to JP marinating Stuart in the red wine the Awash Breweries produce in Addis Ababa if he'd just promise to let me live.

We landed at Korem and were welcomed by the Irish nurses who were working there and had become used to the media circus that invaded their work every day. I watched as Jean Pierre got back into the pilot's seat and turned on the ignition. The engine misfired for a moment and I heard a 'Fucking thing' before it roared into life and the plane rumbled along the grass strip, hesitated, flung itself into the air like a flying lawnmower and wobbled its way over the mountains and back to Addis Ababa.

The European nurses in that area had just come unstuck in their dealings with an American journalist who was less than sympathetic to their work, and who had turned up all smiles and smarm one day to say 'hello'. They had been as generous to him as they were to us, inviting him to join them for their pretty basic lunch while they did their best to brief him on how tough the situation was. The low-life ratbag had said his thankyous, taken a few pictures of the nurses smiling at him and got back on his flight to New York, where a few days later a double-page spread appeared consisting of that photograph of the nurses all smiling, sitting at their long communal lunch table. 'Nurses live high on the hog while millions starve' was the nub of the caption above a story that babbled about the inadequate food supply for the Ethiopians in the refugee camps as opposed to the three square meals a day that the nurses were able to command. Conveniently, of course, the story ignored the fact that if the nurses were to suffer malnutrition then there'd be no one there to look after the refugees, no one to administer what medicines there were and to pressure for more.

A few days later, we spent a while in a field hospital set up by some Americans. The row of tents looked to me as though they were in the middle of nowhere, sheltering at the foot of a range of mountains, but they were there for a reason. The camp was set on one of the old trading routes and anyone in the area who was in trouble would walk to the Americans, if they could get that far. When we arrived, the latest innovation had just been unveiled, a malaria-free lavatory and the staff were chuffed to bits with themselves. Although it looked like any lavatory anywhere in the Third World, this lavatory was a breakthrough designed by the UN. It was as though Terence Conran had just declared a new building open and Stuart and I were the staff of *Vogue*. We were asked to admire the bit of funnel that seduced the flies into going up and out of the pit that had been dug for the refugees. I had to go in, take a look and a crap just to realise how sophisticated and contemporary this piece of architecture was. We all proudly took photographs of each other standing outside it.

In the evening, I watched as the staff made their rounds and dealt with the living and the dying. Earlier that day a man had brought in his wife. Lying on the ground, surrounded by European doctors and nurses in jeans and denim shirts she was obviously desperately ill, malnourished and coughing up blood. There was a shortage of medicine and the almost inevitable decision was made that there was sadly no point in treating her with desperately needed antibiotics, as her chances of survival were slender. There was no soap-opera drama and no callousness in the decision, it was made because of the lack of medication, and for no other reason, and only after a hasty consultation between the staff. It was also a decision made everyday but always with immense sadness. The man was given a cup of water for himself and his wife, and she was made as comfortable as possible. Some time during the night she died and in the morning as the camp began to show some signs of activity the husband came over to the medical staff and with immense dignity embraced each one, thanked them in Amharic for their efforts and went to carry his wife's body away.

'He will bury her not far away,' said the minder, 'he has not much strength.'

I have been lucky and travelled through Ethiopia quite a few times in the last ten years. It is like its people, a beautiful and extraordinary country which is vastly self-aware.

Once when I was staying in a crossroads town called Jijiga there had been some fighting in the hills. The British mechanic working for Oxfam and Save The Children's joint trucking operation, running relief supplies into some of the worst areas, had gone back to his little house to find some rebels setting up a machine gun. Eric had a naturally ruddy complexion which had exploded with rage and all his Yorkshire stubbornness had surfaced. 'You buggers can just take that bloody thing,' he exploded, pointing at the machine gun 'and bugger off. Go on.' And of course they did.

If God was a member of IATA, Ethiopia would be one of the great tourist destinations, but he isn't and very few people have had the chance as I have to tramp virtually from one end of the country to the other. It is riddled with echoes of the centuries. Certain villages and towns have long been crossroads for the traders of Africa and the Arab countries and still operate almost independently of the rest of the world.

'You've got to realise,' said an Ethiopian who has subsequently become a close friend, 'just why we call ourselves the British of Africa. We are cunning, conniving bastards.'

There are occasions when I realise how deep the BBC culture is imprinted on those who have been steeped in it. Stuart and I got ourselves arrested in as pleasant a way as one can be under these circumstances when we turned up in the wrong town at the wrong time. We were fairly close to Tigre and it turned out that the town was patrolled by government forces in daylight, but at night they disappeared into their fort as the rebels came back into town to spend time with their families. This arrangement worked perfectly well, but our arrival would compromise it and embarrass everyone, so we were arrested. A fairly innocuous old chap in a Mao jacket, accompanied by a squad of under-trained, under-uniformed soldiers carrying Lee Enfield rifles, asked us rather apologetically to accompany them. There really wasn't anything else to do and we spent the night locked up in their compound. The government forces were very helpful, we were provided with red wine and got drunk enough to try the harmonies on 'I'd Rather Go Blind' with the soldier responsible for our security.

Come the morning, though, we wanted to move on, but here we came up against a chicken-and-egg situation. There was a weekly bus through the town which would get us on our way back to Addis Ababa, but the problem was that because we'd been arrested, we'd committed a crime, and because we had committed a crime we'd have to go to court. That was going to take for ever, and however good the wine was, neither of us wanted to spend the next month sleeping on straw and singing with prison guards. It was obvious that judicious palm-greasing would be the order of the day, so our Mao-suited friend was called for and the Lee Enfield rifles all gathered round to negotiate. Eventually, Stuart, who took the responsibility of care placed upon him for the money issued by the BBC cash office extremely seriously, handed over the equivalent of about ten pounds in bribes and all was well. It was only when we were on the bus and heading towards Addis Ababa that I noticed how thoughtful Stuart had become.

'What's wrong?'

'I should have got a VAT receipt off that bloke, God knows how I'm going to reclaim that ten quid.'

By the time we got back to Addis Ababa it was time to take off again in a Polish helicopter, to meet the RAF and watch as their Hercules dropped food aid in the more inaccessible regions. The Poles had their own area behind some bushes at the airport and kept themselves well away from the Russians, whose presence was much more obvious.

'Is bad enough we have to fly their shit,' said the helicopter pilot, 'without we drink their crap as well.'

The helicopter had seen better days. There was a bullet hole in the canopy and the rotor blades wobbled ominously. Stuart and I got in the back and as the engines started, the helicopter began to rumble towards the runway. Immediately, two of the crew hurled themselves at the fuel tank – a drum Velcroed to the webbing on the walls of the helicopter – and held it down while the machine trundled along the tarmac and then sort of threw itself into the air.

'Is shit. Is Russian sardine can,' yelled one of the crew, and the others nodded, smiling.

We bounced across the now familiar scenery. Deep, wide chasms followed by flat table-tops with clutches of straw huts surrounded by brushwood fences scattered across them. On board was a British liaison officer whose job was to use the Polish communications system to guide the RAF Hercules to the right spot and make sure that the area was cleared of tribesmen before the drop began.

After we landed, the Polish wireless officer began to get really cross with his walkie-talkie. He talked into it, pressed a few buttons and then listened. Nothing. Then he shook it and banged it on the ground and went through the whole ritual again.

'What's wrong?' I said, adding, 'Russian shit?'

He nodded, adding, 'Is bad Russian shit,' as he gave the walkie-talkie a pasting on a handy rock.

After a while, the British officer walked over and proved another of my theories, that wherever two 'sparkies' are gathered, language becomes irrelevant. On this occasion my theory was proved correct and eight years later in a different part of the country the principle would be tested once again. On this occasion, the Polish soldier handed over the equipment to the British soldier, who took the walkie-talkie looking sympathetic. The Pole shrugged his shoulders. The Brit pointed at part of the machine and the Pole raised his eyebrows and looked quizzical. The Briton held out his hand and a screwdriver appeared from the Pole's pocket. The two crouched over the walkie-talkie and both grunted slightly in sympathy as the Briton undid the screws. The back came off, each looked at the other and into the mass of wires and laughed. Polish fingers reached inside and replaced a wire while British hands snapped the back into place. The Pole tested the walkie-talkie and it worked. They looked at each other and then with contempt at 'the Russian shit'. Both roared with laughter. Not a word had been spoken.

Stuart and I spent a little over a week in Ethiopia before flying to Khartoum and spending another week in the Sudan. To anyone brought up as I was on *The Four Feathers*, the word Khartoum breathes romance. It wasn't like that at all, of course. Like the rest of Sudan, the place was silting up as the desert, whipped by vicious winds, crept in and down the streets of the city.

As soon as we had checked in at the hotel and been told cheerfully by the desk clerk that there had been an attempt on the life of the American Ambassador as he crossed the foyer of the Hilton that afternoon, we went for an evening stroll by the Nile. Stuart disappeared almost at once. By that, I mean he disappeared downwards. One minute we were walking calmly side by side, the next Stuart gave a little grunt and vanished down the most enormous storm drain I have ever seen. The only thing that was damaged was his dignity, but later, when there was a sudden torrential downpour, I could understand the reason for the storm drains.

We took ourselves back to our hotel to realise one awful aspect of Sharia law – the complete impracticality of asking for a whisky – and then went to bed with the television and an extremely practical programme made by the BBC in the seventies on how to drive safely in Milton Keynes.

The following morning, we were due to meet up with our contact in the Sudan, a British aid worker responsible for administering his charity's funds throughout the vast country. We took a taxi and found his address, and having knocked on the door both of us stood outside the small house practising our best 'we know you're busy so we're very grateful for any help you can give us poor chaps from the BBC' speech. There was a lot of damning and blasting from inside the house as someone made their way to the door and yanked it open from the inside, scraping it squeakily along the tiles of the hallway, and a black beard appeared, topped by an accusing stare.

'If you're the blokes from the BBC come in, for God's sake, if you must, I haven't all bloody day.'

The beard turned and disappeared, and we sort of trailed along behind into the kitchen, where the beard, his wife and child were having coffee.

'Look, I'm bloody busy and you're a nuisance.'

Neither of us spoke, but we tried to look as inconspicuous as possible. He was busy and we were a nuisance. We were the latest in a line of nuisances. Ethiopia and the Sudan had become a media circus after Michael Buerk and Geldof, with everyone trying to steal a little of the tragedy and cover themselves in glory, and Chris was pissed off about the self-centredness of the visitors he was getting. It was the classic dilemma. Back in London, New York and Paris, the agencies, who relied on donations to fund their work, were thrilled to be fashionable for once. Broadly, the more people who went and saw for themselves the desperate need and reported back to their audience what they saw, the more people would care and dig deep into their pockets. The problem was that people like Chris were trying to balance carrying on the business he was employed to do, with the demands of yet another bunch of media hangers-on.

Christopher was that rare thing, a radical right-winger who was working on getting desperately needed food to the almost impossibly inaccessible areas of this vast country. There wasn't a trace of the leaflets about Nuclear Free Wales that you usually found in aid workers' houses. Old copies of *The Economist* lined the walls and Chris launched into a quick lecture on why Margaret Thatcher had the right policies for Britain. This was not a typical product of his trade, but he was no fool. We talked about why nothing seemed to work in the city and for a moment Chris almost appeared to be resigned.

'We do our best, but it's an impossible task. Politics, decay and more politics. Take a look around yourself.'

We took a look around. This was back in the eighties when Khartoum was a moderately safe place and one could go almost anywhere, and here were two middle-class Britons trailing after the myth of Empire. Inevitably, we found a whiff of it in the little Christian church and the plaque erected by the British before they left, commemorating the place they say General Gordon fell as the Mahdi's forces took over. We walked in the market and were offered a hundred 'Mahdi swords', most of them suspiciously shiny, and we looked, just looked, at a great city on its last legs, where the infrastructure was collapsing around its ears. The decay and sense of failure were tangible. The electricity didn't work regularly, the water supply was periodic and an international call on the telephone was considered a miracle. There was nothing quaint about Khartoum, it was a sad and bitter city full of memories and with little hope for the future.

'I get my son out of here to America,' said the taxi-driver, 'soon there will be worse and the fighting will come. Peace will never win here.'

Chris was as generous and helpful as he'd been blunt, and sent us off to Port Sudan with more introductions than we needed. I've learned over the years that trusting first impressions can be dangerous, but on this occasion as the UN truck took us over the desert road to Port Sudan, the first impression was the right one, of the collapse and total decay of a nation. As we drove, the road gradually disappeared into the sand and the desert grew up the side of the telegraph poles, and as the miles passed, so the sand rose around these poles and seemed to suffocate them. After a while, the drifting process had become so total that we followed the road by driving alongside the top halves of the poles, which stuck out of the sand with the wire trailing uselessly – ripped from their moorings by the camel trains.

We were staying at the Port Sudan Country Club, which sounded impressive, but which had also been invaded by the desert. The ground floor, resplendent with a board recording the winners of the annual Polo Cup from 1921 to 1948, was close to silting up. There was nothing that people could do. No money for public works and no money for equipment so, like the other guests, we stayed on the second floor.

In Port Sudan the Red Cross, and Unicef, and Oxfam, and Save the Children, and all the rest were fighting to save the lives of so many forgotten people. Here I met one of those extraordinary women that you come across so often working under conditions like this. They are so often presented to the world as saints, but that is too easy, and it is also wrong. They are heroes, but to canonise them is to underestimate them, and reduce the impact of what they do. This one was a nurse in her early thirties with a bright red tip to her nose from the sun and a wisp of hair falling from her cap, Jane was from Wiltshire and had been working in Port Sudan for a couple of years. Every now and then she would get a bug and be laid low with it for three days. Then weakened she would rise like the phoenix from the ashes and start all over again, marching to her clinic and making sure that whatever she had was fairly and sensibly distributed, that as many babies as could be were inoculated and that the family-planning classes that she was running with the women didn't upset the men too much. She was the voice of authority writ large, and though she wasn't a big woman I can't imagine any man besting her.

We sat one evening and talked about why she lived there. It's a lonely life, after all, so why not come back to Britain and work in a nice clean clinic for a good salary.

Jane smiled and shook her head. 'It's not that easy. Here I'm the boss and I do what I think is right.'

She had been working for aid agencies for six years, heading her own projects, bulldozing her way through local bureaucracy and getting things done. She said she was almost afraid of going back to the UK and becoming an inflexible part of another bureaucracy. When I met her, she had a howling cold and stomped about the town with a handkerchief held to her nose most of the time. But above the hanky was a pair of eyes, bright and watchful, that were a warning to anyone who messed with this lady that you could come off second best.

We drove out of Port Sudan in a UN truck and headed towards the Ethiopian border. The desert here consisted of scrub, but the sandstorms, when they were whisked up by the winds from the sea, weren't so severe as they'd been a few days earlier. Every now and then along the trail we'd come upon a camel train, some heading out of Port Sudan and some towards the city, with twenty or thirty camels, and maybe half a dozen men and some boys walking alongside, carrying the sticks that are always there to remind the camel who's boss.

'They are themselves,' said the driver. 'They go where they want and do what they want.'

The war over the border being waged by the Eritreans was supplied by the huge Mercedes trucks that would pass us from time to time, but these camel trains were doing what they had done for hundreds of years, trading whatever they wanted and whatever they could get. They were their own men and not limited by borders invented by the British and the French and not controlled by anyone. We stopped for coffee with them and sat as they put two or three tablespoons of sugar in the tiny bowl before adding the coffee and handing it to us, smiling toothless smiles.

After a day or so we reached a small windswept town in the desert, and stayed the night. But we were visiting celebrities and a party of a kind was thrown for us by the locals. Two rooms of a house with electric light-bulbs hanging naked in the middle and an endless supply of Vimto made up the ingredients. In my childhood in the Midlands, Vimto was our champagne while dandelion and burdock was the normal pop we swigged by the gallon. I hadn't seen the stuff for years, but of course it was logical that it should have had a revival. Sharia law had outlawed alcohol – in Khartoum, when the fundamentalist government had taken over, crates of booze had been taken down to the Nile, crushed and buried.

I stood as a group of girls sang for us, and talked to a huge Nubian local policeman who asked me if I liked alcohol. I shook my head, concerned that he might be setting me up, and he laughed.

'No, my friend,' he said, pointing to his glass of Vimto. 'You see, this is a secret Vimto.' And he held it out for me to try.

It tasted exactly like Vimto with whisky in it. It turned out that, like good Catholics, some fundamentalists were less fundamental than others, and when the instructions to destroy local supplies of booze had come up from Port Sudan, the people out in the desert had decided to take a broad view of them. They had bulldozed great holes by the roadside and carefully, very carefully, stacked the alcohol into the holes for a time when traditions would change.

'But sometimes, on special occasions, we make arrangements with the whisky,' said the policeman, handing me a large tumbler with a half-and-half mix of Bells and Vimto. 'We are the same you and I, yes?'

And of course we were.

A week or so later, Stuart and I got back to London. He began his long-term relationship with the Hospital for Tropical Diseases, and I went back to the daily regime of nine to twelve thirty and began to lace together the twenty-five hours or so of recordings that Stuart and I had made. The programme developed a life of its own as these things tend to do and dominated my life for a while. There is a great joy in sitting in a production studio fiddling with bits of recording tape and trying to create the sound and the feel that you're after. It's the model-train enthusiast in us all I guess. The tapes eventually became a two-and-a-half-hour special that was broadcast on a bank holiday. It wasn't a bad programme, but a lot of effort had gone into

it and I thought that it mattered so much, and I was deeply disappointed that somehow it wasn't the earth-shattering special that we'd
both hoped it would be.

I had been to Ethiopia and the Sudan and we'd made an adequate
programme that was very acceptable by BBC standards but it didn't
convey the sensation of actually being there. All the facts were there
in roughly the right order, but it lacked a heart. I was no essayist and
certainly not a broadcaster of the standard of Tully or Cameron.
Besides, we weren't broadcasting to an audience that wanted to hear
what they were trying to do over on Radio Four.

Getting tangled up abroad, which had happened to me years before when I'd been trotting around South-East Asia and the Pacific,
had left an indelible mark. I adored travelling, but I wasn't a journalist. I didn't want to explain how things could be solved in a four-
minute pre-recorded piece. I'd travelled enough to know that that
was bullshit and worse it meant that the audience had come to expect, over the years, a neatly wrapped, pre-digested segment, offering
a background to the problem presented in a distant way and with a
neat solution at the end.

Then I kept thinking, as we finished the dubbing and the mixing
and the technical fiddling that always accompanies big productions,
that the programme also lacked an air of immediacy and closeness.
There was something self-defeating in these carefully edited tapes
that were almost six weeks old when they were transmitted. Wasn't
there something terribly old hat in keeping tapes for six weeks before
we transmitted them? Didn't the simple delay almost turn them into
archive pieces before they were broadcast? It was all too predictable.

There must be a way of making radio less stodgy and more flexible when covering the kind of thing we had seen. It would be a
hybrid of course, certainly not news and certainly not current affairs,
and therefore, because it would be neither, a programme that could
afford to be more adventurous technically and editorially. Wasn't it
right to take a few more risks with the medium, to push a little and
see not only if the system would support a different approach, but if
it could work technically. It was just a toe in the water in the endless
quest for difference.

Chapter 12

I T IS AN INCONTESTABLE FACT that a least one BBC producer has devoted his life to attempting to bump me off and if he dares to sue, I shan't hesitate to apologise. The fact that he has not yet succeeded is a tribute to my caution and instinct for self-preservation and symptomatic of his incompetence. But as it's almost inevitable that he'll get me one day, I want the world to know the truth.

I first bumped into Jonathon Ruffle at 'Live Aid' and then again when I was doing a couple of programmes for BBC World Service in the Strand. In those days he was a young golden-haired engineer who had absolutely no interest in the technical side of things, but he did have an obsession with making programmes. Besides being pretty bright, he was also hard-working and funny and had somehow avoided that glassy-eye sterility that can be part of the BBC staff *oeuvre*.

I mentioned J to a few people at Radio One and a year or so later, when a job came up, he applied for and got it. I marked him as a man after my own heart. Despite sad periodic attempts to prove some kind of musical credibility, his heart really lies in plotting to get out of Britain and go almost anywhere just so long as it is abroad and he doesn't have to pay for the flight. In recent years he has become more and more desperate in his determination to end my life. Jonathon's schemes usually start with a phone call and a cynical attempt to engage my interest by saying something along the lines of 'I've just had a great idea'. Who can resist that?

This ploy has ended with me being thrown around the sky in an RAF fighter-plane. I was brave, but lost the cheese sandwich I had eaten earlier within seconds. He has lured me into a shaky Liberator that was scheduled to fly from the USA to Britain via the Arctic Circle, on the grounds that it was a great idea. Of course, by the time we had completed half our journey and lumbered into the air over Equilit on our way to Iceland, it was patently obvious that we were doomed. One engine failed entirely, another was intermittent, the navigation system packed up and oil seemed to be leaking everywhere. It was pretty obvious, as we got lower and lower over the ice-pack, that this incident was not on the schedule. There was a strange calm amongst the elderly crew which at first I couldn't understand. Then I grasped it: they were so damned enthusiastic about this rumbling, creaking old aircraft that they were happy to die in it.

We were flapping over Greenland, where the chances of surviving a crash and being found were nil, and the pair of us looked gloomily through the canvas windows at the rocky terrain below as the Liberator flew lower and lower. At least they'll never find our bodies, so there'll be no funeral expenses, I thought, though I didn't really fancy being smashed to pieces on those damned rocks.

The temperature sank way way below zero and J and I fell to arguing about whose fault this was. The saner Fergus Dudley, sensing that something was going desperately wrong, had hitched a lift to Iceland with an RAF Nimrod. When he had reached Reykjavik, he had, as a matter of tact, bought a case or two of beer for the crew of the Nimrod, and when they explained that they couldn't drink it when they were on duty, he'd knocked back the lot and was roaring drunk when we crash-landed.

'I thought that you were dead, loves,' he burbled drunkenly, flinging his arms around us beerily as we got out of the wretched aircraft.

Yet again, when J and I drove across Syria together after having visited Tadmur, it was J who thought it was a good idea to pick up a nondescript figure in a long coat who was standing in the middle of nowhere. This stopped being a good idea when the man spoke briefly in Russian.

'He's got a gun,' J mouthed dramatically at me while I was driving.

Great, I thought, I'm either going to die with a bullet in the back of the neck, or I'm going to die wrestling with this Russian spy in the middle of the Syrian desert. Either way it's all J's fault. We did as the Russian told us and dropped him on the outskirts of Damascus.

J is always great company, but whenever I'm with him, I know that something is going to go hideously wrong and that if I don't die, at least he'll try to shift the blame on to me. But when we first got to know each other well, it was through the bottom of Mr Adnam's glasses in the Yorkshire Grey or the Crown and Sceptre that we put the world to rights and agreed that to be in Britain when the Roadshow was on, would ruin both our lives. We had to get out and to do that we had to produce an idea. For a while we edged round the subject of travel, working on the basis that one of us would come up with an idea so good that Johnny Beerling, the Controller, would fall on his sword rather than pass up the opportunity.

Our first scheme was rejected out of hand and callously at that. Both J and I thought that 'Great Restaurants of the World' had a certain cachet, but for some reason we weren't taken seriously by the powers that be. But time was on our side, and management, as someone in Australia once said, is always getting older and weaker.

Towards the end of 1988 I was flying back from New York on an Air France flight. I'd requested seat J26 as usual. The advantage of this seat is that it is stuck away round a corner by the bulkhead and is unquestionably the most comfortable seat in economy. The disadvantage, if that's a proper definition, is that you can't see the movie screen and have to entertain yourself. Coincidentally, if you're trying to pick up a member of the cabin crew, which I was not, this seat is ideal because having no line of sight with the screen, one of them has to do a special safety advisory just for you. On this particular red eye I couldn't sleep and ran out of books, so I found myself desperate enough to read the in-flight magazine. There, in a fairly vague advertisement, was a picture of a satellite telephone and my rudimentary French translated the copy line as 'use anywhere in the world'. I felt like kissing the steward, but he looked a little suspect and might have wanted to follow it up, so I limited myself to a little hiccup of joy.

A couple of nights later, I was sitting in the Yorkshire Grey with Jonathon and the subject of the summer and what we should do came up. I pulled out the advertisement I'd clipped from the in-flight magazine, Jonathon looked at it and produced a rather grubby Letts schoolboys' diary, and we started to plan where we would like to go using the map at the back and the company's assurance that we could use their system 'anywhere in the world'. Half an hour and a few beers later, we had lots of candidates and no reason to visit them.

Then Fergus Dudley arrived, at the time a blameless and junior producer, and suggested 'Around the World in Eighty Days'. It was obvious, simple and immediate. What we didn't know was that Michael Palin was planning his epic film series around the same time.

When we found this out, our spirits sank, until someone said quite rightly, 'Totally different enterprise. He's doing it with a film crew observing it for later transmission and you're doing it live, just the two of you.' We both perked up at this and carried on plotting and planning. This wasn't too easy as neither of us had the faintest idea how we would actually achieve our goal, but obviously the first job if we were to offer up the idea of a series of live programmes was to discover if it really was technically possible.

We talked to an extremely important BBC engineering boss, who listened gravely and went away to think about it, before returning a few weeks later to deliver his opinion which ran roughly thus, 'If God had meant you to broadcast live from inaccessible points around the world he wouldn't have invented the bicycle. It will never work.'

This was a major blow, until we realised that our extremely important engineering person hadn't thought about it at all. He'd simply walked round the block a few times thinking, 'This sounds like a lot of work for me so let's squash the idea before I end up working weekends.' Once we'd grasped that, there was no stopping us.

We phoned and faxed the world and his wife and found some wonderful people at GEC who were enthused by the project. It's my experience that if you become enthusiastic about a ridiculous idea and look hard enough you can always find someone whose eyes light up at the thought of it the same way yours do. They agreed to lend us the two suitcases full of technical gear that we would need. This consisted of the satellite system and a small generator and, as we came to understand, it weighed a fair bit. The two suitcases actually weighed about eighty kilos when you were healthy, but if you had a touch of montezuma's Revenge, as we did from time to time in the succeeding months, they weighed four tons.

Things were going pretty well and both Jonathon and I spent a good deal of our time reassuring management that everything was hunky-dory, even when it was close to catastrophic. 'Don't frighten them, they're not up to the strain,' Jonathon would quite properly advise.

Jonathon at that time was producing Steve Wright and introducing new comedy ideas into the show, and I was still chuntering away between nine and twelve thirty every day, so our workload increased dramatically. Neither of us had any assistance on the project (we didn't dare ask, just in case someone realised how full of holes the operation was), so apart from the technical aspects, we were getting permissions to travel through countries with equipment that looked as though only the CIA would issue it, working out our travel arrangements and researching ideas that might, or might not work as we travelled around the world.

A few days before we left, we had a dry run with the equipment. We both drove out to Cambridge and together with half of Marconi's boffins we stood around in a group putting plugs in here and attaching leads there. When the moment came to shoot the signal up to the satellite and back to Broadcasting House in London and we pressed the button, it didn't work. As the only non-sparkie in this gathering, I wanted to scream when this highly motivated bunch of Britain's top communications experts gathered round Jonathon and spent an hour looking at the satellite system before agreeing that 'it didn't work, but they couldn't understand why'. To make the quality of the sound a little better we had bolted on some electronic gismos and they were behaving like a rejected heart in a transplant. Nothing worked, even the generator went at the wrong speed.

I looked at Jonathon and he at me and we both silently agreed that we were in so deep now that whatever happened we would have to go. Like all sparkies, J believes that some strange engineering god will reach down at the last possible minute and it'll be 'all right in the end'. I didn't have the same belief or confidence.

Oxfam came on board to give the project a fund-raising angle and we were almost there. Well, not quite. We didn't actually have any transport, but that problem would surely be solved. The fates sent us a lady called Jenny from Thomas Cook who was one of those extraordinary ladies who know the train timetables for almost every service in the world including the seasonal service to Machu Picchu in Peru. And from out of nowhere came John Crichton from the Cunard Elliman line whose knowledge of the world's shipping schedules was equally encyclopaedic. They both agreed to advise us on how to get to A, when we were stuck in B.

We took our package to the Controller, adding the magic words 'and it's incredibly cheap' and we were off, or nearly so. That odd British negativity raised its head with some of the management being less than helpful. Roger Lewis – then a newly created executive and for a time my never-present producer in time of need – displayed a total lack of understanding of human nature by declaring loudly and generally that Bates and Ruffle would fall out within ten days and go no further. Nothing could have been more designed to cement us together like lifetime brothers. Still, who gave a damn about him?

Roger had always been an interesting man. He was one of those people who could barely keep his hands off you, although he harboured absolutely no sexual designs whatever on the men he worked with. His favourite trick was to reach out, grab your nipples between his two fingers and twist them painfully. I've often wondered why.

We really had no idea what the hell we were doing, but we did have a pair of trusting natures and the *Radio Times* had announced that we were going round the world, so it must be true. By this time, massive overwork doing daily radio and working on RTW had reduced the two of us to blundering, exhausted ciphers, so when the first of many real problems surfaced, we nearly panicked.

A week before we were destined to leave, the ship that was scheduled to provide berths for us on the first leg of our journey took a turn to the right and failed to enter British waters. We had no way at all of getting across the first ocean. John stepped in and the Geest line offered us berths on their boat going to the West Indies. It meant leaving three days early, but that was hardly a problem. The difficulty was that originally we had scheduled our farewell for a Friday, which gave us two days in which to get used to the equipment and do a series of technical tests with the studio in London that was being run by Fergus Dudley and an engineer called Brian Thompson. If we took the berths offered us by Geest, we would have to be on air the following day from out in the Atlantic when we weren't absolutely certain that it was possible to transmit from a ship at all without stabilisers (I hadn't actually told management about my worries on this point, no use alarming them!). Still, it was either go or face the slings and arrows of the rest of the department when we would have to own up that we couldn't achieve what we'd said we could achieve.

So after a bit of a send-off from Broadcasting House and weighed down with technical gear that we needed and thought we might need, we set off in a borrowed car for the Welsh coast. Producer Malcolm Brown had delivered the vehicle to us and forgotten to point out that he hadn't filled the tank before he said goodbye, but that unscheduled walk for petrol was a brisk two-mile warm-up for both of us. I've since forgiven him, but I don't think that J has got round to it yet.

Our first ship was the *Geestport* and I'm afraid I must own up to our very first broadcast being a half-truth. We set sail on time and most of the night was spent with J and I settling the equipment in. Now Jonathon is an ex-sparkie, an ex-engineer if you prefer, and like all of his kind the only way he can control a rising stress level is to get a reel of gaffer tape and gaffer things to each other. It doesn't really matter what is being stuck to what, it's an engineering version of worry beads. By the time the first real 'live on air' test of the equipment was scheduled, there were little bits of gaffer tape stuck all over the ship. You could tell where J had been just by following the grey patches attached to the companionways and walls in the crew area.

The two of us struggled with the SatPac. We weren't used to it and it most certainly wasn't used to us, but eventually all the right bits went into the right holes and after some fiddling about we made contact with the studio back in Broadcasting House. They could hear us and we could hear them. This would be considered a miracle under normal circumstances, the fact that J and I had achieved it confirmed that the feeding of the five thousand was hard fact.

'Hello, Fergus, we're standing by,' I said.

At that moment, the ship's engines failed and the *Geestport* stopped dead in the water. There was much tramping of feet as various men were sent down into the engine room to find out what had gone wrong, but that couldn't disguise the fact that we were silent and static. Here we were, our first broadcast on an epic journey, and we weren't going anywhere.

J and I consulted and I went on air; both of us had our fingers crossed. He whipped out a tape recording we'd made of the engines that morning when we'd been testing our recording equipment. A slight pause and then from the machine came the reassuring sound of pre-recorded ship's engines.

'Yes, we're steaming ahead at twelve knots, the bows of the *Geestport* slicing through the waves of the Atlantic . . . ' and so on and on.

The *Geestport* was our home until we reached the West Indies. The crew were quite wonderful to us and we ate far too much and did far too little on the Atlantic crossing. Remember we were both exhausted so the rest did us good and we divided up the duties we had and learned how far we could push the equipment. By modern standards, I am talking about 1989, just after the dawn of satellite time, our system was primitive and the quality of sound we were providing to London wasn't the best, but we were going to air live and we weren't being forced into that 'here's one we made earlier' mode that had so concerned me in Ethiopia.

We left the *Geestport* and hitched a lift with a little German trader that spent its days pottering around the West Indies and would eventually get to Trinidad, where we would meet up with our next host for the crossing to Panama. The first day was sunny and J and I sat on the deck as the trader unloaded its containers in a tiny port, going through the equipment list. He was less stressed by this time and could go for an hour or two without the need to hold a reel of gaffer tape.

'Look,' he said, 'we've brought far too much stuff. Let's get rid of what we don't need.'

So as the sun went down, we two hideously non-ecological broadcasters threw overboard everything we didn't think we'd ever use and went below. Half an hour later, sitting in the tiny mess drinking coffee with the Filipino crew, who all spoke better English than us having learned it from the BBC World Service, we both went white simultaneously and rushed up on deck. One of us, and it's been the subject of intense debate ever since, had thrown over the side our handset which enabled us to talk to London. Each of us hurling the blame for such stupidity at the other, demanded that the other jump over the side and dive for it.

Eventually, one of the Filipinos excuted a perfect dive from the stern of the trader grubbed about in the water for a bit and produced the handset.

'It says waterproof,' I said, praying.

'Don't be so bloody stupid, they all *say* waterproof, it doesn't mean a thing,' said J.

I have never been so nervous as when we dragged the SatPac on deck, rigged it and experimented to see if we could get a signal to Britain and back. When the familiar voice from Portishead said, 'Yes, that's fine', both of us came as close to having someone else's children as it is possible.

We arrived in Trinidad on a beautiful, crisp, sunny morning, the hill behind the town sloping upwards was a deep dark-green and there at the next berth, towering above the little trader, was the container vessel that would take us to Panama. The vessel was old for a container. She'd been built eleven years before and as the Yugoslav captain cheerfully said, 'She breaking up, but no worries, hold together for quite a bit yet maybe.' Every part of her creaked and strained. In the mess room, the engine noise coupled with the heaving of the metal plates combined together to do Stockhausen out of business in the Caribbean.

The captain was a delight, but when he heard that we intended to drive up the Central American Highway from Panama City to Mexico and then across into California, his face darkened. 'Don't go, boys, don't go! Is a very bad place, they try to kill you.' Then he perked up a bit. 'Come with me, we go round the world too, all the time.'

We tried to explain that we really had to get off at Panama and that it would be difficult to explain to our bosses back at the BBC just why we were swanning it around the globe on a container vessel when they were expecting us to be hacking our way through some unfriendly jungle, but he wouldn't be persuaded and even when we'd berthed and the two of us were huffing and puffing as we unloaded all our gear, he was softly saying, 'Don't go, boys, come with us.'

Waiting on the dock in Panama, and a picture of sartorial elegance too, was Barry Wigmore, the *Daily Mirror* feature writer. Barry has been all over the world and wherever you meet him, in a jungle or in the Arctic, he always looks immaculately turned out. He has a couple of secret compartments in his suitcase and goes to endless trouble to make sure that his sweat-shirts and slacks are always clean and pressed. Being a pair of grubby, ill-kempt tramps by this time, J and I grew to dread our first view of Barry every morning. He is never less than well kept. But don't get the idea that Barry is a milk-sop, he's made of strong stuff. Driving through Panama City we were stopped by a traffic cop who was after some easy money.

'You, speeding. Is fine twenty dollars.'

'No, we weren't,' said Wigmore.

'Yes, you gimme twenty dollars.'

'No,' said the representative of Her Majesty's press, whispering, 'It's a matter of principle' to my urging to just hand over the cash to the obviously crazed idiot who was cradling a machine-gun.

The idiot was getting nasty. 'Gimme dollars and you licence,' he screamed, bringing his machine-gun, which I noticed wasn't cocked, level with Barry's tummy-button.

This was too much for Wigmore, who leaned forward aggressively and said, 'That's it, look here, my man, I want your number and I'm going to report you to your superior officer.' He turned and walked away.

The psycho with the machine-gun looked baffled at Wigmore's retreating back and I waited for him to blow Barry's head off, but he just shrugged, spat in the dust and stomped off in the opposite direction.

On one side, the confrontation had been a classic South American one, on the other, it had been worthy of Miss Marple. The result had been Noriega nil Agatha Christie one.

J and I drove with an Oxfam team from Panama to Mexico and we learned a lot about each other, most of it good. But one always has to remember that he is a highly intelligent tactician. There was one problem, represented by our comparative sizes. Both J and I can sleep like logs anywhere. Earth floors, concrete floors, hammocks, they're all grist to the mill, with the exception of sitting in trucks. I am six feet one inch long. J is about five feet five. His is the perfect size to curl up in the passenger seat of a truck or a Cessna, and like a doormouse he has driven me mad by doing that wherever we have travelled together.

He also claims to be a bad driver . . . 'Oooh, can't drive at night/in a sandstorm/over big bridges/through long tunnels, I'm afraid I've brought the wrong specs.'

'Take a look at the view, J,' I will say, eyeing a magnificent sunset/sunrise/gorge or whatever and there he'll be, curled up foetus-like in the corner of the truck/Landrover/half-track, mouth open, eyes closed, snoring like a buffalo on speed.

In my experience, it has usually been me who has driven, though J is only too willing at moments of stress to offer advice. 'I wouldn't have gone that way myself/Are you sure that speedo's right?/Did you check the tyres before we left?'

The Nicaraguan civil war was going on at the time and there were countless small disagreements between the countries the Central American Highway ran through, so virtually every border crossing became an epic. Of course we had documents a go-go from embassies in London asking local guards to let us through, but a good number of border guards were nervous fourteen and fifteen-year-old boys toting Kalashnikovs and intimidated by the arrival of a bunch of gringos with a truckload of electronic gear. But behind the kids there were usually a few adults lounging around in one of the huts that lined the barrier to the next country, and here J and I would, if necessary, go into our act. This consisted of being incredibly chummy with the grown-ups and dispensing pencils and pictures of Princess

Diana to the kids with the AK47s. These border posts were lonely places and after the initial surprise of seeing us and thinking that all their Christmases had come – 'Aah, a bunch of gringos with fat wallets' – the colonels and the lieutenants would usually settle down for a chat.

We never owned up to what we did and who we worked for, it seemed unnecessarily inflamatory, or rather I never owned up. On one occasion on the Costa Rican border, when I'd been chatting up a junior and J had been saddled with the colonel, Jonathon walked across with a mad, staring look on his face.

'I've told the colonel what you are, sir,' he said.

'Sir?' And what the hell did he mean 'told the colonel what you do'? The sun had got to the poor boy.

'No, no, no, *sir*,' said J, grabbing my arm in the traditional vice-like grip and trying to wrench it off at the elbow. 'The colonel explained to me that he is an avid listener to the BBC World Service and I have explained to him that you are the boss of Bush House.'

This was crazy talk, but there was obviously some sub-text that I was missing, so I stood there in the dust trying to look important and as though I was in command of the situation, while my idiot colleague jumped up and down, glaring at me as though I was a simpleton.

'The colonel listens to the World Service,' he bellowed in my ear. 'He likes it, but he doesn't like the pop programme introduced by Dave Lee Travis.'

J had lost me somewhere along the way, I just waited for the denouement. J was desperately trying to get some message or other across but I simply couldn't grasp it. He glared at me.

'I've told the colonel that it has been in your mind to stop the programme for some time, *sir*, and he seems very pleased!'

Ah, now I got it, all the centavos fell into place. If, in my new position as Head of World Service, I promised to have Travis removed the moment I got back to the UK, the colonel would stamp our passports and we'd be on our way.

I looked the colonel straight in the eyes. 'The man is as good as finished on my radio station,' I said.

The colonel grinned, up went the barrier and we were waved through with a flourish.

'God, you can be dumb,' said my soul mate.

'Thanks, you know how to hurt a man,' I said.

As we travelled on and crossed more borders and met more and more people, J and I began to develop a sort of cabaret act that would fill in embarrassing moments, or provide, when needed, a performance that might get the two of us whatever we required. It was pretty poor stuff and I knew if J was running out of material when he trotted out the King Haakon story, which went like this.

King Haakon went into Bush House during the war to do a propaganda broadcast to his people back home in occupied Norway. The commissionaire asked King Haakon who he was and called the studio to tell the producer that 'Your Mr 'Awkins has arrived'. When he entered and gave the producer his script, it became immediately obvious that it was too short and there would have to be some kind of filler. A nervous secretary was deputed to go to the gramophone library and get a fanfare. In the meantime, the clock ticked on and King Haakon began his speech. As the speech droned on, the producer began to panic, the secretary hadn't returned with the fanfare and then just as His Majesty reached his climax, 'Arise, ye Norwegians, and strike the dreaded foe' the secretary rushed in with the disc, which was slammed on to the turntable unheard. The King made a final plea to his people, 'Forward, brave Norwegians, your King is with you', the button was pressed and the record went to air. 'Roll up, roll up, lovely ripe bananas.' The poor girl had been given a recording of a funfair.

I'm sure my stories were just as lame, but at least I knew when J was in deep trouble the moment I heard the fatal words, 'Well, way back in the Second World War when the Norwegian King Haakon went to Bush House . . . '

The drive to Mexico City was spectacular, from the plains of Panama, up into the mountains of Honduras and then down again on roads with hairpin bends into the lush valleys on the Mexican side.

In Honduras we bumped into Alistair Cooke. That's not entirely true, we didn't bump into him, we stopped off at a hotel which turned out to belong to a Welsh expatriate who sounded very familiar. As we sat down to a meal of dog – 'It's good, I'm telling you' (it wasn't) – the Welshman came over and started talking to us about his life. He was a lonely man, whose living was the six-bedroom hotel out in the middle of nowhere, but who also made night flights to Miami once a month for reasons that we could only guess at. But it was his voice that fascinated us. Close your eyes and block out the sounds of the drunks in the bar and you could be listening to the younger Alistair Cooke as broadcast twenty years ago.

It turned out that the man had left Cardiff in the fifties and travelled a good deal, always with his short-wave radio packed away in his duffle-bag. When he was a kid, the family would listen to Alistair Cooke's Friday evening broadcasts religiously and he was always told to shut up and pay attention. The sound of Cooke's voice had been for him the sound of home, the sound of quality, the sound of class, and gradually as he'd got older and spoke English less and less, his own tones and accent had disappeared and vocally he had become Alistair Cooke. The man looked like any other who has lead a long and hard life; he was tall and tough with greasy hair, and he'd married and settled in Honduras. The whole town knew him and left him alone when he wanted to be alone or when he made those trips to and from Miami. But he had never stopped listening to those weekly broadcasts on short wave, and like most ventriloquists, he'd eventually come to assume the personality of his own dummy.

We crossed the border into Nicaragua. The civil war was grinding onwards and the road was rumoured to be mined, so when the heavens opened and the rain blanketed any view that we could expect to get through the windscreen, we pulled over into a small town and looked for somewhere to shelter. Just off the highway and down a back street from a magnificent church set amongst the poverty in its own elaborate square, there was what appeared to be a village hall. The door was open and inside people were dancing to what sounded like a band. We dashed in out of the rain and asked if we could stay until it stopped. Inside the hall there was a party going on that the villages had laid on for themselves. There was paella and music and Coca-Cola to drink and that was about it. 'Yankee?' then 'Inglés?' We nodded and said 'sí, sí'. There was much laughter and we were welcomed into their private party, food and drink were forced upon us and we even danced a little with the old ladies with their smiling, lined faces and their laughter at our clumsiness. We stayed for an hour or so and then had a whip-round to pay for our food. As we expected, getting them to accept anything was almost impossible, but we forced our money on them as they had their hospitality on us. It wasn't a fair exchange, but we all felt better. And then we drove on towards Mexico City.

Every day we stopped wherever we were to do our half-hour link with London. Sometimes the stop was a convenient one and we could plug into a local power supply, sometimes we'd use the small generator. It was in Managua, or just outside it, that the extraordinary nature of what we were doing struck us. We'd spent the night in a Managuan suburb and in the morning we were scheduled to drive out into the country and record some material at a water project funded by Oxfam. This coincided with our scheduled transmission time, so we decided to kill two birds with one stone, and loaded the two suitcases that made up our satellite system and the generator on to the truck and drove off.

The traffic at that time of the day was pretty heavy, added to which some farmers were driving some cattle into the capital down the main road, so inevitably we were held up. By the time we got to the bottom of the hill where the water project was being built, we were fourteen minutes away from airtime. The driver kicked the truck into first and it clawed its way over the stones that made the new road and up the hill. At the top was a small church and a row of stand-pipes, but looking at the work being done by Oxfam would have to wait. J and I sprinted out of the cab and round to the back. We pulled the pegs from the trailer and lowered the flap. Eight minutes to go. I grabbed the two suitcases and pulled them open, took out the petals as quickly as possible and started attaching them to the main body of the satellite transmitter while J was pulling on the generator starter. It roared into life at about five minutes to go and J snapped the power cable into the SatPac. A moment's pause and then the distinctive 'beep' that told us the system was ready.

J, guessing where in the sky the satellite was, swung the dish in a circle, while I watched the read-out on the dials and listened for the sustained 'beep' that would tell me that the system had locked on. For thirty seconds, nothing and then the strongest signal we'd had in days. One minute and twenty seconds before we were due to be on air and we could hear the dial tone that told us the handset in the London studio was ringing. There was a click, followed by a series of clunks as the system at the London end locked on, followed by Brian Thompson's voice, clear and calm, 'You're cutting it fine, stand by for theme and then you have some guests who've just come in, Fergus will brief you while you do the intro, stand by, four, three, two, one, theme coming.'

On that hilltop in Nicaragua, there was a moment of sheer beauty as the pollution from the city dissipated the sun's rays and the plain beneath seemed to go on forever. I could hear the theme that Vince

Clark had composed for us coming from London and then it was cut as Fergus said in my ears, 'Twenty seconds, Simon, and Bros are in the studio, you'll have to talk to them so that they can respond, stand by,' and the theme was back and starting to fade.

I stood on the hillside, breathing pretty heavily after the exertion of getting the satellite system going with Jonathon, who was also panting and pulling out as many pairs of earphones as he could find so that the Nicaraguan kids could listen to what we were doing, and wondered for a moment. Down on the plain a few miles away, a war was going on. We had fetched up in one of the poorest areas in one of the poorest countries in Central America. We had been made to feel welcome and here we were on a hilltop, above the filthy city air, talking to one of the most popular groups of the day. It was crazy, both J and I felt entirely removed from everything that was happening in London. Bros and Radio One and even Fergus and Brian seemed a million miles from any kind of reality. They were off the map somewhere in an unreal world that we didn't have anything to do with, except for our commitment once a day for half an hour to talk to them and play some of the tapes that we'd made. For us, for the first time, we felt totally free and entirely independent of everything and anything at Broadcasting House. We would continue to feel that way until the moment we landed back in Britain sixty days later. That day, on the hilltop, was the day that we realised that to get the job done we would have to operate in our own way and stop thinking like BBC people, which is what we did.

After leaving Nicaragua there was a *frisson* when we turned right instead of left and ended up in a war zone in El Salvador, but we made it to Mexico City just in time to miss the train to Guadalajara. We mooched around that great sewer of a city until we found the equivalent of a milk train that would take us to the American border. The journey wasn't uneventful. The train took twice as long as scheduled, the Mexican Army raided it for cocaine and the lavatories got blocked in the most specific way.

We crossed into the USA and were met by Barry Wigmore and Brendan Monks, his photographer. No, that isn't entirely true. Barry was there OK, looking irritatingly spick and span, the photographer was laid low in a motel with a vicious dose of the trots and had entirely lost his legendary sense of humour.

From Los Angeles we crossed the Pacific aboard a Chinese freighter to Tokyo, where the Controller met us and we nearly brought his life to an end. It had been a good crossing but we had no time to waste and a new freighter was to take us on to Singapore the same day. The vessel was empty and riding high at her moorings with the stairway to the bridge towering above the dock. Neither of us wanted Beerling to think that we were tiring or that we weren't both extremely fit, so, taking a deep breath, we each grabbed an end of one of the suitcases and working on the principle that the quicker we got to the top of the companionway the less pain would be suffered, we sprinted up the stairs. By the time we got to the top we were both puffing in the Tokyo humidity, but rather than leave the job, we ran downstairs and did the same with the second suitcase. This time we were both knackered and paused for a moment at the top of the stairs, only to hear, 'Jesus Christ', and see a bright-red face streaming with sweat and crowned with ginger hair stagger into view. It was the Controller, who being a macho little fellow had decided that if we could do it, then so could he. He'd grabbed the generator and run up the stairs after us and nearly collapsed in the process. He didn't stay long for the goodbyes, but tottered off, gasping something about brandy.

There were pirates and there was a hurricane in the South China Sea. The former were less frightening than the latter. To stay on the air for our feed to London someone had to hold on to the wireless mast with one hand and the SatPac dish with the other. Since I was talking, that job fell to J, who stood directly in the satellite's line of sight for a full thirty minutes getting the full value of the transmission just below the waist-line. Sparkies will tell you that this is a guaranteed way to lose your potency and your ability to procreate. J hasn't felt it necessary to discuss this with me and I regard the whole thing as very much his business, but he has a full social life with a fair number of girlfriends, yet he's never married. Strange that.

Then on to Singapore, where we met our Yugoslav captain and his rickety old container vessel once again. 'My boys, I thought that you were dead. Good, good, we have some beer, yes?' And it was good to see him and his crew and to share an hour before they sailed out of the harbour. We stood on the dock waving and waving at the grinning figure of the mate standing in the stern shouting incomprehensible good wishes in broken Dutch. Then from Singapore to Madras, and on across India by train and car and outward bound from Victoria Dock, Bombay. An astonishing sight as the ship was physically hauled through the mouth of the harbour by hand, or rather by lots of hands pulling on the most elaborate rope system I've ever seen. To the Arab Emirates and Egypt, and then down from Alexandria by sea to Greece and a European landfall in Venice.

There is so much to tell you of what happened to us, of what we saw and where we went, but as Fergus Dudley said when we returned to Britain, 'They don't want to hear all that stuff again.' So, I'll be brief. By the time we reached Venice, J had a horrific dose of tummy trouble and had taken to walking in a peculiarly straight up and down sort of way. He had also, as in my experience most sufferers of this horror seem to do, lost his sense of humour.

After we landed, we took a launch to the moorings by the Doge's Palace. Once again we were very close to transmission time and J wandered cautiously off to find somewhere we could transmit from, while I stayed with the equipment. He was back in a couple of minutes and said that he'd found a café that had agreed we could use their forecourt. So, for the last time, we pulled up our back packs and swung them on to our backs. Or rather I did, J swung his a little too vigorously and its weight took off and turned him into a very small jet-propelled missile, which hurtled across the cobblestones for a moment before landing. I was fairly weak myself and reached J to find that he had fallen on his back and that the back pack, being strapped to his back, was preventing him from standing up. He lay there like a dying fly, his arms and legs making wheeling motions as he tried to regain his footing.

'It's not fucking funny, you bastard, get me up!'

I was helpless with laughter.

Our very last 'Round the World' programme came from a little café which would normally have ripped us off rotten for the price of a cup of coffee. But when they saw the state of us, the coffee was on the house and so were the croissants. It had been like that all around the world. People helping and people giving.

The next day, a car drove us back to Calais and the crossing to Dover. We'd run out of all but a few quid, and I thought that I would have to talk long, loud and hard to get on board the 4 a.m. sailing.

'Oh, 'ullo,' said the purser, 'I know what you've been up to. You two must have had the best summer of anyone in the bleedin' world.'

The two of us had travelled together for three months and barely been out of each other's sight. We'd also spent most of our time either talking to foreigners or to each other, so getting back to Britain and having any kind of social contact with the mass was a bit of a shock. When we arrived in England at Dover, we were picked up by Neil Ferris, an old friend, who realising that we were in a bit of a daze poured the most dreadful coffee down our throats.

Radio One management had suddenly gone bananas and decided that rather than just turn up at Broadcasting House, the station would provide a twenty-gun salute, or rather a live outside broadcast of our procession up the Thames in a boat. You must remember that J and I had worked so closely together for the last few months that we didn't need to talk a lot to anticipate what the other would want to do next. Equally, I suddenly found myself back in the confusing world of switchable talk-backs with a couple of good-natured producers yelling down my earphones telling me what to do next. J was pushed to one side and by the time we reached our mooring, just below the House of Commons, both of us had had enough. We'd both wanted just to get back, make sure that our equipment was OK and then be about our business – which meant going to work the next day.

The final straw was seeing our beloved SatPac lifted over the side by a couple of BBC producers, who thought they were being helpful, and watching as they clumsily tried to pack it away, a job that would have taken us about five minutes. This was our baby. So we tried to escape and legged it up on to the Embankment and hailed a cab.

'Take us to a pub,' said J, and then looking at me, 'Got any money?'

The cabbie recognised us and joined us in the pub, just around the corner from the House of Commons, while we discussed our next move. Neither of us really wanted to go back to Broadcasting House, but it was the cab-driver who brought us to our senses.

'If you ask me, lads' – we hadn't – 'I'd go back and then get out of it as quickly as you can.'

Which is what we nervously did. The cab-driver dropped us round the corner from the Langham Hotel and we walked across the road to Broadcasting House at midday, to a huge welcome that neither of us expected and neither of us felt we deserved.

There was an odd moment after our management had stopped being cross about our escape attempt and we had said thank you to everyone and anyone, and that was when we had to go our separate ways. Neither of us are particularly demonstrative and we just said, 'See you', and then each got into his own taxi and drove off in opposite directions. A few months afterwards both of us wondered

whether we should have staged some dramatic and emotional farewell, but of course it would have been tacky and ridiculously over the
top. In retrospect, I think 'see you' was a pretty good thing to say after
a long journey and a lot of hassle. But it wasn't as simple as that.
When he got back to his flat, J was extremely tired and did what all
male animals do when they get back to their lair, went to the lavatory.
He pulled the switch down and nothing happened, the light had fused.
'Fucking Bates,' he thought, and then, before he could stop himself
called out, 'Simon, you've broken the bloody lamp,' before tailing off.

Since we completed this journey technical standards have improved and I would wince now at the sound quality of some of the
material we broadcast back to Radio One. I would probably find
some of the material we produced pretty wince-worthy as well. We
won a few awards for the series, which was nice and for which I am
grateful, but that wasn't the object of the game. We are both infinitely proud of the fact that, with enormous help from Fergus Dudley
and Brian Thompson in London, we got on to the air every day
except one, when we were arrested in Mexico, and stayed on the air
for our allotted transmission time. It is not a smug pride and I hope
it isn't a nostalgic pride. That sort of thing would reduce us both to
reminiscing about the Golden Age. It is the pride of two people who
will now admit what they never for one moment admitted to the
management at the time – 'Don't tell 'em, it'll only frighten them' –
that they hadn't the faintest idea whether or not the project would
work technically or physically when they left London.

The project was titled a 'challenge', and that presupposes that we
knew what it was all about and that we were involved in a well-
planned media exercise. Nothing could be further from the truth.
There was no agenda and for our sins there was no forward planning. We were totally reliant on two people for technical contact and
two others, both holding full-time jobs, for advice on where and
when to catch a ship or a train in the middle of nowhere. Neither J
nor I really knew how the SatPac operated. We'd even forgotten to
take a circuit diagram with us.

On one horrifying occasion we opened the SatPac and something
fell out of the bottom. It looked like one of Frankenstein's bolts with
a pair of wires coming out of it, and J sat contemplating it for a long
time before he could even speak about it. It took us eight hours of
fiddling to find where the something fitted, but with the help of a
non-English-speaking ship's engineer we replaced it and it worked.

Over a Chinese meal in Kuala Lumpur, J looked at me and said, 'You know, I sometimes sit and look at that SatPac and a feeling of total fear sweeps over me, because I know that if something goes wrong, I wouldn't know where to start fixing it.'

After we'd been back for a week or two, we suddenly became aware that almost everyone else on the other networks was charging off on projects involving either SatPacs or use of the technical add-ons that we had experimented with. There was a sudden rash of these programmes. That was something we were both quietly pleased about.

We had operated as a two-man crew and found that it worked extremely efficiently. There was no time at any stage of the journey for either of us to sit and sulk, or to worry about this or that. We were simply too busy and by the time we'd had a couple of weeks on the road we had organised ourselves to the point where we really could be an efficient programme-making unit. The ideas that we developed on this project to make programmes quickly and under the most spartan conditions, I used again and again in programmes that I worked on in subsequent years from Brazil, Jordan, New York, Moscow, Africa and the Gulf. At that time though, we didn't know what the hell we were doing and we didn't achieve much more than that toe in the water, but that was infinitely more than J or I had hoped for.

Chapter 13

TO INTRODUCE YOU TO the matter of broadcasting from the Gulf, I must first tell you about Mildred. Mildred is a highly respected and thoroughly married broadcasting executive with nothing but heterosexual thoughts in his head. He is also extremely good company. But when he gets together with Johnny Beerling, the two of them, both of an age, develop a sort of duality, which meant that they were nicknamed George and Mildred after the ITV sitcom.

Mildred is no fool and when British forces were deployed to the Gulf, was one of the first to argue for the British Forces Broadcasting Service to establish a radio station there. The American forces of course had arrived complete with TV station, movie theatres et al. Our government places everyday welfare well down the list, so it took a good deal of pressure from high places to get a radio station, all boxed up nicely in a container, delivered to Dahran. But finally success was achieved.

By this time, Fergus Dudley and I were working together as a team with Claire Sturgess. Now Fergus is not normally a man who likes roughing it, his idea of raw adventure is the cocktail bar of the Hilton. But he's a radio man to his fingertips and if it is logical to do the programme from the moon, he will quietly and efficiently set about organising it. I'd broadcast from the Middle East some years before with Sue Foster as my producer when we'd done a couple of programmes from Royal Navy ships in the Gulf. Fergus on the other hand thought the Middle East was a restaurant.

The opening shots of the Gulf War had already been fired and were continuing to be fired as Scud missiles left Baghdad heading for Saudi Arabia or Israel. I was invited by the British Forces Broadcasting Service to go and do some programmes from unspecified locations in Saudi Arabia and Fergus, Claire and I agreed that this would be an excellent idea. I also had a personal motivation for going to Saudi Arabia. The government had refused to let J and I cross their country when we'd been going round the world, causing both of us a good deal of heartache, and I was under strict instructions from J to take a shovel with me and go and 'crap on their desert like they crapped on us'.

At the time it looked as though this could be a major conflict and the supposition was that gas would be used, so Fergus and I were packed off to a location somewhere in southern England to be briefed on the use of NBC (Nuclear, Biological and Chemical warfare) suits. We were met by a sergeant whose opening line was, 'Gentlemen, I have an hour with you that just may save your lives. I doubt it personally but I'll do my best.' He then demonstrated how to put the suit on and how to use the pens that were attached to the suit. 'Nifty things these. If you smell gas, then use 'em. If you notice the symptoms of gas, twitching and loss of muscle control, then use 'em, they will give you an hour or so survival time. Of course there is a problem, Mr Bates, as twitching and loss of muscle control is also a symptom of naked fear. If you use the pens under those circumstances you will die.'

We rolled and unrolled our NBCs and headed for a plane and for Riyadh, all the usual paraphernalia of broadcasting safely stuck in the hold. The RAF jet swung over Riyadh with me sitting in the jump-seat peering out.

'If you're thinking they're bonkers to have all their lights on,' said the pilot, 'then think again. This isn't World War Two, Scuds can see in the dark.'

We stayed the night at the airport, sleeping on the concrete floor of the area that had become a staging post for incoming forces. In the morning, Fergus and I drove down the vast motorway to Dahran. There was nothing on the flat desert road bordered by scrub on either side but long lines of ordinance, mile after mile of American tanks and transporters and trucks. In our little jeep we looked up into the cabs of the vehicles we were endlessly overtaking and often a female face would grin down at us, and I wondered where they were from and if they knew what the hell was going on, because we certainly didn't.

That night we stayed outside Dahran in a small hotel and it was there that naked brutal war struck us for the first time. Both of us were exhausted and went to bed early. I woke at about one in the morning with a high-pitched alarm going off and leapt out of bed stark-naked. 'God almighty,' the Iraqis were bombing us. Now what did the sergeant say. Yes, that's it, you've got seven minutes to get on your NBC suit. Oh God, the NBC suit is in the car. I dashed hither and thither in the room as the alarm rang in my ears, trying to find my clothes so that I could get the lift and retrieve my NBC suit which would save my life. Then I remembered that the jeep was in a compound outside the main hotel area. 'I'll call reception and they'll get me the key and I can unlock the compound and go to the jeep and get my NBC suit . . . Oh my God, Fergus has got the key to the car. OK, I'll call him and then he can get the key to the car and we can both go down to the compound . . . I'm going to die!' The phone rang.

'Hello, Mister Bartesh,' said the voice.

'Yes, yes, yes!' I said, trying to sound cool.

'You have left your door on the latch, sirrr. The door alarm, it is going off. Please to stop it by closing the door so that others may sleep.'

The following day, we were in the British army base in Dahran when a Scud alert was called. We'd erected a makeshift studio for Fergus on an oil drum and he was busily editing a piece of tape, headphones covering his ears which made it impossible for him to hear the alert.

'Should we take it seriously?' I asked.

The lieutenant answered, 'Yes, don't do anything but be prepared to if the Tannoy confirms that it's heading this way.'

I thought it only fair to warn Fergus that he might be blown to pieces in six minutes, twenty-five seconds, so I lifted up one of the earpieces and said, 'Fergus, a Scud alert's just been sounded for the camp.'

Fergus waved his hand irritably. 'Tell 'em I'll be with them as soon as I've finished this edit, will you.'

We broadcast several programmes from Saudi Arabia as the Scuds whistled over our heads harmlessly and went on to wreak havoc elsewhere. At this time it looked as though the war when it came would be quite horrific. I kept meeting pale-faced young soldiers and wondering what to say to them. We recorded their requests and tried to do the right thing, but neither Fergus nor I could come to terms with the fact that these young people were really in the firing line.

There was a huge hospital at the base. Everything was under canvas and there were air locks at all the entrances to keep out the gas. To a stranger there seemed to be mile after mile of dark tunnels opening out into wards and operating theatres, all with dozens of young nurses and medics. I found the concept that these people could be wiped out in such a dubious cause sickening, but of course it wasn't my job to say so.

Just down the road was the journalists' mound, from where the great and the good would regularly deliver to a waiting and anxious world that they knew next to nothing. We watched as one perfectly ordinarily dressed hack slipped into a flak jacket and army hat before delivering that hour's non news. Fergus got a call from one of the British Sunday papers asking him to arrange for me to wear fatigues for a photo spread they were planning. Fergus didn't even have to ask me, he said 'no thanks' on my behalf.

Back in Britain, the machinery of the BBC had moved into top gear and Radio Four FM had turned itself into a rolling news service, which almost immediately earned the soubriquet 'Scud FM'. There *was* a need for a continuous news service, but although essential listening, this one quickly lapsed into a series of tedious round table discussions with the inevitable experts sitting in London speculating on the next move to be made by the protagonists 'out there'.

Because there were only a few members of staff at the Dahran BFBS base, there was a limit to the number of hours they could transmit to the troops. Some bright spark in the MOD had decided that when they were off the air, BFBS should rebroadcast 'Scud FM' which was beamed out to the Gulf by satellite. Bob, a minor technical genius, had managed to rig up what looked like a dustbin lid with a sausage sticking out of it, which served as a reception system for the BBC network.

On one occasion, I was in the desert somewhere bouncing along in an army truck when we came across a British forward position with a heap of sandbags, some corrugated iron and a tiny Union Jack. Sitting sweltering in the heat was a soldier, muscle from the ankles up, tattooed everywhere and who looked thoroughly cheesed off with everything in general and, when I approached, with me in particular.

'Oh, it's you is it?' he said unenthusiastically, and when I agreed that it was indeed me and asked him if he'd like to record a message for his family back home, he consented with pretty bad grace.

Simon Bates

I got my tape recorder out and he said what he wanted to and then, the recording having finished, spat angrily onto the sand. For want of something better to say, I suggested that he looked pretty pissed off.

He gave me a look that Alf Garnett would have been proud of. 'Pissed off, pissed off? I should fucking say so. I'm burning my arse off in this God-foresaken hole. There's no beer, the bloody Americans have all got fridges and Coca Cola and all I can get is fucking BFBS and bloody Radio Four with a bunch of idiots yakking on all the time about the fifty different ways the Iraquis are going to blow my fucking head off. You could say I'm pissed off.'

Once Fergus and I had done our half-dozen programmes it was time to fly back to London, so we packed up the gear and loaded it into the back of a New Zealand Airforce Hercules for the trip to Riyadh. Leaving Dahran was difficult. I had friends in BFBS, one of whom was an ex-Para by the name of Dave Boyle; aside from being quite mad, he was also a wonderful, larger-than-life character. There were also the young nursing staff in the hospital, not only worried about whether they would survive, but also terribly nervous about whether they would be able to cope when the casualties started coming in from the front in what everyone agreed might just be 'the mother of battles'.

For us it was easy – we were passers by. For all these people and the military personnel, it was for real.

The New Zealand Hercules clambered into the air just after dark and flew low over the desert. I was sitting in the jump seat once again and as the aircraft droned on towards Riyadh I looked out across blackness where, every now and then, a string of tiny lights marked some small community. Suddenly, ranged right across the desert from one horizon to another, a thin trail of intensely bright light shone out. It was hard to judge just how long the strip was, but I'd guess about eight miles of this illuminated narrow corridor was strung out over the desert.

I had lost all sense of perspective, so I pointed down to the desert and shouted at the pilot, 'That can't be a road can it, the street lamps are all in the wrong place?'

He laughed and pushed the stick so that the Hercules engines growled and the aeroplane dipped low over the sand.

'No mate, that's the Yanks.'

And it was, wheel to wheel from one side of the horizon to the other, mile after mile of tanks on transporters driving up towards the Kuwait border.

When we reached Riyadh, there was an air raid warning in process, so Control had sensibly postponed the return flight of the RAF aircraft on which we were hitching a lift, until the morning.

Fergus and I went back inside the elaborate airport terminal, took a left turn and began to climb the stairs to the floor that had been designated as a British staging post. One half of the bare concrete hall had been made into a canteen and the other half was an area with very little lighting, where anyone who was waiting for a flight could get some rest. We unrolled our sleeping bags and went to sleep, using our DAT machines as pillows (the only time I found the blasted things totally reliable).

At about three in the morning, a soldier shook me awake. The sirens were going off, but we'd been so tired that we'd slept through the warning alarms. 'Get up mate quick, there's a Scud coming in. Suit on.' I rubbed my eyes and shot out of my sleeping bag.

The army loudspeaker system was issuing instructions by that time to suit up and get down to the air raid shelter. Fergus was already starting to zip his suit on and I followed his example, fumbling with the zips and wondering how long we'd got before the Scud hit.

I pulled on my gas mask. Wearing a gas mask is a nasty business; there's a foul, rubbery stomach-churning stench and the moment you put it on, you feel as though you're separated from the rest of the world. Your vision is restricted and you become very aware of the sound of your own shallow breathing as you adjust to the mask and the noise that it makes.

We followed the 'buddy' system as we'd been instructed by the sergeant back in Britain and checked that the seals on each other's suits were effective. It was an amateur effort, but it gave the passing soldiers a laugh.

Fergus and I followed the other soldiers, quietly making their way down four floors, to the airport basement. When we arrived we simply sat, row upon row of us on benches, listening for the moment the Scud would hit.

Conversation was almost impossible with a gas mask on, so we just waited. I remember thinking how bloody stupid I was being, sitting at the bottom of a structure built out of steel and concrete and wondering how the hell I would explain all this to Fergus's mother if things went wrong and I went back home alone. Lexa is a tough and delightful woman not given to accepting lame excuses.

The seconds ticked by and there was a tap on my shoulder. I looked round and there were half a dozen faces staring at me, all asking me through their gas masks if I was Simon Bates. I've always been a bit cautious about answering this question, because you never know what the motive behind it is, but since it looked as though we were all going to be blown off the face of the earth I put my thumbs up and nodded.

The half-dozen faces grinned maniacally and then began to hum the theme to 'Our Tune'. It was a ridiculous moment, a sort of augmented barber's shop quartet in fatigues leaning together in the poor light provided by bare electric lamps. Little more than their eyes were visible through their gas masks and their voices were muffled, sounding as though they were coming through a ton of cotton wool.

Those six were the only people I've ever come across who could sing the whole refrain from beginning to end apart from Ian Hislop, but that's another story.

Exactly one and a half minutes later (you get to notice things like that in these situations) the Scud whistled harmlessly overhead and buried itself in some rough ground a few miles beyond the airport. There was a loud bang, but that was about the extent of the damage. It was a long night with endless alarms and frequent treks up and down those concrete stairs, before we caught the flight back to the UK in the early morning.

We returned to Saudi Arabia several times, to the little BFBS camp in the middle of the desert, with its home-made satellite dish and washing hanging on the transmitter lines.

On the last occasion we drove up to Kuwait City with a British Army officer who also wanted to take a look. The pall of smoke that hung over the city after the retreating Iraquis had set fire to Kuwait's oil wells was visible for miles. There was very little wind which meant that the smoke and the fumes hadn't dispersed much: they just hung in the air a shapeless, black mass.

One minutes we were driving in relatively clean air, the next we were plunged underneath the canopy of oily smoke and the windscreen became spattered with huge black droplets.

We spent a day and a night in the city, looking at a little of what had happened. Although the Kuwaitis were cleaning up as fast as they could, the roads were still littered with Iraqui tracks and tanks and the trenches they had dug on the beach – 'stupid, badly built defences' according to our friend from the British Army – snaked across the sand. The sheer scale of the stupidity and cruelty of it all was overwhelming. The murderous behaviour was visible, but so was the small-mindedness of a bunch of fools.

There was a breathtaking incompetence in the looting that had taken place. They had stolen a good many of the country's best race horses and shipped them to Baghdad, but had left the rest with an armed guard watching over them as they died from thirst and starvation.

As they had pulled out the Iraquis had smashed up the children's funfair at the zoo.

In the afternoon, we drove the mile or so out to Mutla Gap, the point where the road to Baghdad narrows and where the retreating army, having commandeered every vehicle imaginable, had come to a halt in a traffic jam that provided a perfect opportunity for an aircraft strike.

The planes had stacked up over Kuwait and, one by one, had gone in and systematically bombed the convoy to hell. There was nothing that any of the Iraquis could have done: they were ten thousand or more rats in a trap, unable to avoid the death that rained down on them.

No one knows or will ever know quite how many people were killed in that action. The heat had been so intense as the vehicles exploded that some lorries had simply melted and now consisted of little more than a wrecked chassis with a cold pool of metal forming a circle around them.

Some vehicles had left the road and tried to drive for safety across the desert, but had got no further than a hundred yards. The bodies of a few soldiers who had tried and failed to escape on foot lay beside them.

There were personal letters and photographs and mountains of military files blowing across the desert. There were also televisions and radios, fridges and cookers. But one wonders what madness it was that made the soldiers risk and ultimately lose their lives for plastic flowers and notebooks and cheap Hong Kong-made GI Joes, shrink wrapped toys which were now lying on the road.

The Americans had got there first after the horror was over and covered the shells of vehicles in graffiti, nearly all of it obscene.

When I was last in Saudi Arabia, the British forces had been sent home and the BFBS radio station was being packed away into its container.

Simon Bates

As the crane swung the container onto the back of the lorry for transportation to the nearest port, six of us toasted the outbreak of peace in Fanta orange. The hospital had gone and the base camp that had been home to the British forces was nearly deserted. Things for the Saudis were getting back to normal.

There was a distinct change in atmosphere. The Europeans weren't so welcome now that the Iraquis were no longer a threat; the little kids in the street didn't smile and wave any more, they watched the adults to see what kind of reaction was expected.

Down the road in a small town, there had been a couple of public executions and the religious police were back on the main road outside the camp gates, patrolling in their American police cars. I was glad to leave.

Chapter 14

N THE MIDDLE OF 1992 I got a call at home from Allan, a BBC journalist I knew slightly. He was back at home after several months in Sarajevo and he sounded tired and angry.

'Do you realise how bad things are there at the moment?' he asked me.

I said I thought that I had a rough idea but I didn't know enough. He spent an hour on the phone trying to knock into my head what I later learned for myself, that this was a genocidal, cruel and unacceptable war and that straight, dispassionate journalism had, in his view, failed to get the message across. He wanted me to get someone, almost anyone, to make a record à la Band Aid. I called a few people, but understandably after all the nit-picking that the weasels had done about charity records over the last six years, no one was prepared to stick their heads above the parapet and commit themselves. All the artists I called were enormously sympathetic, some of them even offered to make a donation to the Red Cross, but all of them were nervous of being castigated as publicity seekers. I found their attitude very easy to understand and I had to admit defeat.

Allan's point about journalism was that it had failed to get the message that this was a genocidal war across to a wide public, and generally everyone had become bored with the intense coverage of the political issues behind the war, and had forgotten that this was happening in Europe and had resulted in the largest and most miserable movement of refugees since the Second World War.

In 1993, Fergus had moved to another department before being brought back into Radio One to give the Mark Goodier show a real shot in the arm and I had a new producer, Christine Boar. Christine is another of those rare and joyful people, a woman who when challenged won't back down. A few years before when I had decided it would be a good idea to do some programmes from Moscow, my male then producer had nearly shrieked with horror at the idea. Not so much I suspect because he was nervous of possible unpleasantness, but because it would interfere with his social itinerary. Christine is made of stronger stuff and when I told her I thought we ought to go to Croatia, she agreed at once. Then I added that she'd have to learn how to operate the technical equipment and she went a little quiet, but still agreed.

I called the endlessly patient Peter Beardo, who said, as always, yes, of course we could borrow another of his satellite dishes and yes, he would show Christine how it worked. Christine, who had never changed more than a plug in her life, spent a day with Peter and came back, a little glassy-eyed but almost certain that she knew how to work the equipment, and we headed off to Zagreb.

Our first night was a disaster. After dinner, Christine suddenly got an attack of the worries about the SatPac. 'I want to give it a trial run,' she said.

'It's after midnight, for God's sake.'

'I know, but we're travelling tomorrow and I'm worried stiff about it.'

So, unwillingly, I dragged out the SatPac and the generator and all the little fiddly things, and hauled them into the open where we could get a good line to the satellite. We both stood in the pitch-black and freezing cold in some open space or other in the middle of Zagreb and waited as the machine warmed up. It didn't work. What's more, it continued not to work. Christine and I tried everything, we coaxed it, moved it, put our arms around it, gave it a little slapping, but nothing would induce it to deliver the little sign on its read-out saying 'correct'. We were there for four and a half hours before we gave up and went to bed.

The following morning when we got up, depressed at the idea of not getting through to the London studio as we always had done before, I saw the reason for our failure. There was the biggest multi-storey car park I've ever seen right in between our little satellite dish and the satellite itself hanging a hundred and seventy-odd thousand miles away in space. Moral: when you feel like panicking, do it in broad daylight.

We drove as far as we could from Zagreb, to Karlovac and then to Bihac, an almost magically beautiful town nestling in a valley. From a distance Bihac looked like something from Tolkien's Middle Earth, but as we drove through the checkpoints and across the bridge and into the town, there were the tell-tale sandbags up against walls and the slag heaps that had once been houses. Bihac was under siege.

We drank coffee, and that evening a local Moslem family asked us to join them for a meal. Their house was a couple of miles away and when we got there the family had laid out a spread that was impossibly generous. Pancakes, jam and beer, on a table set up outside their house. Christine asked about the noise that the crickets were making and was told sadly by the old lady that that was gunfire from the hills.

I had just got back from Croatia when I heard the news that a convoy due to carry fifteen hundred women and children out of Sarajevo had been cancelled. They had been scheduled to leave the city after a ten-month wait amid the shelling and the brutality. It's impossible to imagine the despair these women and children, many of them sick and old, must have felt when they heard the news. To most of them it must, I suspect, have seemed as though they had been condemned to death. God knows what caused the cancellation. This vicious civil war is a dreadfully cynical business. It's so easy travelling around to see how ordinary people are used daily as pawns in the political chess game, and of course they are the victims.

On a cold grey morning in Zagreb, I turned a corner and bumped into a Red Cross officer who had been transferred from Afghanistan.

'I was dealing with unexploded land mines there,' he told me.

'A bit dangerous?' I supposed.

'Yes, but mines are a lot more predictable than this place.'

Drive through the Croatian countryside (avoiding the main motorway where there had been a 'bit of trouble') and the bitterness of this war is there for you to see. It has nothing to do with the checkpoints or the soldiery. In each town and village are houses that have been destroyed as the result of an unlucky shell and houses that have been deliberately dynamited, leaving their neighbour's house standing intact side by side with a heap of rubble.

'The people who lived there were maybe on the wrong side,' said the driver, shrugging his shoulders.

'Did they get out before the building was destroyed?'

He looked at me quickly for a moment, 'I don't know.'

When I got back to the UK, I was predictably angry and disturbed by what I had seen. Christine, my producer, was equally upset. But the response was easy to understand. People back at base didn't want to hear what we'd seen. The truth was that they were bored with Bosnia and all the others. It wasn't fashionable or politically correct to give a damn. Earlier that month, a leading Dutch daily newspaper had carried a telling cartoon. It showed an ingratiating salesman flogging a TV to a young couple: 'And a special feature, the moment anyone mentions the word "Bosnia", it changes channels.' Pretty funny! I can't help wondering if our daily dose of media death and cruelty in the papers or on TV, whether it be in Northern Ireland or the former Yugoslavia, made us immune to evil? Do we now accept murder, rape and starvation on our back doorstep as 'just one of those things'?

When I first went to Croatia and Bosnia it was summer. The countryside looked glorious, a chocolate-box world of undulating hills, beautiful forests and small farms. Karlovac was a huge rambling old place, which had been a barracks in the days of the Austro-Hungarian empire. In Britain the imposing three-storey brick building would have been a protected building with officials from the Heritage Ministry crawling all over it.

When I arrived, Alessandra Morelli, an Italian woman of about thirty with deep shadows under her eyes, was the UN official in charge of finding countries willing to take the detainees. Most of them had been in concentration camps and had suffered dreadfully.

'You British think of a concentration camp like the Second World War, big and with barbed wire,' a Red Cross official told me, 'but here it can be anywhere. In a garage, a disco even. Anywhere that cruelty can be done in secret'.

Over the last two years the Red Cross have uncovered countless numbers of these centres of cruelty and Karlovac was full of victims: A boy whose leg had been blown off by a mine. For three days he was left untreated, because he belonged to the other side. A man whose behaviour was, by any standards, erratic. Easy to understand when he took his shirt off and you saw the wounds. Someone had held him down and systematically shredded the flesh on his back with a razor-blade. And of course the women and the terrible, unrepeatable stories they have to tell.

In August 1993, when I was there, Karlovac was a pretty safe place. The church had been shelled a few weeks before, but no one was expecting trouble. In fact, the worst that had happened was when the church collapsed. Half a dozen old men had been enjoying their coffee and the sunshine when the spire fell into the square, missing the group by a few feet. The story was that they crossed themselves and went back to their gossiping.

Alessandra was at home in Italy on leave, but she flew straight back in September when she heard the news that Karlovac had come under fire.

'I went at once, of course, what else could I do?' she told me.

She found nearly a thousand people close to panic.

'They were frightened of the shells and then of course they were frightened of what would happen to them if the soldiers came into the barracks. They knew they would be killed.'

Together with friends from the Red Cross, Alessandra managed to find enough buses to transport the detainees to safety.

'But the drivers would not come into Karlovac, it was too dangerous. So the United Nations drove them from the centre to the meeting point with the buses on the outskirts.' Then she smiles. 'We got them all out in seventy-five minutes, I am very proud of that!'

After a nightmarish drive, they arrived at Garsinci and relative safety, although, because of the speed of their evacuation, there was no accommodation for them. But for the detainees, there was no slackening in their fear of what might happen. For ten days, they insisted that Alessandra had to sleep alongside them on the ground to reassure them that things would be all right, that they would be safe and that soldiers wouldn't round them up in the middle of the night. Their arrival, though, added to the logistical nightmare for the authorities at the camp, who had no choice but to add nearly a thousand people to the number they had to feed, shelter and provide for.

Dieter Mathes was the camp manager for the Red Cross. He smiled a good deal, but his face was heavily lined and he looked twice his age.

'At home I am a paramedic,' he said. 'But here I am everything.'

And he was. Part-diplomat, part-logician, he wheedled and cajoled as much material and food as he could out of almost anyone. It was Dieter who kept the camp running and Dieter who negotiated with the Croatian government when there was a problem.

'It is hard for them too, you know. After all, they have half a million refugees in a country with a population of only four million.'

On the evening I arrived, he'd just taken delivery of twenty-five hundred pairs of shoes donated to the Red Cross and was struggling through his exhaustion, trying to work out a fair means of distributing the shoes to the most deserving of the three and a half thousand inmates.

Dieter had been scheduled to go home six months before and had got as far as taking the flight back to Germany. But when the plane touched down and he met his wife, he changed his mind. 'I took her

for a cup of coffee and told her that I was sorry, but I would have
to go back.' He was on the next flight back to Croatia. 'It is for them,
you know,' he said, pointing through the window of his office at the
grey, muddy camp. 'Someone has to help.'

And it is the people who matter of course, the people who live in
Garsinci. Or rather the people who exist in Garsinci. It is a pretty
unpleasant place. Formerly a military firing range with the entrance
still guarded by Croatian soldiers, it is a muddy and barren hillside
surrounded by woods. At this time of year it is cold and damp. Most
of the refugees live in the wooden huts that stand in rows, each of
them providing sleeping space for eight people. Some are still in the
ragged military tents that were hastily put up for the arrivals from
Karlovac. Each tent provides just enough room for ten beds and a
stove. But don't for a moment imagine that each tent or hut contains
the members of just one family.

'I am here with my son,' a woman told me, 'there are six others
sharing with us. They are strangers. I don't know who they are.'

I asked her if she got any privacy, and she winced and answered,
'Not since the soldiers ordered me to leave Mostar eight months ago.'

There is nothing to do in Garsinci but learn to tolerate what life
there is. A refugee has no money, no country and little hope for the
future. The day is broken up by meals. As a refugee you may find
yourself queuing outside, in the cold, for up to an hour for a plastic
bowl of pasta. Then there's the washing to do. A walk of maybe a
third of a mile, down a steep slope to the latrines. That's fine if you're
young and fit, but if you're getting on a bit you'll have to allow
yourself extra time to negotiate the icy path. But then, you might be
in your seventies or eighties and frightened of falling? That means
you will have to wait for a neighbour or a friend to help you. And
even neighbours and friends can run out of time and patience to help
an old lady or an old man. There's a line of concrete sinks in the
open air where there are washing facilities. There is no hot water, so
when the temperature drops and you wash your hair, you'll find it
freezing to your scalp before you get back to your tent.

It is particularly tough for the old people. Miska Yacupovic was
seventy-one and in poor health when she arrived at Garsinci. In the
chilly dampness of the camp, her health rapidly got worse and she
died within a week. Her health certificate said her death was due to
natural causes, but what was natural about the way she died?

Another woman was a mystery to the Red Cross officials at Garsinci. They knew her name and her age. She was Fikreta Mustafi and she was forty-three when she arrived. She was sick and hallucinating. She couldn't eat, sit up or communicate. Finally a camp inmate recognised Fikreta as a woman from her own village. She had been a mother to five children who, when the Serbs arrived, had been butchered in front of her, after which she had been raped. She was at Garsinci for four weeks and the Garsinci nurses achieved quite a lot. They managed to feed her soup and even managed to get her to walk a little. But in the end Fikreta gave up and withdrew into herself. Her temperature soared and after four days she died. The nurses wept of course and so did many at Garsinci, but they also said that maybe it was for the best. So many seem to give up and when they do, the reality of life in Croatia denies them any dignity at their end. An elderly man was taken to Zagreb hospital a hundred kilometres away for an operation on a tumour. His wife remained in the camp. Sadly the old fellow died following the operation. He died alone because the camp lacked the transport to take his wife to visit him.

Everywhere you go in Garsinci, you heard the tell-tale hacking cough.

'We have seven people here with TB,' Kreet told me, 'But many others are coughing now and I'm worried. It's early in the autumn and this shouldn't be happening.'

Kreet believes that two years of war and deprivation have left these people with very little resistance to disease. 'But, we do our best whatever happens,' she said.

I met a hollow-eyed, sad-looking woman called Saira who'd been a clinical psychologist in Sarajevo. She and her husband had managed to escape from the city but had been separated in the process. He made his way to London, Ontario in Canada. She had found herself in Karlovac camp and wrote to her husband to reassure him that she was OK and would join him as soon as she could get her papers in order. A few days later, the shelling started. Her husband safe in Canada, was watching CNN and saw the reports of the chaos. After five frantic hours, he managed to get through to Zagreb on the telephone and find out that his wife had been evacuated to Garsinci. She is still there, still waiting. The trouble is that Saira now has TB. That makes her an unattractive proposition as an immigrant. When I met her, she was helping to organise remedial work in the camp with children who were suffering the emotional effects of being under fire. She is still hoping that one day she will rejoin her husband. But when you ask her when that will be, she is silent.

Some are not silent. There is a frightening eagerness on the part of many, who want to tell you what has happened to them. It is as though by telling you their story, they can in some way reduce the effect it has on them. To listen for several days to such a catalogue of fear, suffering, tragedy and sadness leaves me, when I'm alone, with tears as the only outlet.

One woman put it succinctly when she said, 'I have lost everything. All I have left is a brain to think with. God gave it me, to make me suffer.'

And they do suffer. And it is getting worse. Refugees are still pouring in to Croatia. The camp authorities at Garsinci hoped that all the refugees would be in proper accommodation by the time the winter arrived.

'But then there will be more coming and if there are too many they will have to go into the tents,' one official told me with a defeated shrug of his shoulders.

I don't pass on these stories to you for effect. They aren't horror stories to make you feel warm and safe when you snuggle up in bed tonight. Neither are they threats that the bogey-man will come and get you if you aren't good boys and girls. They are simply things that I observed before a kind of peace came to some areas of the former Yugoslavia.

More than three million people were on the move last year, the biggest movement of humanity in Europe since the Second World War. The emotion I felt constantly was shame. Shame when the little old lady and her husband came out of their house situated almost in the middle of the firing line and shouted at me to 'bring the Americans and the English. They will stop this madness.' Shame when I was told that despite the efforts of the Red Cross there simply wasn't enough food, and this in Europe. And shame that we, here in the cradle of what we call Western civilisation, should allow this horror to be even considered, let alone happen. In the years to come, people will go on dying as a result of what has happened since the collapse of communism and the outbreak of fighting. What should have become a unity of ideas and ideals has become a crucible of horror. More will die simply because of a lack of food, but maybe they will also die because of a lack of will on our part. The last programme I produced for the BBC was a series of diary readings recorded by a refugee girl from Sarajevo. I was pleased about that.

Chapter 15

Back in the early seventies, the shortly to become Controller had been in France on some occasion or other and had watched the summer roadshow broadcast by Antenne Deux. It had for Beerling been no less than a transformation. He would talk about it in the years to come as though he had had some kind of personal conversion at Lourdes. He returned to the UK and introduced the Roadshow to Radio One. In its initial phase it took the physical form of an elaborate version of those travelling exhibitions you can see at any large agricultural show. There was a stage for the presenter and a reproduction of the studio DJ desk, behind which some hapless soul like Alan Freeman or Noel Edmonds would try and mix a live radio show aimed at a listening audience with kind of workers'-playtime-audience-participation element. It started off in an apologetic way as a series of broadcasts from a glorified caravan; within what was then called rather quaintly 'tea-time' and more accurately would become known as 'Drivetime'.

By the time that I joined, it was a vital part of the summer schedules, going out in the late morning from a purpose-built vehicle for nine weeks, before an accumulated audience of three-quarters of a million and being broadcast to God knows how many listeners. The Corporation billed it as the greatest free show of the summer and I was always amazed that Radio One actually paid a facilities' fee to the seaside towns for permission to broadcast from their car park, beach, or whatever. As a free show it had its value to the seaside resort in pulling tourists into the town. When in addition the BBC paid for it to be there, I thought the mayor and corporation should be dancing with joy. But often we got a surly welcome from a council annoyed at having all those people in one place with the resultant litter/noise/nuisance or whatever. The silly buggers would wander around holding noise meters ostentatiously, or they would appear from nowhere to grumble about the fact that the Roadshow was plugged into a thirteen-amp plug at the roadside and draining the town's power supply.

After a particularly bad week of harassment by local officials in the north-east, I lost my cool one Friday morning, and sticking my chin in the council representative's face asked him if he wasn't pleased that the Roadshow was there bringing light, joy and a few extra thousand holidaymakers and their wallets into the town.

'Certainly not,' said the worthy, pulling his overcoat up around his neck to protect himself from the sunshine, 'it's nothing but an administrative nightmare having you here disturbing our system. And you can be certain, young man, that your superiors will be receiving an extra bill for them crash barriers.' And so they did.

Although the vehicle was purpose-built and mighty glamorous, with a fold-out stage and speakers big enough to land a 747 on, the Roadshow itself was only a part of the circus. There were also two articulated lorries, a portable ground station and plenty of support trucks. The upgrading of the image never really affected the content which was strictly 'kiss me quick', with the 'Mileage Game', 'Bits and Pieces' and ludicrous jokes usually involving buckets of water.

The Roadshow's economic usefulness peaked at a vital time for Radio One, when the network was introducing the idea of FM to an audience brought up on medium wave or AM. It was and is critical to the survival of the network that its audience makes the transition before Radio One loses its AM frequency. The use of the Roadshow as a piece of visual propaganda helped get the message across immensely.

I was always baffled that fifty thousand people would hang on to the cliffs at Newquay and watch an event that consisted of a disc jockey playing records, but they did. All around the coast in the summer months, holidaymakers would plan their holidays around the Roadshow. Beerling was right, the magic of it had nothing to do with the disc jockey on duty or even the music, it was something that the thousands who sat and stood around the Roadshow for the sixty-minute warm-up and then the ninety-minute broadcast injected into it. Whenever I was on stage, and looking back I spent more time than I care to think of wondering desperately what to do next, I was always aware of the audience working immensely hard at enjoying themselves and succeeding. It was as though we up on stage were a great blank and they were painting the picture for us.

For the crew, the Roadshow was a nine-week nightmare of logistics and hard work, arriving at a location, rigging, doing the show and then derigging before driving to the next town. For them, engineers, drivers and outside broadcast people it was long hours and total commitment. The damn thing was always getting into trouble through no fault of its operators. Once, the tide moved too fast and caught the vehicle and the engineers unaware. They were sitting safe inside while the water lapped around their ankles. Once, it got stuck in the seaside sand and began to sink. Visions of quicksand appearing beneath their feet and having to explain themselves to Broadcasting House gave its operators renewed strength and they pulled the vehicle out with their bare hands. It was also forever coming across corners that were just too small or bridges that were too low.

We DJs in our little protected world were cosseted and fed in the local hotels. On one occasion when I was staying in a lovely B & B in a small town in Wales, I got out of bed naked and stepped to the window to admire the shore-line. My only misjudgement was not realising that even though my bedroom was on the second floor, the hotel was on an incline, so the Women's Institute ladies on an outing in their double-decker bus got a perfect view of my wrinkley bits as they cruised past. Bless 'em, they tried not to show their disappointment.

Once, on some crazed outside broadcast that someone had suggested, the Roadshow and I were reunited in Berlin for a programme from the Brandenburg Gate. We rigged in the sunshine as the salesmen offered us everything from a Kalashnikov ('It's new, see!') to a box of grenades ('I have not got here, we go get!'), when out of nowhere PC Plod in an old East German policeman's uniform appeared and said in so many words, 'Sorry, mate, you can't park that here.' He was right, too, so the guys had to derig, pack up and drive the vehicle ten yards through the Brandenburg Gate and set up all over again in fifteen minutes. That they succeeded is a testament to their commitment, but I wish they hadn't bothered.

Fifteen minutes later, sitting on stage in front of a paltry crowd who wondered what the hell we were doing, I suddenly realised that someone was shooting at us. It took a while for the reality to sink into my dim brain, but when it did, I took a really silly decision, I cleared the stage and stayed on it myself. God knows why I did this, perhaps some crazed sense of duty, 'the show must go on,' that sort of nonsense. But by the time I had come to my senses the engineers had sensibly locked the door to their little cubicle and I couldn't have left if I'd wanted. (They, by the way, claimed afterwards that they took this course of action to defend themselves, not to place me in jeopardy, but I've often wondered.)

I looked into the crowd and saw the shootist reloading what looked like a shotgun and, all bravery having deserted me, I yelled at the local police to grab him, which they did. As a social liberal, I have been subsequently appalled at my reaction to the fact that in grabbing the sniper, the police jumped up and down on him vigorously, probably breaking a bone or two. I couldn't have given a damn about his welfare at that moment. He turned out to have a grudge of some kind, not against me but against the BBC. I just happened to be in the firing line. I carried on with the programme, though the heart had gone out of it, and of course it took an age to persuade the engineers to unlock that door.

These were the occasional Roadshows, the special programmes that were done for some reason or another, usually at the behest of an embattled management who thought that by appearing in Europe we'd please the politically correct element on the fourth floor of Broadcasting House. I've often wondered if they cared a jot about what we did.

The real Roadshow, though, took place between June and September and was broadcast every day between eleven and twelve thirty to an astonishingly high audience. For the DJ and the producer it was a week's commitment in the middle of the summer, and for those who enjoyed performing in front of an audience like Gary Davies, Steve Wright, Mike Read and Dave Lee Travis it was a joy. For others it was a chore. For some, for those who didn't care to be in front of an audience at all, it was an agony. I fell into that unique category of just not being very good at it really, thank you. I always felt that the audience deserved better than I was giving it, but I soldiered on like a loyal fellow and tried not to cock it up too much.

There were of course the good times and the funny occasions and then there was Roger Lewis. As part of the warm-up, the producer had to introduce the entire circus and represent the BBC at the very beginning of each day at ten o'clock, and on Roger's first day he was, I thought, rather quiet for a man whose instinct was to be at the centre of everything. After doing a very straightforward 'Good morning, and this is what's going to happen', he watched first Smiley Miley and then me do our warm-ups and get into the live segment of the show.

The following morning at a different location, Miles and I sat in the tiny room that acts as a sort of catchment area for those about to go on stage and listened bemused as Roger walked out and filled the air for a good fifteen minutes with material that Smiley and I normally used. Not only had he nicked our emotional props, but he was using them in front of their owners as a crutch for himself and it has to be said he got a few laughs into the bargain, which drove the nail into his coffin. When he came off stage sweating slightly, death threats were issued and his face, from being the mask of Demetrius, became a picture of injured innocence. The following day he reverted to his own material and we allowed him to live! He was referred to ever after, on the rare occasions when anyone was trying to be polite about him, as 'The thief of bad gags', with thanks to Barry Cryer.

After a few years, tramping round the stage of the Roadshow lost what charm it had ever had. I was simply not the stuff that was required, so I wrote to Johnny Beerling and asked to be excused any further public humiliation. He quietly agreed that I had served my term and I set about filling my summers in other ways, but the Roadshow was always there, lurking in the shadows like something from a Stephen King novel waiting to get me. Maybe those of us who had qualms about it were being far too precious about the Roadshow. Maybe we should have accepted the animadversions of the Controller and the fact that three-quarters of a million people enjoyed every minute of it, and that the audience at home, if figures are to be believed, drank it in like the elixir of life. In later years, the producer Fergus Dudley tried and in part succeeded in updating the Roadshows' image by introducing live bands, but in the end it was still the DJ, the celebrities and the 'fun element' that the audience came to see.

A member of the audience said to me last year, 'I can get worked up about Jason Donovan and Steve Wright up there on stage, but, Blur, do me a favour, I want a bit of fun!' Maybe Johnny was right and 'kiss me quick' is still valid.

There was an extension of the Roadshow back in the eighties that was part of a strategy by the management called 'Weeks Out'. In this strange form of torture we happy band of DJs would all go to a hotel in one particular town or city (oddly there would often be a commercial station about to open for business in the area), and for an entire week, the nation would hear nothing but Leeds, LEEDS, LEEDS, or Manchester, MANCHESTER, MANCHESTER. Radio One, its DJs and its radio cars would be everywhere. You couldn't get away from us. Open your front door and Gary Davis would pounce on you. Try to escape through your back door and Steve Wright would be there. Catch a bus and you'd find me ambling about interviewing merry passengers. We flooded whichever town or city had been chosen for the honour and we squeezed every drop dry.

I was working for Malcolm Brown, who had two things going for him. First, he was extremely able when he wanted to be, second, he was a drinker. Malcolm nearly always managed to make our last call of the day on these extravaganzas an outside broadcast from a pub or brewery. Malcolm is a complex man. He is a quite brilliant musician, given to tossing off the odd cantata for his local church choir, and when he'd been planning one of these extravaganzas he'd asked permission to broadcast for a moment or two from Bristol Cathedral. When he'd heard what station was going to do the programme, the bishop nearly split his gaiters and said the equivalent of 'no way'. Malcolm was incandescent with fury and went stomping about the office complaining, 'I'm a church-goer, that bugger's got no right to stop my show coming from his bloody cathedral.' Malcolm couldn't believe the decision had gone against him, he even tried explaining to the bishop that there wasn't a conflict between God and Mammon, this was the BBC, the nearest thing to the Anglican Church on the air in Britain.

So we 'codded' a few moments from the transept. That is, I took a look inside, walked back to the outside broadcast vehicle, and while Peter Powell played in some organ music from the studio in London, I described an entirely imaginary walk I was taking towards the altar. I thought it went well as a radio piece and Malcolm was cackling with delight at the idea of getting one over on the bishop. We both thought that we had a winner, until the shadow of the Controller, Derek Chinnery, fell over both of us. Derek was furious, not because we had told a white lie to the audience but more because we'd dragged the Church into it. We were made to do penance.

Malcolm was one of broadcasting's great producers. That is not to say that he was a model of efficiency, or even a model of anything really, he was a classic BBC product. Massively intelligent and dumped in entirely the wrong department. If there ever was a God, then He would have seen to it that Malcolm worked in Radio Three or produced strange television programmes featuring an awful lot of plainsong. But He didn't and Malcolm ended up working with me on some of the most ambitious programmes I've ever been involved with.

He took it into his head once to do a live broadcast from Bath and since Beau Brummell was associated with Bath, he thought it a fine idea to dress both of us up in eighteenth-century costume, and to do the programme from a sedan chair. I looked rather dashing, he looked like a footpad. In vain, I said to him time after time, 'Malcolm, it's radio, can't we pretend?' But he took no notice and when the day dawned, there I was in my sedan chair, with a couple of idiots ready to walk me round Bath, and there was Malcolm in his cloak and tricorn chatting up a traffic warden.

There had been a row and for some reason neither of us was talking to the other, so Malcolm addressed me through the engineer. 'If he's ready, let's go.'

The engineer said, 'Malcolm says if you're ready let's go.'

'Tell, Malcolm,' I said through gritted teeth, 'that I'm as ready as he is.'

'Malcolm, Simon says he's—'

'Yes, yes, yes ... I heard him.'

The DJ in London handed over to me, I introduced the idea of what we were going to do and cued in the first record. The two sedan-chair men heaved, and off we went, for ten yards, before coming to a bumping halt. Feeling vulnerable, and looking ridiculous in my little box with BBC aerials sticking out of it, I waited and then heard a peel of laughter from Malcolm, who stuck his head discourteously through the window.

'The two blokes have said they're not carrying you any further, you're too heavy, so you'll bloody well have to get out and walk.' He was grinning all over his face.

A year or two later, another of his great ideas nearly came off. It sounded wonderful in the pub, which was where we plotted these exercises in absurdity.

'You ride up The Royal Mile on a horse' (the Edinburgh Festival was in full swing) 'and we end up at the Castle. Lots of history, blood and gore. Have another one.' Put like that, who could argue?

Come the day, the horse turned out to be a rather ordinary-looking animal whose normal duties were to draw a milk float. I was a little miffed at this, I'd rather had Shergar in mind, but I hopped on board and off we went, a strange procession of man on horse, followed by producer carrying a hundred or so sheets of handwritten research, and two outside broadcast engineers sprouting aerials and microphones everywhere. People did stop and stare.

The programme went well, until a couple of hours later we reached the Castle. It was here that to his horror, Malcolm realised that he had forgotten to bring the last three pages of research about the what, when and where of its history. Blissfully unaware of this, I was sitting on the horse rabbiting about what an extraordinary history Edinburgh had and what a wonderful day it was. Rather than admit that there was no research, Malcolm thought quickly and then began to walk in front of me, beckoning me and the damned horse on over the cobblestones and under the arch into the Castle. I thought for a moment that he had gone mad and then realised from the way he was leaping up and down, grinning frantically and waving his arms at me that he was guiding me to some kind of denouement for the entire show. He was about to show me the reason for life, the universe and everything. My commentary began to reflect this, without Malcolm being mentioned, of course. I was building to a big finish.

Malcolm lured me on, never taking his eyes off me, like some Guinness-drinking siren, and I and the horse followed. He suddenly stopped by a wall and staring at me hypnotically flung his arms wide in a gesture that could only mean 'look over this wall and you will understand everything'. In a crescendo of excitement, my voice trembling with anticipation, I kicked the horse on and looked over the wall ... at nothing. All I could see was mile upon mile of what appeared to be cotton wool. What should have been a perfect view of Edinburgh was covered in fog!

Of course all this was massively patronising, but we seemed to get away with it, more because of our enthusiasm and their local tolerance than anything I suspect. The object was obvious and for the most part successful – to increase awareness of the station and to present the DJs as one happy family, which of course they weren't. As in the world of gigs, sex was always on offer, though drugs were conspicuous by their absence, but the disc jockeys tended to be too tired for much in the way of shenanigans. Strangely there were one or two Radio One producers who were more determined to be bedded than any of the disc jockeys and the squeals of joy were more likely to come from the production bedrooms.

On the Leeds week, I was up and about early one morning and

sat transfixed with joy in the reception area as three of the producers appeared out of the lift with their paramours for the night, took one look at me sitting there in my silly Radio One jacket, went pale and vanished up to their bedrooms. I drank free for a week on the alcohol bought to ensure my silence by those three.

The weeks out were an opportunity for the good, the bad, the ugly and the downright dumb. The good – Peter Powell acting as peacemaker after I'd accidentally stubbed my cigar out on the end of Paul Burnett's nose. 'I warned him, I told him he was waving it around too much.' The bad – a barking-mad woman trying to hunt one hapless DJ and cover him in the paint she carried in a bucket. The ugly – one notoriously eccentric producer late for a programme, driving a BBC Range Rover on the wrong side down the motorway, lights full on and horn blaring. The downright dumb – I have only ever seen a broadcaster terminate his own contract once, and that was on one of these events when one poor chap had a little too much to drink and threw up over an executive producer. He was gone within a month.

Chapter 16

'THERE IS NOTHING Like a Turn'.
(Rodgers and Hammerstein)

Allow me to pause and dwell for a moment on the subject of those whose self-importance surpasses everyday hubris. I will first define the term and then follow the switchback career of your typical turn.

'Turn'.
Untalented self-obsessed opportunist who parades his/her ego for re-muneration, however poor the pay.
Often exists in a vacuum of uncertainty.
Derivation – Northern England Club Comics.
See 'Mummer'.
Usually unwilling to surrender central stage to anybody.
(Although the term refers to broadcasters it also fits journalists, pro-ducers, executives, voice-over artistes, lavatory attendants and Direc-tor General.)

'He's a great turn'.
Compliment paid to enthusiastic young thing who still has the energy to kneel or bend over when selected members of management pass him/her.

'What a turn!', 'Now, there's a turn', 'He's a bit of turn'.
Resentful compliment usually paid by middle management while waiting for career down-turn to popular broadcaster who is felt to have a few more years in him/her.

'Turned'.

Term of derision for once-popular broadcaster who hasn't long to
go.
Terminal condition often accompanied by bouts of self-pity, fête
opening and after-dinner speaking.
Periods of deep depression made obvious by a tendency to weep and
blame others for everything.
This condition is rarely recognised by the sufferer but often develops
into helpless sobbing on air and a declared ambition to 'tell the
punters what it's really like'.

'To have turn', 'He has turned'.
To become ridiculous, a figure of fun.
Elderly broadcaster struggling in the twilight of his/her years.
Not being recognised by BBC canteen lady.
Being ignored by management when throwing monumental wobbly
over some imagined slight.
Downward spiralling career, aka slippery slope.
See also 'Bum's Rush', 'Big E', 'Employment Hiatus', 'Resting', as in
'No, it's going really well. I'm working on some great ideas for the
Beeb, let's do lunch.'

'Terminated turn'.
Standing outside Broadcasting House at nine in the morning greeting
commuting executives with frantic smile.
Appearing as guest without requesting fee, on almost any pro-
gramme, regardless of suitability.
Being spotted in Sainsbury's on Sunday mornings buying pet food for
newly purchased small dog.
Posing willingly for photograph with Su Pollard at charity function.
Dying alone in small flat in Blackheath.
Ill-attended memorial service at the Langham church.
Blurred photograph next to obituary in *Anoraks' Guide to Great
Radio Stars of the Past*.

Of course you will probably think that the word 'turn' refers only to
performers. Sadly, this is not true and I suspect it never has been.
   A turn is almost anyone in media who can't quite understand why
he, she or it is not the absolute and total centre of attention. (The 'it'
by the way is relevant, as anyone who has worked with animals will
tell you.)

Simon Bates

There are some basic rules to follow if you are to survive as a turn.

Rule 1. Everybody is so self-obsessed that you've got to be pretty tall, wide or ruthless to get noticed. You must also get used to people talking to you while looking over your shoulder. This is perfectly normal and enables them to keep an eye out for anyone more important than you.

However, in the never-ending chase for attention, dignity and eternal youth must always be preserved. This explains why generation after generation of height-deprived, balding broadcasters have invested in personality lifts and rugs to make themselves larger and hairier than in real life. To my eternal shame, along with a few others I stalked one of the more mature DJs back to his hotel bedroom one evening years ago and waited till he'd settled down for the night before setting off the fire alarm. There was a crashing sound from behind the door before it was wrenched open and a frantic face holding a hairpiece on the wrong way round charged into the corridor. We nearly didn't recognise the superstar because he was at least six inches shorter than usual.

In the mid eighties, one much-loved Radio One DJ was broadcasting from a children's rowing boat and tumbled out of it. He sank like a stone as his wig lifted gracefully off his head and floated into the rescuing arms of a bunch of jeering kids standing on the bank.

In New York I rode along with a distinguished broadcaster and a film crew to the top of the Empire State Building for a couple of shots. We filmed high up in the open air for about half an hour and our D.B. refused to take his hand away from his head for a moment. 'If he does, the shmuck's wig'll be flying down Fifth Avenue faster than a speeding bullet,' his personal assistant told me.

Five or six years ago at a recording for 'Top of the Pops', a chart fave arrived the worse for wear and was dragged straight to his dressing room by his two minders. Both had been with him for nearly a decade and had grown to loathe him, so when they returned to the dressing room and found the star passed out on the floor there was a moment when their hearts lifted at the thought that he might be dead and they could at last release the Greatest Hits album and make a fortune. 'Then the bugger came round and we had to pretend that we hadn't noticed that his rug had come off.'

If you're a 'turn', still have your own hair and are tall enough to be noticed, yet people are still ignoring you, then maybe a well-placed tantrum will solve the problem.

One particular Radio One disc jockey was (and still is) superb in his ability to stand on his dignity and roar at the middle management. In fairness they usually asked for it and when they did, he gave it to them from both barrels. There would be a sort of stoking up of the boiler followed by a thunderous, 'How dare you, I've been in this business for twenty years and no one has talked that kind of crap to me before.' If this wasn't enough, he was pretty good at running through the poor victim's dubious background before stomping off in a 'rage'. But the outrage wasn't what it seemed.

'It's all for show,' he told me once; 'a lot of hot air and as I get older I have to work harder at doing it. One day they're going to see that it's all a performance.' But they haven't yet.

There are different ways to pull this stunt and it is very important to know exactly where you stand in the scheme of things before you do. Miscalculation can spell disaster.

One broadcaster on Radio Two got himself into a state over the music policy a few years ago, stomped off to the Controller and announced that unless things changed, he would have to resign as a matter of principle. When he was told that things wouldn't be changing, he was reduced to blushing, giggling nervously and saying 'Er, oh, um, well, I'll be off then, hurrumph, see you all tomorrow then!' Of course he didn't last; the management had spotted a weakness and he was doomed.

Then again, there's the business of dealing with management when they become self-important, tantrum-throwing 'turns' themselves.

The aforementioned Roger Lewis was an unpredictable old thing when it came to the matter of a consistent approach to life. Ruffle solved this problem not long before Roger moved on. Whenever he was called into Roger's office for a confrontation, J would mimic Lewis's body language. If Roger leant forward and slightly to the left, J would do exactly the same thing. If Roger leant back and put his hands behind his head, he would notice Ruffle imitate the movement exactly. It was the kind of dumb insolence that drove Lewis crazy and reduced the staff to hysterics. Not long after one of these confrontations, Roger moved on to become a bigwig at the classical division of EMI.

This business of being a management 'turn' but desperate for status and attention can lead to absurd behaviour from normally civilised people. One member of Radio One's élite could never quite tear himself away from his earlier life as a 'turn' and continued to write a pop column (together with a suitably youthful portrait) and present programmes on a local radio station. This would have been fine had not the programmes been so grindingly mediocre, leaving the poor man bereft of any authority when it came to criticising less-experienced Radio One hands and their work.

One new member of a commercial TV-managing élite checked on the model of car his predecessor was given, so that he could make certain that his company car was one mark better! And the head of a news division used to call the office at seven every morning 'to find out what time it is'. He once called to see what day it was and when challenged by an overworked sub editor, burst into tears, sobbing 'You don't know how lonely I am.'

Another broadcasting manager new to the hurly-burly of commercial life insisted that, 'I must fly Concorde to New York because it's quicker,' and then stayed an extra day in New York to recover from the jet lag.

Drawing attention to yourself is as important for the management 'turn' as it is for the performing 'turn'. One bloke I worked for scored a bull's-eye by waiting until his immediate superior was away and then changing the staff list. Previously it had been in order of seniority with our hero at the bottom of the list. Now, changed to an alphabetical listing, his name and his prestige rose magically to the top, or near enough to guarantee promotion! Watch this space.

The odd thing is that, surprisingly, performing 'turns' are often more generous to each other than management 'turns', certainly in public. I once had to introduce some event or other at a theatre in London and to my horror found that Stephen Fry would be introducing *me*. The fact that Fry is extremely witty and has a Tomahawk missile for a brain had not escaped me and I sat on the stage gloomily awaiting execution, prepared for him to take me apart. In fact he was charm and kindness itself, and I shouldn't have been surprised.

The same is true in my experience of all really talented 'turns'. Maybe it's their realisation of their own talent that makes them quietly confident, but it's the overwrought, drunk, messianic, drug-addicted or self-important management that can spell disaster.

Yet there are some things that even a relentlessly ambitious management 'turn' would find unacceptable. For example a former head of department at the height of an IRA bombing campaign received a package, sent for a commissionaire and ordered him to 'step outside the door, will you, and open that parcel.'

Most management 'turns' are pretty well behaved when they are out for the day with performing 'turns'. They may bite their lips at not being given full recognition, but sometimes, under great strain, they can snap. At one great British summer event, a BBC management figure was stopped when trying to enter a hospitality tent.

'I'm sorry, sir, but you haven't got a pass.'

'I'm with him, you fool,' gesticulating at Noel Edmonds's retreating backside.

'Ah, but you see, sir, I know Mr Edmonds, but I don't know you, so I'm afraid you can't come in.'

'Listen, you whimpering oaf, I am Mr Edmonds's boss.'

'Oh are you, indeed? Well, you're the fourth person to come up to me and try that one on, so be off with you.'

Sometimes, though, management are justified in their fury. A few years ago, 'The Brits' were memorably staged at the Albert Hall. I arrived at the main entrance to find the doors locked and the rain pouring down. Standing in a miserable heap were the then Head of Light Entertainment, his wife and his child, soaked to the skin and minus umbrella. As he had commissioned the programme from the makers who were busy inside and who had locked him out in the torrential downpour, I predicted then that the company would find it hard to get commissions from the BBC in the future and I was proved right.

Then again, management as 'turn' includes the kind of person who is so insecure that leaving the office is well-nigh impossible. This type usually follows the example set a while back by a senior broadcasting official who took a holiday and a portable phone up a Swiss mountain at a fairly difficult time and left strict instructions that 'any decisions must be referred to me.' And they were; at four quid a minute.

While some have absolutely no sense of humour about their position in life, others can be almost endlessly good-humoured about the absurdities of being top dog. Fergus Dudley and I were doing a series of programmes from Hong Kong and he had managed to persuade the airline to give us a free ticket for the Controller. Dudley is an inspired negotiator and at Heathrow he spent an hour convincing the PR officer how important our Controller was in the scheme of things, before coming back to me with a smug grin on his face. 'Full result,' he said. 'They're going to upgrade Beerling to First Class.'

'And us?' I asked.

'Oh, I forgot, we're still at the back!'

The flight was pretty uneventful, though Beerling did good-naturedly tease us about the quality of first-class service versus that provided for us mere mortals.

Our retribution, though, was sweet and swift.

We had an overworked and tired Controller to look after on our return journey to London, so it was quite easy to extract his ticket from him and change his flight. We popped the poor soul onto a different plane out of Kai Tak airport, telling him that this was the only way we could get him an upgrade. Johnny sat back in first all right, but it was only when the 747 was taxiing to the runway that he learned the flight was non-stop to Paris!

After the flight and on our way back into London on the tube, Fergus became a little thoughtful. 'D'you think putting the Controller on a flight going to the wrong country is a sackable offence?'

'No, JB's got a sense of humour,' I said, but I wondered if he was right.

It's a tribute to his lack of pomposity that Beerling *did* think that the incident was funny, when he could bring himself to talk to me a week or so later.

Management as 'turn' sadly deprives the sufferer of the greatest joys in life. A couple of years ago I trotted up the stairs at Radio One on my way to the fourth floor. As I passed the third-floor landing I noticed that familiar whiff of marijuana coming from one of the offices. In the nineties there was something almost comforting about it and I casually mentioned the fact to one of the Radio One executives who was coming down the other way. He went white, leapt for the fire door and began to swing it frantically to and fro, trying to create some kind of draught. 'You idiot,' he gasped at me, turning bright red with the unaccustomed exercise, 'the Board of Governors are coming round on a visit in ten minutes.' He never forgave me for being reduced to helpless laughter.

On the subject of drugs, I was in a Miami recording studio six years ago with the now retired Doreen Davis, who always kept abreast of things and never missed a trick. The engineer was puffing on a pipe full of hash and not knowing Doreen terribly well, I wondered how she would react. She looked at me knowingly and smiled the sweetest but firmest of smiles; 'I do think these herbal tobaccos smell nice, don't you?'

As to hard drugs – well, I'm sorry to disappoint you, but I've seen the after-effects and I haven't cared greatly for what I've seen. Like Aids, addiction is a rotten and painful way to go. In the early eighties I went to a showbiz party and, walking into one room, saw a couple of glass bowls full of white powder. Truth to tell, I was more excited at the idea of seeing what I'd read so much about in the tabloids than actually indulging in the stuff.

This was also the party where I opened a door to find a much-loved comedy star lying semi-naked on a bed wearing nothing but his socks, while a rather bored groupie tended to his every whim. At least he had the style to wave and say 'Good evening, old chap.'

I made my excuses and equally I never got round to trying to stick half of Bolivia up my nose. I always feel I have to be cautious when I'm commenting on hard drugs because I've never got as far as sticking anything up my nose or in my arm. I did however have a brush with the heavy stuff in the early eighties.

I was in Peru for some reason and I'd decided to visit Machu Picchu in the Andes. To get there meant a long train ride to Cusco which is high up in the mountains, and by the time I reached the city the shortage of oxygen had left me exhausted and panting for breath. 'Here,' said a passing Australian, 'drink this and you'll feel better.' I took a mighty gulp from the glass he offered and then another, and felt a great deal better.

By the time I had drunk several of these magic potions I had turned into everybody's favourite furry animal, and had to be prevented from capering around the city square shouting 'the drinks are on me!'

What I'd been busy guzzling was coca tea, which sounds pretty inoffensive and tastes that way until you learn that it is made from coca leaf, the same leaf that makes cocaine. The way it made me feel that day made me want to make it available through the NHS, but please, always check with your parents first before you go to Peru and drink coca tea. And don't forget not to make a mess in the kitchen.

Rule 2. Everybody, without exception and no matter how successful they are, believes that God intended them to be somewhere else, and that the job they're doing is the next step on the route to something bigger.

Hence disc jockeys want to be *Panorama* reporters and *Panorama* reporters want to be disc jockeys, or at least music reviewers. Newsreaders want to be journalists and journalists want to be on air longer than newsreaders. Game show hosts want to be respected and pop stars want to be taken seriously and get OBEs at the very least. Deep down however they're usually hoping that the endless presents sent by them to the Palace will at least gain a knighthood.

Members of Parliament want to get on radio and TV as often as possible presenting sports quizzes and other shows that have nothing to do with politics.

Sports personalities will burst into song at the drop of a five hundred quid note.

And everyone wants to do *Have I Got News For You*.

In other words, nearly everybody wants to be and do something they're not doing or being. The fact that they're trying to do something to which they're probably totally unsuited hasn't occurred to them.

It's not so much ego tripping, though that's always a good motive; more realistically the reason is the age-old insecurity of trying to keep one step ahead of the game.

Very few 'turns', bless 'em, have ever understood precisely what their value is or where they really shine. That is why agents exist. They try to keep their 'turns' on the money-making path, while allowing them to indulge themselves occasionally.

'Look Harry, I think it's great that you want to try for the Christ at the next Oberammergau, but what's the band going to do without a drummer?'

But everyone wants to be someone else.

Johnny Mathis wants to be a golfer.

Almost every contemporary comedian I've ever met wants to be an actor and simply can't grasp that it would be impossible for them to subdue their egos and personalities enough for them to assume another character convincingly.

Paul Simon wants to play football for the NFL.

Billy Joel wants to be a stand-up comedian.

In fact sometimes I think that Joel wants to be almost anything other than the superb musician he is. The first time I met him, we ended up having a heated but friendly argument about the US involvement in Vietnam. Predictably I was against, and my perception was that he was for. It wasn't until years later that I realised the reason for his sensitivity on the subject. He'd escaped the draft and friends of his hadn't. There is what one might call a 'guilt thing' involved and Joel is never one to carry any kind of weight lightly.

Back in the sixties, the Australian actor Chips Rafferty was be-moaning his fate. He was finding it hard to get parts for long, rangy Aussie tough guys.

'Why not do a cameo part?' suggested a friend in the pub one night, 'like Laurence Olivier has just done at the National in London. You come on, do a couple of minutes and then bugger off to rave reviews.'

'Aaw no mate,' came the reply, 'I couldn't do that, it's different for me than for Olivier. I'm a star.'

Rule 3. Victims. The victim in all this 'turning' is the producer. He or she on radio or TV is the person who has to keep everyone happy and therefore has to deal with both management and the 'turns' themselves.

The basic rule for the producer who has any sense is to keep saying to everybody, 'It's all going frightfully well.'

If the programme is a Roadshow and an audience of twenty-eight has turned up where last year there had been twenty-eight thousand, the producer must say, 'Yeah but that was for Travis and look at the kind of people who showed up for *him*! This lot is class.'

When an interview has gone wrong and a rock star has stormed out, it is the producer who must return to the studio crying, 'He thought you were great!'

When the management descends *en masse* for a photograph with some visiting celeb, it is the producer who must purse his or her lips and say, 'He really wants to, but there's a time problem here.'

It is the producer who must tactfully fend off drunken manage-ment bent on firing or making love to their 'turn'.

When the artist hasn't learned his or her lines, it is the producer who must lock the 'turn' in their dressing room and berate them, but at all times tactfully! It is never enough to say, 'You're terrific and it's going frightfully well really,' to a 'turn'. Producers must always be aware of heightened sensitivity caused by paranoia.

Earlier this year a first-rate political journalist got what he'd always wanted, his own show on BBC TV. The farewells done, he left the local TV show he'd been fronting and, wishing his replace-ment well, moved on to greater things.

Any sensible soul would have immediately forgotten the local show, but not a 'turn'. This one called his old producer with whom he was close friends after the following night's show to find out how the replacement had done. He isn't a venomous man, but he wanted to hear what a rotten job his replacement had made of the first show.

Instead, 'He was great, brilliant,' blurted the producer before realising that he had made a dreadful mistake and then, in the giant pause that followed, added, 'But not as great as you were.' Honour was satisfied and their friendship survived.

One performing 'turn' got married earlier this year and, giving his management 'turn' the date of the nuptials, sat back to wait for the obligatory congratulations. The management 'turn' looked up at his wall chart and scowled, 'You can't, there's no one here who can deputise for you. Oh, well I suppose you can get married on the Friday, just so long as you can be here to introduce your programme in the evening.' Then he brightened up, 'Or maybe we could send down an Outside Broadcast Unit and you could pre-record when you come out of the church.'

It was the producer of course who stepped in and prevented the performing 'turn' from slaughtering the management 'turn'.

It should be a rule for all producers, whether they're looking up or down, that 'an unhappy turn is a dangerous turn'.

Chapter 17

D ON'T GET ME wrong, but for some of the best entertainment of your life, there is nothing better than a good graveyard. I'm selfish enough to enjoy being on my own from time to time and wherever I am I've always enjoyed wandering through the churchyard and taking an hour or so to look at the headstones. If you're hunting for the end of Empire anywhere in the world it's in the regimental graveyards full of teenage subalterns and clerks who left their native country with their dreams and never survived to see them realised.

A year or so after J and I went around the world, we drove across the States, down through the South and across to California. The headstones there don't have the majesty of those in India, Australia and Asia, they are much more basic, but they are just as telling about the kind of people buried six feet under as a full-page obituary in a national newspaper. There are classic epitaphs like, 'I told you I was sick', and 'She lived with her husband for fifty years and died in the confident hope of a better life.' Or 'Dead and good riddance', and 'Thankfully gone before his wife.'

Walk, as I did, through the cemetery in Paris, Texas and you'll find the memorial to cowboy Bose Ikard. It's more like a celestial reference. Mr Ikard was buried in an unmarked grave until his long-time friend, cattleman Charles Goodnight erected a marker to the old pioneer. It read, 'Served with me on the Goodnight Loving Trail. Never shirked a duty or disobeyed an order. Rode with me in many stampedes, participated in three engagements with Comanches. Splendid behaviour.' Then there's the memorial to Willet Babcock. It's a lurid statue of Jesus Christ. Nothing original in that, you might think, except that this particular JC wears, along with his flowing robes, a pair of cowboy boots! There is something very consoling about all this kitsch.

Sitting reminiscing one spring afternoon in a bar on Christopher Street in New York with an old Australian friend, we came up with a bang against the subject of death.

'I guess,' she said, 'that it's a sign of encroaching middle age when you turn to the *New York Times* obits before you look at the jobs' page.'

Gordon Elsbury, one-time director of *Top of the Pops* had died the week before in Los Angeles. It was one of fate's rotten tricks, once Gordie knew that he had a limited amount of time left, he'd made plans to fly back home to die, but his disease caught up with him before he could settle his affairs in the States.

Endlessly kind, Gordon had developed an unlikely attachment to the extremely straight band Doctor Hook and the Medicine Show back in the seventies when he worked for the BBC. When he directed the last TV concert, one of their roadies told Gordon that they'd left a present for him in his little Citroën CV. After the show and the thankyous and the farewells, Gordon slipped out of the TV theatre, into Shepherd's Bush and hopped into his little car. There on the passenger side was a carrier bag stuffed with extremely green grass and a note saying thankyou for everything. A member of London's constabulary strolled past and wished Gordon goodnight. Gordon panicked as his BBC career flashed before his eyes. He started up the engine, and as the darkness fell and the lights came on in the Spud U Like, Gordie drove round and round Shepherd's Bush, tossing great handfuls of the stuff out into the gloom. Legend reports that the pigeons had a smug, unfocused look about them for days afterwards.

Aids wasn't an issue when my loins started dictating my lifestyle to me. I used to spend most of my mornings-after locked in a cubicle in the mens' lavatories examining every nook and cranny and wondering how venereal disease showed itself. My paranoia was on how I would explain to the doctor what had happened and whether or not your family was immediately informed. I first became aware of Aids when a young press officer died with terrible suddenness back in the middle of the eighties. More died in the intervening years and at least one had the HIV virus from a blood transfusion he had in the late eighties. Now I always travel with an Aids pack, just in case. Though if I were in a serious accident in a Third World country and unconscious, the last thing anyone taking care of me is going to do is sort through my back pack and find the pack with its assorted needles and syringes.

Another friend died of Aids early this year. A married man, he was one of those who'd received a transfusion of contaminated blood. It took him quite a while to die and leave his kids and his young wife alone in the world with no cash from a pension scheme or hope of a pay-out from the Government. Of course, he realised all this. One of his last and most fervently expressed wishes was that someone would take his ashes and strew them all over Virginia Bottomley's living-room carpet. Sadly, he didn't get his wish. It would have been nice to think of the expression on his face as he watched from up above the Minister of Health coping with the sudden dispersal of one of her ex-clients all over her best three-piece suite!

So, in New York the two of us fell to counting the number of close chums and enemies who have died – from Charlie the nutter in Sydney who persuaded me and a room of half-smashed druggies that he could fly, before stepping out on to the windowsill and proving himself terminally wrong, to the splendid Tony Stratton-Smith, who succumbed painfully to cancer. Tony had taken himself off to Spain, so only the closest of friends knew that he was dying, but a clause in his will left enough cash for a wake and specified that his ashes were to be spread over the first jump at Kempton Park.

On the night of the last transmission by one of the pirate radio ships, the remaining crew and cast of DJs put on a party. They had planned ahead and had smuggled plenty of alcohol aboard, so by ten o'clock in the evening the party had become a very public one. None of them cared greatly, it was their last night after all and they were having a good time. One by one, as midnight and switch-off time advanced, they approached the microphone to say goodbye. One, more drunk than the rest, announced that he was going to swim home and performed a perfect swallow dive into the darkness. His body was washed up a few days later.

Then there was the engineer in New York who worked for the main news network. He was one of those people who live for their work. A sad, ugly, lonely man with a one-room flat and no private life of his own, he developed a passion for one of the overnight newsreaders. She was a young, pretty and impressionable girl who was at first flattered and then, as his obsession grew, appalled. But the two of them still had to work together every night. Everyone in the office knew the story. The kind ones murmured sympathetically, others made no attempt to cover their contempt. As things so often do, his passion developed into hatred and her boredom changed to fear. One night he lost control and lay in wait for her outside the studios. The attack wasn't very effective, but although he didn't hurt her physically he succeeded in frightening the girl thoroughly, so he had to go. The station did its best to make the sacking as painless as possible and they recommended that he get counselling. The engineer went home and stayed there for a few weeks, by which time the story had got around the other radio stations and made him unemployable. So one morning he got up, took the bus to the 57th Street bridge and threw himself off.

Way back in the seventies, the old BBC hand Roger Moffat drank himself to death. He'd left the BBC and gone to work for a commercial station, Radio Hallam. But even *in extremis*, Roger had a sense of his own importance, so after his death the station released an obituary, the one they found in Roger's office drawer, written by Roger Moffat.

Then there was the time I was visiting a TV station out in the country. Their seven o'clock news was a two-handed affair, with a distinguished-looking, silver-haired older man and a young, sprightly girl with hair sprouting from every part of her head. The night I was there, the older of the two cued to some film report or other, went a little grey and slumped forward on to the desk. There was a moment's silence as the floor manager rushed forwards and the gallery went to a commercial break.

'I think he's dead,' said the floor manager on the intercom.

'Christ,' said the director. 'Well, get him out of there.'

So we watched in the control room as one screen offered great deals on the newest Hondas, and the other nine showed three burly men bustling the late newsreader's carcass out of his chair as his erstwhile colleague checked her make-up before looking up, right on cue, smiling at the camera and saying, 'The news continues, in just a moment.' And so it did.

I was travelling around the world for Radio One when the disc jockey Roger Scott announced that he had terminal cancer. A producer, Mick Wilcoiz, was the one person kind enough to think that I should be told. He tracked me down to a ship in the middle of the Pacific and put a call in to the radio operator.

I asked the stupidest question possible. 'What should I do?'

'Nothing,' Mick replied sensibly, 'there's nothing you can do, just carry on with your life.'

Roger was a tall, craggy, extremely able and above all sensible broadcaster who was wedded to radio. It was his entire life and it hadn't always treated him with TLC. He'd been in the middle of a shift on Capital Radio when a call had come through telling him that his wife and child had been killed in a car crash in Canada.

When his cancer returned it can have been nothing less than a terrible blow to both him and his wife. For us it was terribly distressing. He insisted on working for as long as he could, but towards the end he would become desperately tired. He would often come in to Radio One around lunch-time and I would walk out of the studio to find him lying on the settee in the corridor. I never knew what to say, but I always tried to follow Mick's advice, 'There's nothing you can do, just get on with yout life.'

A year or so later, talking to Brian May about the death of Freddie Mercury brought me face to face with a greater understanding of what Mick was trying to say. For more than three years, Brian, along with other members of the Queen family, protected Freddie Mercury by refusing to allow the truth to escape that Fred had contracted Aids. The strain must have been huge, everyone suspected what was wrong and wanted to know the truth. It was something much more than merely prurient interest.

Brian was proud of himself and richly deserved his pride. 'We lied very effectively, didn't we,' he said 'and I stand by it'. 'You know Fred was so in control of himself. He decided that he didn't want any fuss or sympathy or any special treatment when he got Aids. He said that he wanted business as usual until it stopped. And that's what he managed to achieve. And we helped him to do it. My decision after Freddie died was that I would plunge into work. On one level I'm doing all right, but there's another level right down there where I haven't got used to it. There's often a time when I'm in studio and I think, "Oh, Freddie'll do that", and then I realise, of course, that he won't, ever again.'

A while ago now a great Australian actor died, a man I'd got to know quite well while I'd been out there. I'd seen him when I'd last been in Sydney and he hadn't looked well, but he made it his business to keep doing as much as he could until the end. And that included the occasional trip to the bottle shop. He'd died on his way back home from one of these trips and at his wake someone had said, 'Thank God Ronnie was dead before he hit the ground. Smashing those bottles would have broken his heart.'

My Grandmother died that same year. I had found it very difficult to observe her decline, and in her later years I'd used work as an excuse for my infrequent visits to become less and less frequent. I was working hard. There were big money problems and eighteen-hour days. Days when I didn't go to bed at all. But of course I could and should have done more and that bothers me.

My mother, who is an extremely perceptive person, called me one week and virtually insisted that I go and see Queen. 'It's important that you come up to the Midlands,' she said.

Family pressure is family pressure and I bowed under it and went to see Queen, a little old, confused and bent lady, nothing like the strong-minded, strong-willed, autocratic person I had known as a child. For me it was an agonising hour or so. I hope it did something for Queen but I can't tell if it did. Maybe it was too late to say the things one should always say, I don't know. She died a few days later, and thanks to my mother I had some perception of doing the right thing at the right time for once, even if it was at the last minute.

I recorded the Radio One programme and took the following Friday off to go to the funeral in the small village church across the way from the farm. I had been wearing my shades in London to avoid the bright morning sunshine when I caught the train. In my confusion I forgot to take my ordinary specs, so I must have looked like some Mafia head as I settled into my pew in the church. The church was packed with quiet Midlands voices, the Black Country accents mingling with the local ones, so many people whose faces I recognised but couldn't put a name to. They knew me and I couldn't for the life of me remember which of them was which. The service was simple and as I fumbled with the unaccustomed hymn book and Bible, the vicar didn't wallow in sanctimonious waffle but said just the right thing and said it briefly.

I come from a family of farmers and we would all agree that it was a good thing that my grandmother died, and maybe that it would have been better for her if she'd died a few years earlier, so I couldn't regret the fact that she was now dead and buried. There could be no false grieving, it was an overdue full stop, for Queen and for me.

My cousin took me to the railway station to catch the train back to London after we'd all stood around having drinks and making polite conversation after the funeral. It was a curious rerun on a clear, bright, sunny day, of that night twenty-six years before when I'd first left home. As I settled into my seat, I suddenly realised that the Labour leader, Neil Kinnock, along with a coterie of party workers, was in the same carriage. Kinnock is a social man and likes everybody to be happy and on this occasion he was working hard at making sure that they were. He was cracking jokes and they were roaring with laughter. Sunk in my own thoughts at the other end of the carriage, I gradually became aware of the noise and the happiness a few feet away and began to resent it deeply. I wasn't at all in the mood for all that 'in the midst of death there is life' stuff. But then I realised how stupid and self-indulgent I was being and how cross both my grandparents would probably have been at such unreasoned thinking and I began to smile.

Chapter 18

'M A FAN OF THE British music business, I think it is a remarkable forcing house for talent. However, the British music industry doesn't need me as an apologist. It is packed with talented, infuriating, likeable people, who for the most part are palpably off their heads. They make arbitrary decisions which often seem to have no logic whatever to them. The fact, though, that one in every four records sold anywhere on the planet has British content isn't just luck. Neither is it just the product of a profit-obsessed industry. The majority of the people in the business like what they do and they do what they like well.

The people who run the record companies are almost entirely Damon Runyon figures. Put them all in pin-stripe suits and you'd have half a dozen productions of *Guys and Dolls*. But I'd rather spend a day with any present record company boss than thirty minutes with a consultant from Coopers & Lybrand.

It would be silly to select any of the present crop of executives but now that he's retired I can wax nostalgic about Morris Oberstein, boss at CBS/Sony for about fifteen years and then head of Phonogram records. He's not typical of any of them, but like his successors he was a huge and interesting individual. There are a million stories about the man who started off running a small label in New York and ended up as one of the best-known players on the world music scene, many of them true. Obie has made a virtue out of eccentricity. He has the largest collection of outrageous hats of anyone I know. But no one is as successful as he has been without being tough. Obie's bite has always been just as bad, if not worse than his bark. As a kid, his uncle was a ticket tout on Broadway and the tickets that didn't sell went to the boy Oberstein, so he saw almost every great musical to play the Great White Way in the late thirties, forties and fifties. He adores musicals and once took Barbara Dickson to see a

London production of *Oklahoma* and ruined the evening for her and probably everyone sitting within twenty feet. He unconsciously sang along at the top of his voice throughout the entire show!

'I was never more convinced,' said Barbara, 'that in future I should do the singing and he should do the deals.'

This is the man who desperately wanted to contract a band called The The. Their manager would only sign if Obie agreed to sit on one of the lions in Trafalgar Square at midnight when he was doing it. Obie duly sat on the lion and the manager signed. But while he built a reputation as a wildly eccentric and tough negotiator, he also helped create an atmosphere where success at home often meant hits abroad for British pop stars. In ten years with CBS, the company had forty-four number-one singles. That's success.

When I first met him, Obie owned a red setter called Charlie, a dog that was almost more eccentric than its owner. We went horse-riding together once and the moment that Obie mounted, Charlie panicked and started rushing around.

'Fool, dog, he's looking for me, I forgot to teach him to look up,' said Obie.

On another occasion around about Christmas time, he turned up with a smile on his face and said 'I've brought you a present.'

I was a little surprised, but said thank you and he gave me one of his latest albums. 'How come you're not playing this, it's brilliant?'

He was right of course. He's also great company, very tough, likeable and very funny. I've never heard him waste a word, though one Christmas he did take it on himself to dance around my table singing 'HaVaNaGeila'.

I had been doing daily radio shows for seventeen years when I left Radio One. I'd been working seven-day weeks for the last four years and I was pretty tired. Correction, I was absolutely buggered. Surprisingly there had been quite a few offers when I left, all of them well-meant and most generous. But all the radio jobs meant a return to daily work as a disc jockey and the TV work required me to wear a blazer and do quizzes. I'm not against the principle of either, though blazers and me don't go together terribly well, it was just the commitment I couldn't face.

I had some work to do in the UK and in America, which took me through until February 1994 after which, with the exception of my contract with Atlantic 252 and my continuing tiny commitment to

CBS news, I was free. I had no ambition at all to go back to daytime radio for a long time and being absolutely exhausted I desperately needed to sleep for a year or two. So I took myself off to the south of France, determined to catch up on the books I hadn't had time to read and to live a healthier lifestyle. The first couple of weeks were wonderful. It was early spring and the Côte d'Azur was almost deserted. I would listen to the eight o'clock news on Radio Four and then potter down to the *boulangerie* for a baguette and practise my French on the patron who would practise her English on me. Then I would spend the rest of the day drinking instant coffee, reading and writing, and be in bed and fast asleep by ten at night. For the first time in seventeen years I could actually take my time rather than running everywhere. When the need arose I could be back in London within four hours. It was the perfect existence and the only drawback was that my weight exploded.

Then, the phone rang. Robin Malcolm, whose reputation I knew, called with an offer. The journalist Richard Littlejohn had resigned leaving a hole in the schedules on LBC, the London news station and would I like to fill the gap until the station went off the air as it was scheduled to do, in October? I thought about it but not for too long. I'd never worked on a Newstalk station and knew even less about how it worked. It would be a totally new and therefore exciting experience and there was the matter of remuneration that seemed pretty generous for a beginner. 'A beginner', that sounded fun. If I screwed the job up totally or hated it, the contract was only for six months, the agony wouldn't be endless either for the station or for me. I said 'thank you' for the offer and added 'I'd love to do it'. A couple of weeks later I flew back and started work.

There is another book about the travails of London broadcasting and it is for someone else to write. It's sufficient to say that life has been tough for the station and for its employees. In fact, stronger men and women have cracked under similar strains. It was a topsy-turvy outfit in every way. I was expecting the usual wall of indifference and possibly a little antagonism, certainly coming back to a station in flux, I was expecting a lack of enthusiasm. After all, this was a station on the way to closing and I was that final nightmare, a disc jockey! How dare they have their noses rubbed in it by my stepping into their world? On the contrary, the overworked and overstretched staff were totally sympathetic, supportive and enthusiastic. I came from a different world and they knew that, but it didn't seem to bother them greatly. If anything it seemed to make them more helpful. Added to that, now I got free review copies of books! Things looked good.

A couple of days after I arrived, the company went into liquidation. But isn't that the way life always is? You have your good days and your bad days.

Jonathon King got to the nub of it when he said, with I think some affection for me as I left Radio One, 'Bates has been responsible for some triumphs and some dreadful disasters', and that couldn't be more accurate. One of my sins has always been too much quantity and not enough quality. I can't excuse that, but I can try to justify it by suggesting that there is an awful lot in broadcasting generally that should be done and is so often ignored. I am guilty of always hurtling on to the next thing as quickly as I can before someone else forgets to do it. In the meantime I am capable of leaving chaos in my wake because I haven't quite finished what I'm working on at the moment. This can and has resulted in miserable late nights in the studio after midnight with endlessly patient producers and engineers helping me to piece together the bits of tape that I've forgotten to finish off in my rush onward. It is a sin and like most of my other crimes, there are many who have spent a good deal of their time pointing out my faults to me and to others.

I wish that I had developed a philosophy of my own that I can pass on, but that's another of the things that I've been meaning to do and haven't quite got round to yet. I can do no better than quote from Peter Jones, who has quietly been far funnier for far longer than almost anyone else I can think of.

'I decided years ago that it's what one thinks of oneself and one's work that really matters. This simple philosophy has two advantages: critical maulings and public apathy are much less painful and if you're occasionally lucky enough to have a success then you don't get too big-headed about it.'

I've invariably gone wrong when I've forgotten that advice, and then Bob White's words in that dusty office in New Zealand nearly thirty years ago come back, 'Keep it simple and fer Chrissake remember it isn't bloody brain surgery.'

I'll get it right one day, maybe.